P9-AGQ-296

THOMAS NASHE

# THOMAS NASHE

A CRITICAL INTRODUCTION

by

G. R. Hibbard

Routledge and Kegan Paul

LONDON

*First published 1962*
*by Routledge & Kegan Paul Limited*
*Broadway House, 68-74 Carter Lane*
*London, E.C.4*

*Made and printed in Great Britain*
*by William Clowes and Sons, Limited*
*London and Beccles*

# CONTENTS

# PREFACE

WRITING about Thomas Nashe has made me realize, as never before, my debt to others, to the dead as well as the living. Without the help of the late R. B. McKerrow's great edition this book could not have been written at all, and both my text and my footnotes demonstrate, though incompletely, how much I owe to the labours of other scholars and critics—not least to those who have prompted me to active disagreement.

I wish to express my thanks to Professor V. de S. Pinto who encouraged me to undertake this work, read the first chapter in an earlier draft and made valuable criticisms of it. I am also deeply grateful to my colleague, Dr. J. T. Boulton, who read the proofs and saved me from many errors. Any mistakes that remain are my own. Special thanks are due to Miss Sheila Copping and my wife for their patience in coping with my handwriting and producing a typescript from it.

I must thank Messrs. Basil Blackwell and Mott for permission to make use of their edition of McKerrow's *Nashe*.

G.R.H.

# INTRODUCTION

TO have written two lyrics, so representative of their time in tone and manner that many who know them think of them as anonymous, and a pamphlet as wayward, chaotic and eccentric as *Have With You to Saffron-Walden*, would in itself be an arresting achievement, even in an age that tended to take the coincidence of opposites for granted and found an oxymoronic harmony in viewing life as a *discordia concors*. Yet this contrast is no greater than that which exists between the strained, over-written mixture of sentimental bombast and tasteless religiosity that fills the first half of *Christ's Tears over Jerusalem* and the deflating burlesque which provides the staple of *The Unfortunate Traveller*, or between the conventional attitude expressed in the *Anatomy of Absurdity* and the witty originality of *Pierce Penilesse*. Equally ready to dispense moral advice to the public at large and to pander to the vicious tastes of an aristocratic patron, to reflect the most commonplace attitudes of the day and to speak out with an individual voice from a personal and, on occasions, almost a revolutionary point of view, Nashe remains, as I think he would have wished to remain, something of a paradox.

Yet this paradox also has a representative quality about it, for Nashe is in many ways the most Elizabethan of all our writers. Perhaps the most striking feature of the age was its duality. It was a time when, as historians of ideas and literary critics have stressed almost *ad nauseam* of recent years, men believed in 'degree' as the basis of the natural order of things, and in the absolute need for obedience, subordination and discipline in the organization and running of the state, the body politic. But it is perfectly evident, though less often noted, that this belief did not prevent them from being ambitious and enterprising in the conduct of their own lives and constantly on the look-out to improve their social standing. Aristotelians by training and ever ready to hymn the golden mean, they were irresistibly drawn to Platonism and in love with excess. Spenser is nowhere more copious than in Book II of *The Faerie Queene*, where his subject is Temperance, and seems totally unaware of any contradiction between his theme and the manner in which he treats it. In this respect he is like Nashe, and unlike Shakespeare and Donne who were alive to the tension between fact and theory and made it articulate. Nashe remains immersed in his own times and cannot detach himself from them. With the sharpest of eyes for the surface of life, he cannot see below the surface. He reflects the conflicts and contradictions of his age without fully realizing their nature. Filled with respect for the established order of things, he attacks society for failing to provide him with a suitable place and the means of livelihood; always ready to condemn ambition, he prides himself on his singularity and individualism; preaching the virtue of submission to authority, he repeatedly fell foul of authority and lived to see the publication of his works prohibited.

His reputation at the present time is as oddly mixed as his writings. To the common reader he is a lyrical poet, the author of 'Spring, the sweet spring' and of 'Adieu, farewell, earth's bliss', expressing both the gaiety and the melancholy of his age, its joy in the coming of spring and its terror in face of the plague. To a smaller, but still considerable, audience he is the author of *The Unfortunate Traveller*, a composition which seems to speak more directly to the mid-twentieth century than any other piece of Elizabethan prose fiction. On the strength of it he makes a regular, though usually fleeting, appearance in histories of the novel. He also appears in surveys of Elizabethan drama under the guise of a 'university wit', but it is never very clear why he is included, since the only play we have which is indubitably his own was not written for the public stage and was probably never performed on it. The rest of his writings are still substantially the preserve of the scholar. For well over a century they have been recognized as the richest, and, thanks to McKerrow's splendid edition of them, for the last fifty years as the most reliable and easily accessible source from which to illustrate the social life and the linguistic habits of the last decade of the sixteenth century, a mine for footnotes to editions of Shakespeare and of other Elizabethan writers. The scholarly attention he now receives would, no doubt, have flattered Nashe who always prided himself, rather unjustifiably at times, on his learning, but he would not have approved of its antiquarian flavour—he scorned antiquaries—and he would have been puzzled, I think, by its exclusiveness, since he sought to be and, for a brief period, was a popular writer.

The neglect he suffers under as a writer, a creative artist as distinct from a source of information, is due, I think, to two things. First, the varied nature of his work, the rapidity with which he moves from subject to subject, has led to a kind of critical fragmentation in the treatment he has received. As well as turning up, as I have mentioned already, in histories of the novel and histories of the drama he also appears in surveys of Elizabethan criticism, in anthologies of poetry, in works illustrating the social life of the day, in discussions about the Marprelate controversy, about the state of the English language, about prose style, about the position of the professional writer, about censorship and in connection with his quarrel with Gabriel Harvey. But, while no critic of Elizabethan literature can afford to ignore Nashe, he is not a writer who lends himself easily to the elaboration of a thesis. His work does not fall naturally into kinds, nor does it admit of any neat arrangement under topics. Even such a normal line of approach as that provided by a study of the growth and development of his art is of little use in dealing with what he wrote, because he did not really develop. Once he had found himself, as he did with the writing of *Pierce Penilesse*, he was content to go on doing the same kind of thing for the rest of his life.

I have, therefore, in the pages that follow tried to give some account of his writings, treating them in a roughly chronological order, to suggest some lines of approach to them and to make some critical judgments on them, in the hope that others will be spurred to correct my errors of judgment and my misplaced emphases, until Nashe receives the recognition he deserves as a literary artist, and is read for what he made as much as for the miscellaneous information he provides.

All quotations from Nashe's writings are taken from *The Works of Thomas Nashe*, Edited from the original Texts by Ronald B. McKerrow: Reprinted from the original edition with corrections and supplementary notes, Edited by F. P. Wilson, Basil Blackwell, Oxford, 1958. I have, however, expanded contracted forms.

# I

## EARLY LIFE

## and *The Anatomy of Absurdity*

### I

BORN in November 1567, Thomas Nashe came from that middle class to which Elizabethan literature, like Elizabethan life in general, owed so much. He was the second son of one William Nashe, a minister at Lowestoft. The exact status of William Nashe is not known. There is no record of his ever having been instituted as vicar of Lowestoft, and it may well be that, as McKerrow suggests, he was a stipendiary curate there.[1] Nashe mentions Lowestoft as the place of his birth in *Nashe's Lenten Stuff*, 'though', he adds, 'my father sprang from the *Nashes* of Herefordshire'.[2] On the face of it the words seem to imply that the family was well known in Herefordshire and of some importance there, but perhaps Nashe intended no more by them than to point out that, though born in Suffolk, he was not of Suffolk extraction. On the title-page of *Pierce Penilesse* and on that of *Strange News* he is described as 'Thomas Nashe, Gentleman', but he disclaims the title in the text of *Strange News*, where he writes of his family:

> Wee can vaunt larger petigrees than patrimonies, yet of such extrinsecall things, common to tenne thousand calues and oxen, would I not willingly vaunt, only it hath pleased M. Printer, both in this booke and *Pierce Pennilesse*, to intaile a vaine title to my name, which I care not for, without my consent or priuitie I here auouch.[3]

[1] V. 3 and note. [2] III. 205. [3] I. 311–12.

These words are worth remembering in any consideration of what may well appear to the modern reader as the snobbish attitude Nashe was to adopt towards the Harvey family. Much as he was to inveigh against 'upstarts', and much as he disapproved of that element in the middle class which devoted itself wholly to the making of money and was actively hostile towards the arts, Nashe never suggested that his own origins were anything other than they were.

The first six years of his life were, presumably, spent in Lowestoft, and then in 1573 his father was presented to the living of West Harling in Norfolk, some seven miles east of Thetford, a town Nashe was later to describe as 'ruinous and desolate'.[4] William Nashe remained rector of West Harling until his death in 1587, and there Nashe must have lived from 1573 until he went up to Cambridge in 1581 or 1582. The place seems to have made little impression on him since he never mentions it in his writings. It is possible, however, that it provided him with some of the materials, in the shape of country customs and folk-lore, that he was to use in his play *Summer's Last Will and Testament*. With his native Lowestoft and with Yarmouth he felt some real ties. Much of *Lenten Stuff* is devoted to the praise of Yarmouth, and fishermen are the one class of people for whom he expresses nothing but admiration.

It is not known where Nashe went to school or, indeed, whether he went to school at all. The only school of any size in the neighbourhood was at Thetford, too far away to be attended daily by a boy. In the circumstances McKerrow's guess that Nashe was educated by his father at home seems a likely one.[5] Whatever the nature of his formal education was, it proved sufficient to enable him to matriculate as a sizar of St. John's College, Cambridge, on 13 October 1582. Something can, however, be deduced about a less academic sort of education which he was busy acquiring for himself during these early years and which he was to put to good use later in his career. In the course of a rambling and humorous disquisition on the causes and significance of dreams in his pamphlet, *The Terrors of the Night*, published in 1594, he inserts a short autobiographical passage, which runs as follows:

> I haue heard aged mumping beldams as they sat warming their knees ouer a coale scratch ouer the argument verie curiously, and

[4] III. 156. [5] V. 6.

> they would bid yong folks beware on what day they par'd their nayles, tell what luck euerie one should haue by the day of the weeke he was born on; show how many yeares a man should liue by the number of wrinkles on his forhead, and stand descanting not a litle of the difference in fortune when they are turnd vpward, and when they are bent downward; him that had a wart on his chin, they would confidently assertaine he should haue no need of anie of his kin: marry, they would likewise distinguish betweene the standing of the wart on the right side and on the left. When I was a little childe, I was a great auditor of theirs, and had all their witchcrafts at my fingers endes, as perfit as good morrow and good euen.[6]

The boy who listened so eagerly and so carefully to the gossip of old women was never to lose his interest in the things that ordinary people talked about and in the way they talked about them. Much of the effect that Nashe's prose produces comes from his readiness to make use of the popular idiom, the proverbial saying, the vivid slangy phrase that seems to have been caught from the lips of the people. In reading him it is hard to resist the conclusion that he constantly kept his ears open for such things, and it looks very much as though the habit of doing so was formed in these early years.

According to his own account in *Lenten Stuff*, Nashe spent nearly seven years at St. John's and, from what he says of it there, it is plain that he was proud of his college and especially of its reputation for learning. After quoting from Roger Ascham's *The Schoolmaster*, he continues thus:

> Well, he was her Maiesties Schoolemaster, and a *S. Iohns* man in Cambridge, in which house once I tooke vp my inne for seuen yere together lacking a quarter, and yet loue it still, for it is and euer was the sweetest nurse of knowledge in all that Vniuersity.[7]

In another of his works, *Have With You to Saffron-Walden*, Nashe gives the impression that his own Cambridge career was a successful one. Answering a gibe of Gabriel Harvey's, suggesting that his father had been too poor to give him a proper education, he writes:

> My Father . . . brought me vp at *S. Iohns*, where (it is well knowen) I might haue been Fellow if I had would.[8]

It is important to remember, however, that by the time he wrote *Lenten Stuff* Nashe had been away from Cambridge for ten years

[6] I. 369. [7] III. 181. [8] III. 127.

and that in *Have With You to Saffron-Walden* he was more concerned with scoring off Gabriel Harvey than with strict accuracy. He was proud of his college and of its fame, but it is very much open to doubt whether he was either as satisfied with it when he was there, or as successful in it, as the passages quoted above would lead one to believe. A more accurate picture of his reactions to Cambridge is provided by his remarks on it in the preface which he wrote for Robert Greene's *Menaphon*, published in 1589, only a year after he had gone down. There he gives a glowing account of the part that St. John's played in the revival of classical learning in the days of Cheke and Ascham, when it

> was as an Vniuersity within it selfe, shining so farre aboue all other houses, Halles, and hospitals whatsoeuer, that no Colledge in the Towne was able to compare with the tithe of her Students; hauing (as I haue heard graue men of credite report) moe Candles light in it, euery Winter morning before foure of the clocke, then the foure of the clocke bell gaue strokes.[9]

This encomium, however, is merely the prelude to an attack, for, after relating the part played by men from St. John's in spreading sounder methods of scholarship throughout the University as a whole, he voices strong criticism of Cambridge, as he knew it, when he writes:

> But how ill their precepts haue prospered with our idle age, that leaue the fountaines of Sciences, to follow the riuers of Knowledge, their ouer-fraught studies with trifling compendiaries may testifie: for I know not how it commeth to passe, by the doting practise of our Diuinitie Dunces, that striue to make their pupills pulpit-men before they are reconciled to *Priscian*; but those yeares which should bee imployed in *Aristotle* are expired in Epitomies, and well too, they may haue so much Catechisme vacation, to rake vp a little refuse philosophy.[10]

At the time when he wrote these words Nashe was busy establishing himself in the public eye as a satirist, but something more than the conventional lament for the degeneracy of the present, which is part of the satirist's stock-in-trade, is involved in the charge that learning at Cambridge had by this time become superficial and utilitarian. Round about 1540 the enthusiasm for classical studies in particular and for new learning in general reached its

[9] III. 317. [10] III. 317–18.

height in the University and, above all, in St. John's. There followed a natural decline, accelerated by the troubles and difficulties caused by the religious changes of the middle of the century, and by the pressing need of the Elizabethan Church for parsons. As a consequence, theology and its handmaid, dialectic, became the main subjects of study at both universities during the latter half of the sixteenth century, and the study of Greek and Hebrew suffered a considerable set-back.[11]

Both the tendency of the state to see the universities as forcing-houses for parsons and the increased emphasis on disputatious theology were reinforced at the beginning of Elizabeth's reign by the return to this country of scholars who had had to flee abroad during the Marian persecutions. Their period of exile, spent in Switzerland or Germany, had confirmed their Calvinist views, and when they came back they quickly set about the task of winning over Cambridge to their cause. Their power in the University increased rapidly during the first fifteen or sixteen years following Elizabeth's accession to the throne, and they were particularly active in St. John's. James Pilkington, Master of the College from 1559 to 1561, and his brother Leonard, who followed him from 1561 to 1564, were both Puritans, and under them the College became a centre of Puritan influence. From 1574 onwards attempts were made 'to root out Puritanism in St. John's College', but they were not successful, and the faction seems to have made a further advance during the mastership of William Whitaker (1586–95).[12] In such circumstances it is not surprising that the struggle for power between the adherents of the Established Church and the disciples of Geneva should have been the main concern of the University.

Closely connected with the growth of Puritanism at Cambridge was the cult of Ramistic logic there. In the first place Ramus, who perished in the Bartholomew massacre, had himself been a Calvinist. More important, however, as a reason for his vogue at Cambridge was the fact that his *Dialectica*, a simplified and shortened version of Aristotle's *Logic*, seemed to provide a short-cut to knowledge, especially to the understanding of theology, and

[11] See J. B. Mullinger, *The University of Cambridge*, Cambridge, 1884, vol. II, pp. 416–20.

[12] See *The Three Parnassus Plays*, ed. J. B. Leishman, London, 1949, pp. 68–71.

a quick way of mastering the art of dialectical argument. Sir William Temple, a leader of the Ramist movement and a fellow of King's, was a tutor in logic from 1576 to 1585 and in 1584 he published an annotated edition of the *Dialectica*, which enjoyed a great success. The reactions of the more orthodox to the new movement, which met much opposition, are described by Hardin Craig. He writes:

> Men of conservative cast who believed in an established agency for the determination of learned, particularly theological, questions were naturally disgusted by the spectacle; no small part of the censure of Ramus by men like Hooker is due to their resentment at his spreading the plague of superficial and pretentious disputation.[13]

Nashe was no Hooker, but in this matter he was at one with him. There can be no doubt whatever about his dislike of Ramus. He alludes to him on several occasions, twice slightingly in *The Anatomy of Absurdity*[14] and again with scorn in *An Almond for a Parrot*,[15] both of which appeared before he became embroiled with the Harveys, whose approval of Ramus was one of their offences in his eyes. Conservative and traditionalist in his attitude to learning he is always on the side of Aristotle. Whether he really understood the issues involved in the dispute between Aristotelians and Ramists is another matter. For him the connection between Ramus and Puritanism would have been quite sufficient to enable him to decide where he stood. What his feelings towards Puritanism were when he went up to Cambridge we do not know, but by the time he left he was a most determined opponent of it.

More than a dislike of Ramistic logic is involved in Nashe's criticism of his old university in the passage from his preface to *Menaphon* quoted above. It is one of several occasions on which he protests against the use of the university as a kind of parson-factory and against the neglect of the arts which this utilitarian purpose led to. In *Christ's Tears Over Jerusalem* he laments the lack of fire and spirit in the writings of those who sought to defend the orthodox religious views of the time against the Puritans, and then goes on to say this:

> So many Dunces in Cambridge and Oxford are entertayned as chiefe members into societies, vnder pretence, though they haue

[13] Hardin Craig, *The Enchanted Glass* (New York, 1936), Oxford, 1950, pp. 150–1.

[14] I. 43 and 45. [15] III. 368.

> no great learning, yet there is in them zeale and Religion, that scarce the least hope is left vs, we should haue any heereafter but blockes and Images, to confute blocks and Images, That of *Terence* is oraculiz'd, *Patres aequum censere nos adolescentulos ilico a pueris fieri senes.* Our Fathers are now growne to such austeritie, as they would haue vs straite of chyldren to become old-men. They will allowe no time for a gray bearde to grow in. If at the first peeping out of the shell a young Student sets not a graue face on it, or seemes not mortifiedly religious, (haue he neuer so good a witte, be hee neuer so fine a Scholler,) he is cast of and discouraged. They sette not before theyr eyes how all were not called at the first houre of the day, for then had none of vs euer beene called.[16]

It is possible that nothing more than a general reflection may be contained in this passage, but the words do seem to have the bitterness of personal feeling. If this is so, they may well provide one of the reasons why Nashe, after taking his B.A. in 1586, eventually left the university in the summer or autumn of 1588 without taking the M.A. Elizabeth Cooper, writing in 1737, states in her account of Nashe that he 'was designed for Holy Orders'.[17] She gives no authority for the statement, but it could well be true. Nashe's father was a clergyman and the Church was the usual destination of young men who stayed on at the university after taking their first degree. Moreover, Nashe himself says he might have been a fellow of St. John's 'if I had would'.[18] If we replace 'I' by 'they', we probably arrive at the truth. Nashe would have stayed on at Cambridge had his college given him help and encouragement. They did not do so because he had not set a grave face on it and had not seemed mortifiedly religious. In a college with strong Puritan leanings he was not welcome.

The hypothesis fits in well both with what we know about Nashe's other reason for leaving Cambridge and about his conduct while he was there. He needed a fellowship, because his father had died in 1587 and, consequently, he was short of money.[19] He seems to be alluding to his situation at this time in a passage in *The Anatomy of Absurdity* which has much in common with that quoted above from *Christ's Tears over Jerusalem.* Regretting for the first, but by no means the last, time in his writings the decay

[16] II. 122–3. [17] V. 157. [18] See p. 3 *supra*.
[19] V. 11.

of learning and the unwillingness of men of means to help poor scholars, he writes as follows:

> Learning now adaies gets no liuing if it come empty handed. Promotion which was wont to be the free propounded palme of paines, is by many mens lamentable practise, become a purchase. When as wits of more towardnes shal haue spent some time in the Vniuersitie, and haue as it were tasted the elements of Arte, and laide the foundation of knowledge, if by the death of some friend they shoulde be withdrawne from theyr studies, as yet altogether raw, and so consequently vnfitte for any calling in the Common wealth, where should they finde a friend to be vnto them in steed of a father, or one to perfit that which their deceased parents begun: nay they may well betake themselues to some trade of Husbandry, for any maintenance they gette in the way of almes at the Vniuersitie, or els take vppon them to teach, beeing more fitte to be taught, and perch into the pulpit, their knowledge beeing yet vnperfit, verie zealouslie preaching, beeing as yet scarce grounded in religious principles. How can those men call home the lost sheepe that are gone astray, comming into the Ministery before their wits be staid?[20]

Here again a note of bitterness and disappointment makes itself heard. Nashe clearly felt that the university had failed him at a time when he most needed its help, and that it had done so because he was not prepared to be a hypocrite.

Such a view of his reasons for leaving Cambridge does not conflict with the most important piece of independent evidence on the matter that we have. It is contained in *The Trimming of Thomas Nashe*, published in 1597. The work is an attack on Nashe, and in it the author accuses him of 'diuers misdemeanors' while he was a student. Some of the charges made against him, such as the accusation that 'he florished in all impudencie towards Schollers, and abuse to the Townsmen' are very vague and could be levelled at any student of spirit at any time. More specific is the statement that he

> had a hand in a Show called *Terminus et non terminus*, for which his partener in it was expelled the Colledge: but this foresaid *Nashe* played in it (as I suppose) the Varlet of Clubs; which he acted with such naturall affection, that all the spectators tooke him to be the verie same. Then suspecting himselfe that he should be staied for *egregie dunsus*, and not attain to the next Degree, said he

[20] I. 37.

had commenst enough, and so forsooke *Cambridge*, being Batchelor of the third yere.[21]

The remark about Nashe's playing 'the Varlet of Clubs' is obviously a joke, but equally obviously the writer does know something about his university career in general, and there is no reason to distrust his statement that Nashe had a hand in the staging, if not in the writing, of a play. It is exactly what might be expected of one who was always on the side of cakes and ale. It is also the kind of activity which would not have commended Nashe to the authorities of his college. It seems practically certain that he left Cambridge in 1588 of his own volition. Even the author of *The Trimming* does not suggest that he was expelled. The death of his father had left him without support, and his own character and behaviour had ensured that his college, with its strong Puritan leanings, would do nothing for him. He accepted the inevitable and went.

For a young man with some education, a lively wit and a ready pen, but no influential backing, London was the only place offering any prospects at all, and accordingly it was to London that Nashe made his way in the summer or autumn of 1588. In doing so he was following the example of two other Cambridge men. Robert Greene, who had taken his B.A. in 1578, had been there since 1585 and was making a living of sorts out of the writing of romances. Christopher Marlowe had gone there only a year before Nashe, after receiving the M.A. in very unusual circumstances, and had at once made a name for himself with his play *Tamburlaine the Great*. In due course Nashe came to know both of them. Indeed, he may have known Marlowe and even been friendly with him while they were still at Cambridge, since their careers there overlapped for some five years between 1582 and 1587, but we have no evidence on the matter. We do know, however, that the conservative and orthodox Nashe did not share or approve of Marlowe's sceptical tendencies, which he attacks in both *Pierce Penilesse* and *Christ's Tears*. We know also that they had become friends some time before Marlowe's death in 1593. Whenever Nashe mentions Marlowe by name in his writings it is with affection and admiration. In *Lenten Stuff* he refers to him as a 'diuiner

[21] V. 9.

Muse' than Musaeus[22] and in *Have With You to Saffron-Walden* he writes:

> I neuer abusd *Marloe*, *Greene*, *Chettle* in my life, nor anie of my frends that vsde me like a frend; which both *Marloe* and *Greene* (if they were aliue) vnder their hands would testifie, euen as *Harry Chettle* hath in a short note here.[23]

Whatever their differences in religious matters may have been, the two men were drawn together by their love of poetry and their devotion to the liberal arts, as well as by their dislike of Puritans, hypocrites and money-grubbers.

Whether Nashe had Marlowe's example in mind or not when he went to London, there is a strong likelihood that he had already decided on his future career some time before leaving Cambridge. The earliest of his extant works to be written, though not the first to appear in print, was *The Anatomy of Absurdity*. It was entered in the Stationers' Register on 19 September 1588, and must, therefore, have been completed by that date. He describes the circumstances in which it was composed as follows:

> I, hauing laide aside my grauer studies for a season, determined with my selfe beeing idle in the Countrey, to beginne in this vacation, the foundation of a trifling subiect, which might shroude in his leaues, the abusiue enormities of these our times.[24]

This can only mean that the work was written, probably at West Harling where Nashe may well have found time hanging on his hands, during a vacation from Cambridge, so that the latest date for its composition would be the summer of 1588. As he had almost certainly left Cambridge by then, however, the summer of 1587 seems more likely.

## 2

*The Anatomy of Absurdity* is very much a young man's work and has little literary merit. Indeed, almost any bright student with an interest in letters and a certain amount of self-confidence could have written most of it, and no one but such a student would have had the effrontery to publish it. Nashe judges, condemns and dismisses the work of others and, at the same time, purveys platitudinous moral advice with the brash readiness of inexperience.

[22] III. 195. [23] III. 131. [24] I. 9.

The pamphlet aroused no interest when it came out, or at any time afterwards. Only one edition was published, some of the copies bearing the date 1589 and some the date 1590. Even Nashe himself, who was well aware of the value of self-advertisement, mentions it only once in his other works. He contrived to insert a little puff for it at the end of his *Preface to 'Menaphon'*, which appeared late in 1589 a few months before the publication of the *Anatomy* early in the following year. Much of the *Preface* is given over to an attack on bad writers, and at the end of it Nashe makes the following appeal to the reader:

> Reade fauourably, to incourage me in the firstlings of my folly, and perswade your selues, I will persecute those idiots and their heires vnto the third generation, that haue made Art bankerout of her ornaments, and sent Poetry a begging vp and downe the Countrey. It may be, my *Anatomie of Absurdities* may acquaint you ere long with my skill in surgery, wherein the diseases of Art more merrily discouered may make our maimed Poets put together their blankes vnto the building of an Hospitall.[25]

The claim that the *Anatomy* contains merriment of any kind is bogus. Nashe presumably made it, because he had already come to realize that the pamphlet had no positive virtues of its own to commend it and, perhaps, also that its preaching tone and affected moral gravity were hardly consonant with the image of himself as a wit, a humorist and Bohemian man of letters that he was now busy creating. The claim was, in any case, of no avail, and after this one attempt to do something for his first-born he very sensibly forgot it and abandoned it to its fate.

Badly organized, almost entirely second-hand and, alone of Nashe's works, drearily dull, the *Anatomy*, nevertheless, warrants some critical discussion. In the first place it is of interest, because it demonstrates that even at this stage in his career—and he was not yet twenty when he began it—he had already decided that prose was to be his medium, the pamphlet his chief means of expression and 'satire', in some form or other, his vein. In part at least the form he chose to write in, like his title, was the result of a natural desire to be fashionable. As McKerrow points out,[26] 'Anatomies' of one kind and another proliferated during the second half of the sixteenth century, especially after the success of Lyly's

[25] III. 324. [26] IV. 3.

*Euphues, The Anatomy of Wit*, first published in 1578. With its scientific implications that the writer is a surgeon dissecting and revealing, the word 'anatomy' appealed both to those who were interested in the analysis of sentiment and to those who liked to be censorious. Taking the number of the 'anatomies' which preceded Nashe's into account, McKerrow further concludes that it is almost impossible to say which, if any, of them he had in mind when he chose his title, but that Lyly's *Euphues* seems on the whole the most likely, because of Nashe's obvious debt to it for the style he employs.

On this matter it seems to me that McKerrow was mistaken, and that F. J. Furnivall was right, in stating that Nashe was alluding to Philip Stubbs's *The Anatomy of Abuses*, first published in 1583.[27] It is interesting in this connection that, to judge from the reference he makes to it in the *Preface to 'Menaphon'*, Nashe seems to have thought of his own work as the *Anatomy of Absurdities*, a title which would make its relationship to Stubbs's pamphlet even more pointed. This, however, is a minor point; what really matters is that Nashe, in putting on 'this *satyricall* disguise', as he calls it,[28] was not only being fashionable, but was also making a protest that is of some importance in the history of Elizabethan literature. The previous ten years or so had seen the publication of many pamphlets, written from what may loosely be described as the Puritan point of view (the word 'Puritan' implying here moral austerity and not necessarily an adherence to Calvinism), in which poetry in general, the stage, May-games and traditional sports and pastimes had been the object of indiscriminate attack along with real social and economic evils. In fact it would not be an overstatement to say that in this period 'satire' had largely become the preserve of the more ascetic section of the population, and that there was a real danger of the creative impulses being stifled. Apart from Sir Philip Sidney's *Apology for Poetry* which, though written about 1583, was not published until 1595, such defences of poetry as were written were half-hearted and completely lacking in any offensive spirit, such as characterized the works they were designed to answer. Stubbs's *Anatomy of Abuses* had been the most successful of the Puritan onslaughts and had gone through four editions

[27] *Phillip Stubbs's Anatomy of the Abuses in England in Shakespere's Youth, A.D.* 1583, *Part* 1, ed. F. J. Furnivall, London, 1877–9, p. 36.
[28] I. 5.

by 1585. Nashe's title is meant to remind the reader of Stubbs's, because his main purpose in writing the *Anatomy of Absurdity* was, as it seems to me, to produce an anti-satire, to turn the weapon against those who had been using it for narrow and sectarian ends and to make it serve a more liberal and humanistic cause.

The second section of Nashe's pamphlet, which is the core of the whole, is devoted to a thorough-going assault on Stubbs and his like, introduced by a punning reference to the man and his book. Having dealt in his first section with the writers of romances, Nashe continues thus:

> I leaue these in their follie, and hasten to other mens furie, who make the Presse the dunghill whether they carry all the muck of their mellancholicke imaginations, pretending forsooth to anatomize abuses and stubbe vp sin by the rootes, when as there waste paper beeing wel viewed, seemes fraught with nought els saue dogge daies effects, who wresting places of Scripture against pride, whoredome, couetousnes, gluttonie, and drunkennesse, extend their inuectiues so farre against the abuse, that almost the things remaines not whereof they admitte anie lawfull vse.[29]

It is a good beginning; Nashe has picked out the weakest point in the enemies' position, their lack of discrimination and the wholesale nature of their strictures. He goes on to accuse them of being inadequately educated and of relying almost entirely on second-hand material, but he is also aware of the influence they have on the more ignorant, 'whom with a coloured shew of zeale, they allure vnto them to their illusion'.[30]

There is, in fact, a genuine concern in the *Anatomy of Absurdity* about what Nashe felt to be an abuse of the press by the unscrupulous, the narrow-minded and the ignorant, and it was not unfounded. Similar in kind, though, of course, less profound and narrower in scope than Pope's a hundred and forty years later, this concern led Nashe to try to write a sixteenth-century *Dunciad*, as he makes plain at the beginning where he announces his intention

> to take a view of sundry mens vanitie, a suruey of their follie, a briefe of their barbarisme, to runne through Authors of the absurder sort, assembled in the Stacioners shop, sucking and selecting out of these vpstart antiquaries, somewhat of their vnsauery duncerie, meaning to note it with a *Nigrum theta*, that

[29] I. 19–20.

[30] I. 21.

each one at the first sight may eschew it as infectious, to shewe it to the worlde that all men may shunne it.[31]

In the execution of this plan Nashe, again like Pope, finds it impossible to restrict himself to bad writers. Before he has finished dealing with Stubbs books are left behind, and he launches out into a number of topics, only some of which have any close relationship with the subject he had proposed for himself. The Puritans are accused of hypocrisy in their whole way of living; writers of almanacs are taken to task for perverting 'the sacred Science of Astronomie' and misleading the simple-minded; ballad-makers are condemned for prostituting poetry, because they show no art in their writings and are actuated only by the desire for gain. And then, fearing that he may have created the wrong impression, Nashe proceeds to an eloquent defence of true poetry, treating it along familiar Renaissance lines as the most effective form of moral philosophy. There is much of the high-minded and the highfaluting in his insistence that the only real poetry is that which is based on sound learning and studied artifice, but the apology is conducted with a fire and enthusiasm that is reminiscent of Sidney's. The subject of poetry leads on to a disquisition on the value of study, and that in turn to some very didactic and complacent advice to students on the best methods of study.

It is all something of a jumble, but out of it do emerge certain values which were to lie behind much of Nashe's subsequent satire. The two things that matter most to him are learning and poetry. By learning he means the traditional orthodox education of the day, based on the study of Aristotle, of logic and of rhetoric. He sees it threatened by Duncery, Absurdity and Barbarism, which really amount to much the same thing, the arrogant expression of opinion by writers and preachers on matters of which they have only an inadequate and superficial knowledge. There are other enemies as well: first, those who would make education serve practical and utilitarian, rather than humanistic ends; secondly 'money', of which Nashe writes as follows:

Such couetous ignorance dooth creepe amongst the cormorants of our age, who as the *Chamelion* which is fed with the ayre, stands alwaies with his mouth wide open, so these men which liue vpon

[31] I. 9.

> almes, haue alwaies their mouthes open to aske, and hauing felt the sweetnes of Abby Landes, they gape after Colledge liuing, desiring to enrich themselves as much with the siluer of the one, as their auncesters got by the gold of the other.[32]

Nashe is referring in this passage to the proposals made by some of the more extreme Puritans, shortly before his *Anatomy* was written, that the universities should be abolished because of their popish origins; a project which makes one realize how urgent it was that this kind of lunatic fanaticism should be opposed.

Poetry, the free life of the spirit, is menaced, as Nashe sees it, by the same enemies as learning. Duncery, as seen in the work of the writers of popular ballads, whom he always despised, perverts it and brings it into ill repute, 'money' would do away with it altogether as unprofitable, and the Puritans would suppress it as a source of immorality and a waste of time.

It is to Nashe's credit that he saw so clearly that a counter-attack was needed and that he made it. Unfortunately, however, he blunts its effect badly by setting off on the wrong foot and taking up the same kind of indiscriminately negative attitude that he was about to condemn in Stubbs and his like. Their shortcoming as 'satirists' was, as he realized, that they were still writing what John Peter has described as 'complaint', general attacks on general vices, couched in traditional terms and untouched by wit or humour.[33] But, while appreciating this weakness in the enemy, he does not, as yet, see how to remedy it in his own work and does the same thing himself. At the head of his dunces he puts the contemporary writers of romances. Their offence in his eyes is that they do not tell the truth, or write about things as they are, but do their best to keep alive the outworn tradition of courtly love and the mediaeval taste for the marvellous. He accuses them of seeking

> to repaire the ruinous wals of *Venus* Court, to restore to the worlde that forgotten Legendary licence of lying, to imitate a fresh the fantasticall dreames of those exiled Abbie-lubbers, from whose idle pens proceeded those worne out impressions of the feyned no where acts, of Arthur of the rounde table, Arthur of litle Brittaine, sir Tristram, Hewon of Burdeaux, the Squire of low degree, the foure sons of Amon, with infinite others.[34]

[32] I. 36.

[33] John Peter, *Complaint and Satire in Early English Literature*, Oxford, 1956, passim.

[34] I. 11.

The passage has behind it just that arrogant and contemptuous attitude to the Middle Ages which C. S. Lewis has picked out as one of the worst features of sixteenth-century humanism.[35] It also suffers from exactly the same fault that Nashe finds in Stubbs's pamphlet, in that it does no more than 'teare that peecemeale wise, which long since by ancient wryters was wounded to the death'.[36] Nashe has merely expanded the well known denunciation of works of this kind in Ascham's *The Schoolmaster*.[37] Worse still, he has failed to realize that in some matters the humanists, whom he admires for their learning, are on the same side as the Puritans, whom he hates for their barbarism. The only thing in the whole attack that rings true and is not part of the 'satyricall disguise', or pose, is his obvious preference for realism.

The second charge Nashe brings against the writers of romances is that they pervert the truth for the sake of popularity by consistently praising and flattering the female characters in their works in order to attract and please women readers. The accusation is not altogether wide of the mark. Lyly, Greene and those who imitated them were well aware that there was a female reading public, and they did their best to cultivate it. But what Nashe failed to see, or, perhaps, deliberately chose to ignore, was that the effect this preoccupation with women readers had on their work was, on the whole, a good one. Prose became more polished and civilized because of it, stories more concerned with the expression and analysis of feeling. In any case, however, it is very doubtful whether he really cared about whether the romance writers told the truth about women or not. His attack on them on this score is merely the pretext for a lengthy re-hash of some hackneyed anti-feminist matter, much of it deriving ultimately from the Fathers of the Church, which he had culled from his reading and had lying by him waiting to be used. All this is 'complaint' in its worst form and it makes hypocritical nonsense of Nashe's accusation that Stubbs and his like

> that neuer tasted of any thing saue the excrements of Artes, whose thredde-bare knowledge beeing bought at the second hand, is spotted, blemished, and defaced, through translaters rigorous rude

[35] C. S. Lewis, *English Literature in the Sixteenth Century*, Oxford, 1954, pp. 19–31. [36] I. 20.

[37] Roger Ascham, *The Scholemaster*, ed. E. Arber, London, 1932, pp. 79–81.

> dealing, shoulde preferre their fluttered sutes before other mens glittering gorgious array, should offer them water out of a muddie pit, who haue continually recourse to the Fountaine, or dregs to drink, who haue wine to sell.[38]

The author of the *Anatomy* could ill afford to charge any other writer with plagiarism, since his own work, as McKerrow shows conclusively in his notes to it, is a cento of passages taken from writers as diverse as Erasmus and Brian Melbancke.

It is all very dreary, not because it is second-hand—Nashe was a great borrower throughout his literary career—but because it has merely been taken over without undergoing any radical change at all. In his subsequent writings he makes second-hand material his own by applying it in an unexpected way, by jazzing-up its phraseology to give it a new and exciting appearance, or by relating it to the life he knew. But in the *Anatomy* his own voice is hardly heard. Seeking to be fashionable, he adopts the style made popular by Lyly's *Euphues* and works it to death. Later in his career, when Gabriel Harvey taunted him with having modelled his style on *Euphues*, Nashe denied that he had done so, and wrote in *Strange News*:

> *Euphues* I readd when I was a little ape in Cambridge, and then I thought it was *Ipse ille*: it may be excellent good still, for ought I know, for I lookt not on it this ten yeare: but to imitate it I abhorre, otherwise than it imitates *Plutarch*, *Ouid*, and the choisest Latine Authors.[39]

So far as the *Anatomy* is concerned, this statement is false. He obviously had *Euphues* in mind while writing it, and at one point it may well have been in his hand, since he takes a passage from it and stands it on its head.[40]

Much more is involved, however, than any mere correspondence of specific passages. From the beginning of the *Anatomy* to the end there is evidence on every page that Nashe had put himself to school to Lyly and had assiduously learnt his tricks. A passage from the dedication will serve to illustrate the point:

> For my part, as I haue no portion in any mans opinion, so am I the *Prorex* of my priuate thought: which makes me terme poyson poyson, as well in a siluer peece, as in an earthen dish, and *Protaeus*

[38] I. 20–1 [39] I. 319.

[40] I. 11. ll. 22–8. The corresponding passage in Lyly is quoted by McKerrow in his note at IV. 12.

*Protaeus* though girt in the apparrell of *Pactolus*. Howe euer the Syren change her shape, yet is she inseperable from deceit, and how euer the deuill alter his shaddowe, yet will he be found in the end to be a she Saint. I dare not prefixe a *Nigrum theta* to all of that sexe, least immortalitie might seeme to haue beene taxt by my slaunder, and the puritie of heauen bepudled by my vnhallowed speeche. Onely this shall my arguments inferre, and my anger auerre, that constancie will sooner inhabite the body of a Camelion, a Tyger or a Wolfe, then the hart of a woman; who predestinated by the father of eternitie, euen in the nonage of nature, to be the *Iliads* of euils to all Nations haue neuer inuerted their creation in any Countrey but ours.[41]

The unrelenting use of antithesis, the piling-up of instances, the elaborate alliteration, the use of rhyme, the references to mythology and to the Elizabethan zoo all point to the same model. Nashe had little reason to mock, as he does, at those who were fond of alluding in their writings to 'Minerals, stones, and herbes'.[42] He does it himself in circumstances where it is far more inappropriate than it is in the romances of the day. The Euphuistic manner has its virtues as an instrument for the analysis of sentiment, but it is completely at odds with the satirical purpose for which Nashe tries to use it. It weakens the force of his satire and blunts its edge. The sword he waves is sheathed in cotton wool. His complaints only take on relevance and reality when the diction of common speech ruffles the smooth surface of literary artifice and he writes of what he has seen as distinct from what he has read. This happens when he writes:

Young men thinke it a disgrace to youth, to embrace the studies of age, counting their fathers fooles whiles they striue to make them wise, casting that away at a cast at dice, which cost theyr daddes a yeares toyle, spending that in their Veluets, which was rakt vppe in a Russette coat.[43]

Before he could become the satirist he wanted to be, Nashe needed to see life at first-hand as well as through the spectacles of books, and he needed, above all, to forge a distinctive style of his own, capable of rendering his perceptions in a sharp, distinctive and striking manner. In fact, the move from Cambridge to London was precisely what he required, and he arrived in London at the best possible time for a would-be, anti-Puritan pamphleteer.

[41] I. 5–6. [42] I. 10. [43] I. 33.

# II

# LONDON AND THE MARPRELATE CONTROVERSY

## I

THE entry of *The Anatomy of Absurdity* in the Stationers' Register on 19 September 1588 almost certainly means that Nashe had arrived in London by that time. It was a rather propitious moment for a young man who hoped to make his living by his pen. The theatre was becoming popular and there was a demand for plays, while the pamphleteer, provided he was on the right side, was about to find official support for his activities. He certainly needed it. The usual price paid for a pamphlet by the printer was two pounds. This sum secured him all rights in it. The only further profit the author could look for was the reward, either in the shape of money or favour and place, that he might obtain from the patron to whom he dedicated it. As a consequence the great, and many of the less great, were bombarded with dedications, and by the time Nashe came upon the literary scene they were becoming wary of new writers. Seen from one point of view, his literary career appears as an unavailing search for a suitable patron, leading ultimately to the conviction that, so far as he was concerned, there was no such thing and that the only patron worth cultivating was the reading public.[1]

*The Anatomy of Absurdity* was dedicated to Sir Charles Blount,

[1] On the profession of letters at this time see: Phoebe Sheavyn, *The Literary Profession in the Elizabethan Age*, Manchester, 1909; J. W. Saunders, 'The Stigma of Print', *Essays in Criticism*, I (1951), 139–64;

who seems to have had a good reputation as a patron of letters. Perhaps he was a good critic also and decided that it was worth little or nothing. At any rate Nashe dedicated no further works to him, which argues that his reception of the *Anatomy* was not a very encouraging one. *Pierce Penilesse* was dedicated to one Amyntas, whose identity is uncertain, but who was most likely Ferdinando Stanley, Earl of Derby. Like Sir Charles Blount, Stanley was regarded as a friend of poets, but he appears to have been no more friendly disposed to Nashe than Blount had been, since Nashe made no further appeals to his generosity. He was more fortunate, however, in his relations with the Careys. Sir George Carey was in 1592 Captain-General of the Isle of Wight, and in his house Nashe composed *Strange News.* He went on to dedicate *Christ's Tears over Jerusalem* to Sir George's wife, Lady Elizabeth Carey, and *The Terrors of the Night* to Mistress Elizabeth Carey, their only daughter. In the course of the latter work, he writes of the Careys and their home in a way that makes it plain that, until they helped him, he had sought for patronage in vain and that all his hopes of favour and preferment had been disappointed. Here is part of what he says:

> The next plague and the neerest that I know in affinitie to a consumption, is long depending hope friuolously defeated, than which there is no greater miserie on earth; and so *per consequens* no men in earth more miserable than courtiers. It is a cowardly feare that is not resolute inough to despaire. It is like a pore hunger-starud wretch at sea, who still in expectation of a good voyage, endures more miseries than Iob. He that writes this can tell, for he hath neuer had good voyage in his life but one, and that was to a fortunate blessed Iland, nere those pinacle rocks called the Needles. O, it is a purified Continent, and a fertil plot fit to seat another Paradice, where, or in no place, the image of the ancient hospitalitie is to be found.
>
> While I liue I will praise it and extoll it, for the true magnificence and continued honourable bountie that I saw there.[2]

What brought his connection with the Careys to an end is not known, but when *The Unfortunate Traveller* came out in 1594 it bore a dedication to Henry Wriothesley, the Earl of Southampton.

---

E. H. Miller, *The Professional Writer in Elizabethan England*, Harvard University Press, 1959.

[2] I. 374.

It was Nashe's last genuine dedication. At this point in his career he seems to have decided that the system of patronage was of no help to him. He had already complained repeatedly in one work after another about the stinginess of patrons, now he proceeded to make fun of them. The dedication to *Have With You to Saffron-Walden*, published in 1596, is a mock-dedication. Its recipient is not one of the great, but Richard Lichfield, the barber of Trinity College, and its contents are a wild burlesque of the usual fulsome dedication. It is Nashe's farewell to a system which had provided him with so little return. His last work, *Nashe's Lenten Stuff*, published in 1598, is dedicated to 'Lustie Humfrey', as Nashe calls him, a certain Humphrey King, who was a very minor author but, according to Nashe, 'a King of good fellowshippe by nature'. This dedication takes the form of a gay, but nevertheless telling, attack on would-be patrons who promise much and perform nothing, leading up to the passage that follows:

> Wherefore the premisses considered (I pray you consider of that woord Premisses, for somewhere I haue borrowed it) neither to rich, noble, right worshipfull, or worshipfull, of spirituall or temporall, will I consecrate this woorke, but to thee and thy capering humour alone, that, if thy starres had doone thee right, they should haue made thee one of the mightiest princes of *Germany*; not for thou canst drive a coach or kill an oxe so wel as they, but that thou art neuer wel but when thou art amongst the retinue of the Muses, and there spendest more in the twinckling of an eye, then in a whole yeare thou gettest by some grasierly gentilitie thou followest.[3]

By the time he wrote this Nashe had come to realize that the only patron he could rely on was those who enjoyed reading him, but it took him some seven or eight years to discover it.

In September 1588, however, the position of the pamphleteer was on the point of becoming rather different from what it had been before and was to be afterwards. Ever since the beginning of Elizabeth's reign the rift between the Queen and those who supported the Anglican settlement on the one side, and those on the other who wished to push the Protestant reformation still further, had been widening. It is not my intention to trace the dispute in detail. Suffice it to say that with the publication in 1572 of the

[3] III. 149.

*Admonitions to Parliament* by John Field and Thomas Wilcox the controversy became sharper and more copious. The crucial issues were whether the Church should continue to be governed by bishops, and, closely involved with it, as Elizabeth and her Council were quick to see, whether the state should control the preachers, or the preachers the state. Puritan attacks on the episcopacy and the Elizabethan settlement and Anglican defences of the established church followed one another rapidly. The advantage, however, was with the Puritans, especially after the publication in 1587 of the *Defence of the Government Established* by John Bridges. This enormously long-winded and tedious piece of work did more harm than good to the cause of the establishment. Badly argued and so badly written as to be practically unreadable, it asked to be attacked and presented a wonderful opportunity for someone with a sense of logic, a sense of style and the ability to appeal to the masses.

The opportunity was seized on by a writer of genius, the most effective popular pamphleteer of the sixteenth century. In October or November 1588, there was issued from a secret press the first part of a work with the intriguing title *Oh read ouer D. John Bridges*. The author described himself as 'Martin Marprelate, Gentleman' and he soon followed up the first part of his work, the *Epistle* as it was called, with a second known as the *Epitome*. Six further pamphlets were published, ending with the *Protestations of Martin Marprelate* in September 1589. The identity of Martin has never been finally established, though D. J. McGinn has made out a strong case for John Penry.[4] What matters about him, however, is not who he was, but the fact that he could write, that indirectly he supplied work for some of the professional pamphleteers, including Nashe, and that he had a considerable influence on the development of English prose in the last decade of the sixteenth century.

Where Martin differed from the other controversialists both Puritan and Anglican who had preceded him was in his realization that propaganda is of no avail unless it is read and read widely. It must, therefore, be written in a plain direct style. But even this of itself is not enough. The first requisite is to get a hearing by creating a stir and attracting attention. Martin's main aim in *Oh read ouer D. John Bridges* was to make a noise and cut a figure. He knew

[4] 'The Allegory of the "Beare" and the "Foxe" in Nashe's *Pierce Penilesse*', *P.M.L.A.*, LXI, 1946.

that the task of persuasion could be done later. The method he adopted to reach this end was precisely that which Nashe was to use; he deliberately created a literary personality for himself by his use of language.

The part he cast himself for seems to me to have much in common with that of the Vice on the popular stage. The most self-conscious figure in the early Elizabethan theatre and the main-spring of comedy, the Vice, as he appears in such a play as *Cambyses*, is characterized by his rapid changes of front, his love of mischief, the impudence he shows to his superiors, his fondness for equivocation, verbal ambiguity and *double entendre* and, above all, by the way in which he is constantly drawing the attention of the audience to his shifts and manœuvres and to the skill with which he manages them. Now, Martin, Puritan though he was, knew something about plays. In the *Epistle* he refers to *Gammer Gurton's Needle* with admiration. It had been attributed by some to John Bridges. Martin denies the attribution on literary grounds, and tells Bridges:

> You haue bin a worthy writer as they say of a long time, your first book was a proper Enterlude called Gammar Gurtons needle. But I thinke that this trifle, which sheweth the author to haue had some witte and inuention in him, was none of your doing: Because youre bookes seeme to proceede from the braynes of a woodcocke, as hauing neyther wit nor learning.[5]

Furthermore, Martin knew all about the Vice and about the Lord of Misrule, with whom the Vice had much in common. In *Hay any Worke for Cooper* he tells a story about a parson which begins as follows:

> There is a neighbour of ours, an honest priest, who was sometimes (symple as he now standes) a vice in a play for want of a better, his name is Gliberie of Hawsteade in Essex, he goes much to the pulpit. On a time, I think it was the last Maie, he went vp with a full resolution, to do his businesse with great commendations. But see the fortune of it. A boy in the Church, hearing either the sommer Lord with his Maie game, or Robin Hood with his Morrice daunce going by the Church, out goes the boye. Good Gliberie, though he were in the pulpit, yet had a minde to his olde companions abroad (a company of merrie grigs you must think them to be, as merrie as a vice on a stage) seeing the boy going out,

[5] *An Epistle*, ed. J. Petheram, London, 1843, p. 13.

> finished his matter presently with Iohn of Londons Amen, saying, ha, ye faith boie, are they there, then ha with thee, and so came down and among them hee goes.[6]

It is also worth noting that Martin was familiar with the antics of Tarlton, the most famous clown of the age, and refers to him on several occasions,[7] while his opponents, recognizing his affinity with the great clown, often described him as a 'Tarltonizer'.

Even in the *Epistle*, designed though it was to catch the eye, there is no lack of serious matter along with the fooling. Martin attacks the whole institution of the episcopacy, arguing that there is no warrant whatever for it in the Bible and that, consequently, the authority of bishops is a usurped authority like the Pope's. The established Church is taken to task for its neglect of preaching, the most important of its duties in Puritan eyes, and for its persecution of Puritans who, says Martin, are treated more rigorously than Papists. In fact, there is throughout a very shrewd attempt to make use not only of the anti-papal feeling of the time, but also of that undercurrent of general anti-clericalism which was such a strong force in sixteenth-century England.

All these arguments had, of course, been employed many times before the appearance of the *Epistle*, but never so effectively. It is not Martin's ideas that are novel, but his way of putting them over. He behaves like a bull in a china-shop. At the opening of the *Epistle* he announces his intention 'to play the Duns for the nonce'. He goes on playing it throughout and the methods he uses deserve some examination.

Martin, as he appears in these pamphlets, is a distinct personality. Homely in speech, blunt in manner, he is the plain man who is not afraid to stand up to the great and to tell them home-truths. In this respect he is akin to Skelton's Colin Clout and even, in a distant fashion, to Langland's Piers Plowman. But there is more to him than this. He gives the further impression that he delights in a fight and loves to lay about him, that he is something of a swashbuckler always aware of his audience and ready to give it its money's worth. He specializes in elaborate threats couched in homely terms. In *Hay any Worke for Cooper*, his answer to Bishop Thomas Cooper's *An Admonition to the People of England against*

[6] *Hay any Worke for Cooper*, ed. J. Petheram, London, 1845, pp. 20–1.

[7] E.g. *An Epistle*, pp. 1 and 25 and *Hay any Worke for Cooper*, p. 73.

*Martin Mar-Prelate*, he takes his title from one of the street-cries of the time, and prefaces a counter-argument with these words:

> And hold my cloake there somebody, that I may go roundly to worke. For ise so bumfeg the Cooper, as he had bin better to haue hooped halfe the tubbes in Winchester [Cooper's diocese], then write against my worships pistles.[8]

In such a passage religious controversy takes on the character of a street-brawl, with the readers in the position of interested by-standers who may at any moment become participants, which is just what Martin wanted them to become. He seeks to involve them further by appealing to them to applaud some of his shrewder blows. Having proved to his own satisfaction that the institution of bishops in the Anglican Church is regarded as anti-Christian by most of the other reformed churches, he turns to his audience and says:

> And haue I not quited my selfe like a man, and dealt very valiantly, in prouing that my lerned brethren the Lord bishops ought not to be in any christian common wealth, because they are pettie Popes, and pettie Antichristes.[9]

He addresses his opponents as though they were actually present, using direct, colloquial speech, well stuffed with proverbs and slang, deliberately garbling their names and making up punning titles for them with calculated irreverence. 'Sohow, brother Bridges', he writes, and 'Wohohow, brother London', as though he were starting game in the hunting-field, or calling to a hawk. The archbishop of Canterbury is referred to as 'my Lords grease' and 'his gracelesnes of Canterbury', while the children of Aylmer, the bishop of London, are described as 'all his brood (my Ladle his daughter and all)'. The passage in the *Epistle* in which he takes leave of Bridges will give a good example of his usual quality and, incidentally, illustrate Nashe's debt to him:

> I care not an I now leaue masse Deanes worship, and be eloquent once in my dayes: yet brother Bridges a worde or two more with you, ere we depart, I praye you where may a man buie such another gelding, and borow such another hundred poundes, as you be-stowed vpon your good patron Sir Edward Horsey, for his good work in helping you to your Deanry: go to, go to, I perceiue you will prooue a goose. Deale closeliar for shame the next time: must

[8] *Op. cit.*, pp. 23–4.

[9] *An Epistle*, pp. 9–10.

> I needs come to the knoledge of these things? What if I should report abroad, that cleargie men come vnto their promotions by Simonie? haue not you giuen me iuste cause? I thinke Simonie be the bishops lacky. Tarleton took him not long since in Don Iohn of Londons cellor.[10]

The *Epistle* actually takes the form of a burlesque. It is a mock supplication, which Nashe was to remember when he wrote *Pierce Penilesse*, addressed to

> the right puisante, and terrible priests, my cleargie masters of the confocation house, whether fickers generall, worshipful paltripolitane, or any other of the holy league of subscription.[11]

The ribald tone of this opening is reinforced by Martin's insertion of scandalous tales about his enemies into the main body of the work, and by his gift for humorous invective of an alliterative kind. The bishops are summed up as 'proud popish, presumtuous, profane, paultrie, pestilent and pernicious prelates', and Aylmer is told:

> Walde-graue neuer printed any thing against the state, but onely against the vsurped state of your Paultripolitanship, and your pope holy brethren, the Lord Bishops and your Antichristian swinish rable, being intollerable withstanders of reformation, enemies of the Gospell, and most couetous, wretched, and popish priests.[12]

As well as using considerable literary skill to make his own writings forceful and dramatic, Martin is also an incisive critic of the work of others. Bridges is repeatedly taunted for his 'senceles writing', as Martin calls it, and the inordinate length of his rambling sentences is held up to ridicule. 'Lerned brother Bridges', he is admonished, 'a man might almost run himselfe out of breath before he could come to a full point in many places in your book'.[13] Martin is genuinely interested in prose style, both as a critic and as a craftsman. It is one of the main reasons why he proved such a formidable pamphleteer.

The bishops soon came to see that the official apologists for the church were incapable of meeting the Marprelate challenge. Bishop Cooper's moderate and fair-minded *Admonition* was, as McKerrow says, 'too serious, and appealed to those alone who would rather have been scandalized at Martin's pamphlet than influenced by it. Its circulation must have been among an entirely different class'.[14]

[10] *An Epistle*, p. 25. [11] *Ibid.*, p. 1
[12] *Ibid.*, p. 32. [13] *Ibid.*, p. 15 [14] V. 43.

Therefore, at the suggestion of Richard Bancroft, then canon of Westminster, they decided to meet Martin on his own ground by making use of the services of professional writers, capable of catching the public ear with their pamphlets and plays. The arrangement seems to have been a clandestine one—it could hardly be anything else—and the anti-Martinists received no open support from the church. But there can be no doubt that there was an arrangement,[15] which led in due course to such a violent and irreverent anti-Martinist campaign, carried on in the theatre as well as in the press, that many Anglicans were disgusted with it. Among those hired to write against Martin were John Lyly and Thomas Nashe.

2

Nashe's part in the anti-Martinist campaign was restricted, I believe, to one extant work only, *An Almond for a Parrot*, published in 1590; but there is evidence that he was reading Martin with interest and taking up a hostile attitude to him some time before he wrote this pamphlet. The one work from his pen to come out in 1589 was his *Preface to R. Greene's 'Menaphon'*, his first appearance in print. In the course of it he attacks Martin with considerable force in the kind of language that Martin himself had used. The attack is not out of place in the *Preface*, which is a rather miscellaneous piece of literary satire in any case, and it was natural that Nashe, with his deep-rooted dislike of the Puritans, already so evident in the *Anatomy of Absurdity*, should take the first opportunity that came his way to have a bout with their most effective propagandist. I suspect, however, that his motives were not entirely disinterested, and that he probably intended also to bring himself to the notice of Bancroft and others who were organizing the campaign by giving them a taste of his quality. After observing that shopkeepers are often better critics and have a sounder sense of values than those with a university education who set themselves up as judges of literature, he continues:

> yet those and these are so affectionate to dogged detracting, as the most poysonous *Pasquil* any durty mouthed *Martin* or *Momus* euer composed is gathered vp with greedinesse before it fall to the ground, and bought at the dearest, though they smell of the friplers

[15] V. 44–5.

lauender halfe a yeere after: for I know not how the minde of the meanest is fedde with this folly, that they impute singularity to him that slaunders priuily, and count it a great peece of Art in an inkhorne man, in any tapsterly termes whatsoeuer, to expose his superiours to enuy.[16]

The passage shows that Nashe was interested in Martin's style as well as in his matter, and that, in spite of the scorn he affects for Martin's use of 'tapsterly termes', he was not above learning from him. He has not yet done, of course, with the Euphuistic manner of the *Anatomy of Absurdity*; the *Preface* is full of clever cross alliteration, and the panther is still busy about one of the many curious activities attributed to him in Elizabethan prose; but there is a fresh wind blowing over the faded flowers. Nashe is beginning to use a more colloquial turn of phrase and to avail himself of other kinds of experience as well as those to be found in books. The man who writes, 'they smell of the friplers lauender halfe a yeere after', has been into an old clothes shop. He has also caught Martin's trick of calling attention to his own methods and of deliberately mistaking words. Literary criticism cannot be ignored when it is couched in the terms Nashe uses to describe Stanyhurst's translation of the *Aeneid* into English hexameters:

But Fortune, the Mistrisse of change, with a pittying compassion respecting Maister *Stanihursts* praise, would that *Phaer* should fall that hee might rise, whose heroicall poetry, infired, I should say inspired, with an hexameter furie, recalled to life what euer hissed Barbarisme hath been buried this hundred yeere; and reuiued by his ragged quill such carterly varietie as no hodge plowman in a country but would haue held as the extremitie of clownerie.[17]

Enlivened though it is by patches of writing of this kind, the *Preface to Menaphon* does not really amount to much. Yet it has attracted more attention and been discussed in greater detail than anything else Nashe ever wrote. Mountains of scholarship have been piled on what is in itself a trivial and ephemeral squib. Nor is this surprising, for it is one of the most tantalizing literary documents we have. It appears to be full of promising allusions which, if they could only be interpreted properly, would throw much light on the literary scene as it was in 1589. As soon as any detailed exegesis is attempted, however, difficulties arise. The promising

[16] III. 314–15. [17] III. 319.

allusions prove to be vague, uncertain and ambiguous, a smoke-screen rather than a search-light. Some passages in it and, above all, that which seems to connect the *Ur-Hamlet* with Thomas Kyd, have been critical battle-grounds for over a century, and we seem to be no nearer to any solution of the problems they raise. I have no new interpretations to offer, but I would suggest that the confusion might be less than it is, if more consideration were given to the nature of the *Preface* as a whole. We might then know how seriously, or otherwise, the puzzling allusions deserve to be taken.

The first problem posed by the *Preface* is that of how Nashe ever came to write it. It is not easy to see why a young and untried writer with no publication to his name, should have been asked to contribute a prefatory epistle to a romance by one so experienced and so well established as Greene was in 1589. Odder still is the fact that this same young writer should be one who, to judge by the as yet unpublished *Anatomy*, regarded romances as a waste of time and a disgrace to the cause of letters. Faced with these contradictions, McKerrow was driven to assume that Nashe 'had already won some reputation as a wit',[18] but he fails to provide any evidence for the assumption. A simpler hypothesis would be that Greene, already an expert in the art of publicity and also a kind man in his own improvident fashion to those whom he did not regard as rivals, deliberately gave Nashe the chance to make something of a splash and bring himself before the public eye. In other words, the *Preface* was not intended to help *Menaphon*; Greene's name on the title-page could be relied on to do that; it was intended to help Nashe. At the same time, however, Greene may well have found it convenient to use Nashe as a kind of mouthpiece through whom he might pursue some of his literary quarrels.

Several features of the *Preface* lend colour to this theory. As I have pointed out already, Nashe certainly took advantage of the opportunity to write a puff for his forthcoming *Anatomy of Absurdity*, and there is at least a suspicion that the attack on Martin Marprelate, though sincere enough, may also be a bit of touting for employment in the anti-Martinist campaign. Furthermore, there is in the epistle comparatively little about *Menaphon*. It is not a preface, but a general essay of a discursive and provocative

[18] V. 15.

kind on the state of literature and learning at the time it was written, strongly anti-Puritan, distinctly personal in tone—Nashe uses the first person singular throughout—and idiosyncratic in manner, designed to call attention to the personality of its author.

So far as the matter of the *Preface* is concerned, it is an odd mixture of two different things. On the one hand there is a repetition in an abbreviated form of much that Nashe had already written in the *Anatomy of Absurdity*, on the other there is some new material that seems to reflect the views of Greene and to suggest that Nashe had been much impressed by him. A summary of the *Preface* will serve to make these points clearer. It is addressed, not to the reading public at large, but 'to the gentleman students of both the universities', a phrase that may well have been intended to recall the fact that Greene, as he was so fond of asserting, held the degree of master from Oxford as well as Cambridge. In any case, however, Nashe, unlike Greene, is obviously writing with a highbrow audience in mind. He asks the young men at the universities to welcome *Menaphon* as a work possessing the classical virtues of restraint and moderation, especially evident in its unassuming style, a rare quality in an age so addicted to eloquence and the use of ink-horn terms that even the most pedestrian authors have ceased to use plain English. The main reason for this unfortunate state of things Nashe attributes to the influence of tragic actors whose one concern is to shout their heads off in mouthing bombastic speeches. Even the actors, however, are not so much to blame as the playwrights who encourage them in their extravagant behaviour by writing 'bragging blanke verse'. Moreover, Greene's work has the virtue of originality. Unlike plays, which are laboured centos, compounded 'of the crums that fall from the Translators trencher', *Menaphon* is the product of a ready invention and an 'extemporall veine'.

Out of this praise of Greene's originality Nashe then develops an attack on slow-writing plagiarists who borrow plots from Ariosto and the other Italian writers, cull words and phrases from Cicero and the Latin historians and similes from Plutarch; and, as a kind of counter-irritant to the excessively ornate and elaborate style that results from this method of working, he recommends the reading of popular literature, presumably of the jest book variety, since he describes it as 'that *sublime dicendi genus*, which walkes abroade for wast paper in each seruing-mans pocket'. The root cause of bad writing Nashe ascribes to an inability to read; authors have no sense of literary values and are incapable of distinguishing between the sublime and the ridiculous. They can see no difference between a poem by Tasso and such a ribald trifle as 'Ioane of Brainfords will', a work in which, as he writes in his Letter to William Cotton, 'she bequeathed a score of farts amongst her frends'.[19] In fact, in this vital matter of discrimination mere shopkeepers show more sense than the empty-headed, would-be wits from the universities. Unfortunately, however, both classes love detraction and hence are taken in by Martin Marprelate's scurrilous work. Nashe admits that there is something to be said for Martin's style, but objects strongly to his readiness to turn the world upside down.

At this point, feeling that he is now rather far away from his main theme, the state of literature, Nashe returns to it and makes a violent attack on 'our triuiall translators', as he calls them, singling out for special attention those who, having exhausted Seneca as a source for tragedies, have now begun to translate from the Italian, although they are quite incompetent in that language. To balance blame with praise, he then goes on to commend those who have advanced the cause of letters in England in the sixteenth century, drawing up a very 'safe' list of recognized scholars and humanists including Erasmus, Sir Thomas More, Cheke and Ascham.

There follows that lament for the decay of true learning in Cambridge to which I have referred already,[20] leading on to the admission that there are, nevertheless, some good writers and translators such as Gascoigne, Turberville, Golding and Phaer, though there is also the dreadful example of Stanyhurst to be taken into account. As for Latin verse, the only poets capable of writing anything respectable are Thomas Watson, Thomas Newton and Gabriel Harvey. The responsibility for this sad state of affairs lies with the Puritans 'who account wit vanitie, and poetry impiety'. These words come almost verbatim from the *Anatomy of Absurdity*,[21] and here, as there, Nashe asserts his own belief in the value of poetry, holding that every true scholar must be a poet either in whole or in part.

After some jesting on the old commonplace of whether the best source of inspiration is to be found in copious drinking or not, he takes up the challenge of those who assert that the only true poets are the Italians. To Petrarch, Tasso and other Italian poets he

[19] V. 195. [20] *Sup.*, p. 4. [21] Cf. I. 27.

opposes '*Chaucer*, *Lydgate*, *Gower*, with such like, that liued vnder the tyranny of ignorance', and says of them, 'each of these three haue vaunted their meeters with as much admiration in English as euer the proudest *Ariosto* did his verse in Italian'.[22] 'Diuine Master *Spencer*' is held up against 'Spaine, Fraunce, Italy, and all the world' and Roydon, Achlow and George Peele are praised highly, the last named being described as 'the *Atlas* of Poetrie, and *primus verborum Artifex*'. There follows yet another attack on actors, where Nashe writes:

> Sundry other sweete Gentlemen I doe know, that haue vaunted their pennes in priuate deuices, and tricked vp a company of taffaty fooles [the players] with their feathers, whose beauty if our Poets had not peecte with the supply of their periwigs, they might haue antickt it vntill this time vp and downe the Countrey with the King of Fairies, and dined euery day at the pease porredge ordinary with *Delfrigus*.
>
> But *Tolossa* hath forgotten that it was sometimes sacked, and beggars that euer they carried their fardels on footback.[23]

The work then concludes with a few words of commendation for '*William Warners* absolute *Albions*' and the promise that offenders against standards of art and good writing will be further persecuted in the *Anatomy*, which is due to appear shortly.

The summary shows quite clearly that for the most part the *Preface to 'Menaphon'* is the *Anatomy of Absurdity* boiled down and brightened up. Like many a clever young man, Nashe takes it for granted that he and his like are in possession of the truth. Using established figures such as Erasmus, Sir Thomas More and Spenser[24] as his reference points, he makes a verbal assault on all who do not belong to his particular way of thinking. There is the customary wail about the decline of standards, about the incompetence of those who win popular favour and about the disgraceful conduct of those, such as Martin, whom he dislikes. It is all of a familiar kind, and one can well understand why Richard Harvey should have been annoyed by the patronizing tone Nashe adopts in writing about dead scholars. The one thing that lifts the *Preface* above the mere commonplace is Nashe's

[22] III. 322. [23] III. 323–4.

[24] For the rapidity with which *The Shepheardes Calender* achieved recognition see H. S. V. Jones, *A Spenser Handbook*, New York, 1947, pp. 39–40.

fervent belief in the value of poetry and his sturdy championing of the poets of his own country.

Its reliance on the *Anatomy* makes plain that the *Preface* is a pot-boiler, a work put together, probably in a hurry, for a particular occasion. Nevertheless, in some respects, it is something new. In the first place Nashe omits the whole first section of the *Anatomy* in which he had attacked the writers of romance. He could hardly have done otherwise in writing a prefatory epistle to a pastoral romance by the leading romance writer of the day, but it does not necessarily follow that he was cynically suppressing his own views for the sake of profit. His admiration for Greene's facility in writing seems to me to be quite genuine, and the value he attaches to originality and spontaneity as criteria of literary excellence was to have a considerable effect on his own later work.

Secondly Nashe's attitude to the actors is, for him, a very odd one indeed. Three years later in his *Pierce Penilesse* he was to express the highest admiration for the popular stage, for the plays produced on it and for the actors in them, and especially for Edward Alleyn. Yet here we find him putting forward the view that the actors are largely responsible for perverting the English language, and that they enjoy profit and fame, while the scholars who write the plays live in penury and obscurity. These views are very close indeed to those expressed by Greene in his *Groats-worth of Wit*, published in 1592, and, moreover, there are verbal resemblances between the two works which can hardly be accidental. In the passage quoted on p. 32 the reference to the actors as 'a company of taffaty fooles', whom the poets have 'tricked up with their feathers', clearly anticipates Greene's attack on the actors as 'those Anticks garnisht in our colours' and the notorious gibe at Shakespeare as 'an vpstart Crow, beautified with our feathers'.[25] More striking still is the similarity between the rest of the passage and Greene's account of how Roberto meets the strolling player who once carried his 'playing Fardle a foote-backe' and who was 'as famous for Delphrigus, and the King of Fairies, as euer was any of my time'. On top of all which he assures Roberto that 'men of my profession gette by schollers their whole liuing'.[26]

[25] *Groats-worth of Witte*, ed. G. B. Harrison, London, 1923, p. 45.
[26] *Ibid.*, pp. 33–4.

There are two possible ways of accounting for these resemblances. The first is that Greene when writing his *Groatsworth* remembered the *Preface to 'Menaphon'* and what Nashe had said there. The other is that Greene, who, to judge from his writings, had no hesitation about repeating himself, was already talking in this vein in 1589 and that Nashe was influenced by him. This second possibility seems to me to be the more likely for two reasons. First, as I have indicated already, the carping attitude towards actors that Nashe adopts here does not square with what he says about them elsewhere. Secondly, and more important, there are other signs of Greene's influence in the *Preface*. In *Have With You to Saffron-Walden* Nashe says explicitly 'I neuer abusd *Marloe*, *Greene*, *Chettle* in my life, nor anie of my frends that vsde me like a frend'.[27] Yet the fact remains that in a review of the state of English poetry and English drama as it was in 1589 Nashe picks out George Peele for special praise and never so much as mentions Marlowe's name. He appears to me, however, to allude to Marlowe in anything but a complimentary manner at the beginning of the *Preface*, when he writes of those who 'thinke to outbraue better pennes with the swelling bumbast of bragging blanke verse', and who commit 'the disgestion of their cholericke incumbrances to the spacious volubilitie of a drumming decasillabon'.[28] McKerrow, taking Nashe's remark in *Have With You to Saffron-Walden* at its face value, did not think that Marlowe could have been the author aimed at, but he ignores the well known dislike that Greene expressed for Marlowe on more than one occasion. It seems clear that the success of *Tamburlaine* aroused Greene's jealousy. In the preface to his *Perimedes the Blacksmith*, 1588, he had written of men who made their 'verses jet vpon the stage in tragical buskins, every word filling the mouth like the faburden of Bo-Bell, daring God out of heaven with that Atheist *Tamburlan*', and in *Menaphon* itself he again makes an oblique reference to Marlowe as the teller of 'a Canterbury tale; some prophetical full-mouth that as he were a Cobler's eldest son, would by the last tell where anothers shoe wrings.[29] Nashe, I believe, carefully trimmed his sails. Taking care not to mention Marlowe by name, for after all Marlowe had been to Cambridge

[27] III. 131. [28] III. 311–12.

[29] Quoted from E. K. Chambers, *The Elizabethan Stage*, Oxford, 1951, vol. III, p. 324.

and was a scholar of parts, he contrived a reference which would be clear enough to Greene, but which could also be disavowed if he should be challenged by Marlowe.

While taking care to veil his attack on Marlowe, a fellow university wit, Nashe felt no such scruples about abusing another popular dramatist, Thomas Kyd. The author of the *Spanish Tragedy* is the chief of those held up to ridicule as 'shifting companions' who rely on 'English *Seneca* read by Candle-light' to provide them with tragical speeches and who, when they have exhausted Seneca, turn to translating from the Italian, in which they are incompetent, as a way of making a living. Kyd's rendering of Tasso's *Padre di Famiglia* under the title of *The Householder's Philosophy*, published in 1588, is full of mistakes that warrant Nashe's sneers, and includes the unhappy mistranslation of *ad lumina* (*Aeneid*, viii, 411) as 'by candlelight', when its really means 'till dawn'. But, unless Nashe is using plural for singular throughout this passage, the identification of Kyd as one of the 'shifting companions' referred to, does not prove that he was the author of the old *Hamlet* glanced at by Nashe when he writes:

> It is a common practise now a dayes amongst a sort of shifting companions, that runne through euery Art and thriue by none, to leaue the trade of *Nouerint*, whereto they were borne, and busie themselues with the indeuours of Art, that could scarcely Latinize their neck verse if they should haue neede; yet English *Seneca* read by Candlelight yeelds many good sentences, as *Blood is a begger*, and so forth; and if you intreate him faire in a frostie morning, he will affoord you whole Hamlets, I should say handfuls of Tragicall speeches.[30]

When one recalls that Greene was to describe Shakespeare as 'an absolute *Iohannes fac totum*', the words just quoted could apply to him quite as well as to Kyd.

All one can say for certain is that much in the *Preface* seems to reflect views and attitudes that we know Greene held. It has every appearance of having been written for a clique that was jealous of the popular dramatists and of their success. In such circumstances the puzzles in it may well be deliberate. Nashe knew that his veiled references would be intelligible to Greene and his friends and that they would be unintelligible to the general reader, but might, for that very reason, pique his curiosity. With

[30] III. 315.

his instinct for journalism he was already well aware of the possibilities inherent in literary gossip of an allusive kind, and it is not beyond the bounds of probability that much in the *Preface* may well derive from conversations with Greene and his circle. To me it seems to smack of exactly that kind of thing. Interesting as the reflection of the views of a particular group of writers, it has no more value as factual evidence than malicious tittle-tattle in general has.

## 3

If one of Nashe's intentions in writing the *Preface to 'Menaphon'* was, as I believe, to recommend himself to those responsible for the anti-Martinist campaign, it soon brought results. There is some doubt about whether he and Lyly took part in it from the beginning. McKerrow points out that neither of them is mentioned in the passage in the *Theses Martinianae* which gives a list of those writing against Martin in June or July 1589.[31] They must, however, have become involved soon afterwards, since Nashe clearly implies that he was an anti-Martinist writer at the time when Richard Harvey wrote his *Plaine Percevall.* This pamphlet, which cannot have been published later than 1590, is referred to by Nashe in his *Strange News.* There he writes that Richard Harvey

> (a notable ruffian with his pen) hauing first tooke vpon him in his blundring Persiual, to play the Iacke of both sides twixt *Martin* and vs, and snarld priuily at *Pap-hatchet*, *Pasquill*, and others, that opposde themselues against the open slaunder of that mightie platformer of Atheisme, presently after dribbed forth another fooles bolt, a booke I shoulde say, which he christened *The Lambe of God.*[32]

*The Lamb of God* was entered in the Stationers' Register on 23 October 1589 and published in 1590. In it Richard Harvey links Nashe and Martin together in one comment,[33] showing that he thought there was some connection between them. Gabriel Harvey in his *Pierce's Supererogation* writes first of Martin, then of Lyly and finally of Nashe, as though for him all three formed a kind of sequence. In addition to these statements of Nashe and of his enemies associating him with the anti-Martinist writers,

[31] V. 45. [32] I. 270. [33] V. 179–80.

there was also, as McKerrow shows in considerable detail,[34] a strong tradition, dating back to 1640, to the effect that Nashe was a 'Martin-queller' and had played a large part, perhaps the leading part, in putting Martin down.

When McKerrow began his edition in 1903 practically all the anti-Martinist tracts had at one time or another been attributed to Nashe, and he therefore printed the three 'Pasquil' tracts, *A Countercuff to Martin Junior*, *The Return of Pasquil* and *The First Part of Pasquil's Apology*, in his first volume. As the edition progressed, however, he became increasingly doubtful about the soundness of these attributions and, after a most careful examination of the evidence for authorship, eventually reached the following conclusion:

> I fear that the result of this investigation into Nashe's part in the Marprelate controversy has been merely negative. That he had some share is fairly certain, but beyond that I think we cannot go. So far as I can see there is not a single tract produced by the anti-Martinist group of writers which may safely, or even probably, be attributed to Nashe.[35]

Nevertheless, he felt sufficiently unsure about his findings to include one further anti-Martinist tract in his edition. *An Almond for a Parrot* appeared in volume III as one of the doubtful works, because, as McKerrow put it, 'it seems to me that the style of the *Almond* more resembles Nashe's than does that of any of the other tracts'.[36] He would have liked to claim it as authentic, but felt that he could not do so, because certain passages in it seemed to indicate that the author was an Oxford man.

So the matter rested until 1944, when an American scholar, Donald J. McGinn, took up the problem once more and put a strong and, it seems to me, quite convincing case for Nashe as the author of the *Almond* in an article entitled *Nashe's Share in the Marprelate Controversy*.[37] McKerrow concluded that the writer of the *Almond* was an Oxford man, because

> He speaks of 'our Vniuersity schooles at Oxford', and of 'our Beadles'—the Oxford ones—and seems to know the number of students at Cambridge only vaguely: 'in Cambridge they say there is not so many [students] by a thousand'. He several times refers to

[34] V. 45–8. [35] V. 64–5. [36] V. 60.
[37] *P.M.L.A.*, No. 59, 1944, pp. 952–81.

> Cambridge, but never in a way which suggests that it was his own University. A significant fact is his naming Oxford before Cambridge, which would hardly have been done at the date, save by an Oxford man or one particularly wishing to flatter Oxford.[38]

McGinn argues that when the author of the *Almond* writes of 'our Vniuersity schooles at Oxford' and of 'our Beadles' he is taking a national, not a local, view of things, and that for the same reason he names Oxford before Cambridge. McGinn further points out that there are several casual, off-hand allusions to such figures as 'a good fellow in Cambridge', and 'a dreaming deuine in Cambridge', which seem to show a familiarity with Cambridge life to which the passages dealing with Oxford can offer no parallel. The strongest evidence for a Cambridge author is provided, however, by the detailed manner in which John Penry's stay in Cambridge is described, as compared with the ignorance shown about his later activities at Oxford, to which he removed after receiving the M.A. degree at Cambridge in 1586.[39] This fact had already troubled McKerrow to such an extent as to make him suggest that 'this sketch of Penry's life may be a passage contributed by another writer'.[40]

In fact, there are no stylistic grounds for any such suggestion. *An Almond for a Parrot* is all of a piece; it is the work of one hand, written in a distinctive manner, which sets it apart from all the other anti-Martinist publications extant, and by an author whose interests and attitude are not those of the other anti-Martinists. Style, interests and attitude alike all point unmistakably to Thomas Nashe. Here, as McGinn says, is the bridge between the laboured, imitative quality of the *Anatomy of Absurdity* and the confident assurance of *Pierce Penilesse*.

Written in the winter of 1589–90 and probably published in February or March 1590,[41] the *Almond* is marked by two characteristics, apart from its individual style, which distinguish it from the other anti-Martinist tracts. The first is that the author is well informed about the facts of the case. He knows about the Martinist printers, Hodgkins, Tomlyn and Simmes, who were apprehended by Lord Derby's men at Manchester on 14th August 1589; he knows also about some of those responsible for distributing the illegal pamphlets, Mistress Lawson and Newman the cobbler;

[38] V. 60–1. [39] III. 365–9. [40] V. 61.
[41] IV. 460–1.

and he identifies Martin as John Penry. Much of this knowledge is, of course, attributable to the fact that by the time the *Almond* was written the Martinist press had been discovered and, therefore, more information about it was available. But, even allowing for this, the general impression the *Almond* gives is that it is the work of a man who had been taking a considerable interest in the controversy for some time and who had made it his business to read Martin with care, even with a certain fascination, and to collect as many scandalous and discreditable stories about individual Puritan preachers as he could lay his hands on. Yet it is something more solid than mere gossip and scandal. There is in it a deep-rooted opposition to Puritanism in general on humanistic as well as on religious and political grounds. As a result, the *Almond* is an altogether more solid and formidable piece of work than any other anti-Martinist tract. Scandal is so well buttressed by fact that it is often impossible today to say where one ends and the other begins. Nashe's account of Penry is a case in point. The details given of his career at Cambridge are so full that one is disposed to accept the statement that when he arrived there 'he was as arrant a papist as euer came out of Wales',[42] and even the libel that he later became a Brownist and finally an Anabaptist[43] stands some chance of being taken for truth. And, most important of all, both the scandal and the specific facts gain in cogency by being made part of, and subordinated to, a wide view of the Puritan movement in general.

The second feature of the *Almond* that stands out is its literary competence and quality. Alone of the anti-Martinist tracts it can be read, as Martin himself can be read, for its own sake. The others have hack-work written all over them. Their authors mix argument with abuse; they cannot make up their minds whether to take Martin seriously or to laugh at him; they haver and fall between two stools. They try to imitate his style without having taken the trouble to examine it carefully and, as a result, merely reproduce a few obvious features of it with no real understanding of the function Martin makes these devices serve. Figures such as Pasquil and Marphoreus have no reality at all. They are mouthpieces for the official view of Martin as a traitor and subverter of the commonwealth. The face is the face of Mr. Punch, but the voice is the voice of Bancroft.

[42] III. 366. [43] III. 367.

In the *Almond* things are different. From beginning to end it is stamped with a distinct literary personality. The author goes to work with a zest; argument, scandal and abuse are no longer separate and conflicting items, because he enjoys them all and has evolved a manner of writing capable of modulating easily from one to the other. The *Almond* is a work of art as well as a piece of polemic. It has an individual character of its own.

The dedication sets the tone for what follows. Instead of being written to one of the great, in the social or political sense of the word, it is addressed to William Kemp, who was generally acknowledged, after the death of his predecessor Richard Tarlton in 1588, to be the greatest comic actor of the day. The note it strikes is appropriately a comic one. Following the lead given him by Martin, Nashe takes an obvious delight in inventing mock titles for Kemp in a way that looks forward to his fantastic exercise in the same vein when Pierce Penilesse begins his supplication to the devil. The dedication to the *Almond* opens as follows:

> To that most Comicall and conceited Caualeire *Monsieur du Kempe, Iestmonger and* Vice-gerent generall to the Ghost of Dicke Tarlton. *His louing brother Cutbert Curry-Knaue sendeth Greeting.*
>
> Brother Kempe, as many alhailes to thy person as there be haicocks in Iuly at Pancredge: So it is that, what for old acquaintance, and some other respectes of my pleasure, I haue thought good to offer here certaine spare stuffe to your protection, which if your sublimitie accept in good part, or vouchsafe to shadow with the curtaine of your countenance, I am yours till fatall destiny two yeares after doomes day.[44]

To label writing of this kind colloquial and to leave it at that is to do it an injustice. Colloquial it certainly is in the way it smacks of direct, unpremeditated speech and produces an impression of man speaking to man, but there is nothing commonplace about it. It is made arresting by the way this colloquial tone plays over and parodies the set, formal address, an effect that is heightened by the invention of mock titles and the use of the comic simile. Through it the author establishes himself as a personality, a thoroughly good fellow, brisk, lively and open, who will be worth listening to.

And then, as though to sign the work with his name at the very outset, Nashe makes two complaints about the difficulties of the writer's life that he was to go on making throughout his career.

[44] III. 341.

First, he protests against the way in which men of high position promise to reward writers and then fail to carry out their promise. Secondly, he complains about the activities of the intelligencers, or professional informers, who made a living by finding treasonous and libellous statements in perfectly innocent works. The transition from these general statements to the subject of Martin is made when Nashe goes on very much in Martin's own manner, to write as follows:

> Well, come on it what will, Martin and I will allow of no such doinges; wee can cracke halfe a score blades in a backe-lane though a Constable come not to part vs.[45]

The contest is to be a literary brawl, and Nashe gets in a shrewd blow at once by making the charge that Martin by promoting religious dissension in England is helping the cause of the Papacy, a charge that he backs up by an effective, though probably apocryphal, anecdote. This mingling of political argument and fictional illustration is a foretaste of what is to come in the main body of the work.

The dedication does its job; it establishes an intimate relationship between author and reader and sets the tone for the pamphlet proper. This, as the title indicates, is an attempt to stop the mouths of Martin and his supporters and of the Puritans in general by controverting their views and by blackening their personal characters. In Nashe's solid arguments there is nothing new. They occupy only the first third or so of the *Almond* and amount to little more than a repetition, though a lively one, of the official line of attack. Martin is accused of attempting to divide the Church under the pretence of unifying it, and is, therefore, a hypocrite. He is guilty of opposing the lawful magistrates contrary to Christian teaching, as based on St. Paul's *Epistle to the Romans*. And, most damning of all, he and the Puritans in refusing to acknowledge the authority of bishops are traitors, since such a refusal is rebellion against the Queen, by whom bishops are appointed. The activities of the Puritans undermine Church and State and directly further the cause of Satan, since the souls of those they lead astray will necessarily go to hell.

Having faithfully followed the official line, which, it must be added, he thoroughly agreed with and adhered to, Nashe then

[45] III. 342.

devotes the rest of the tract to a series of personal attacks on individual Puritans, some of whom had no connection with Martin at all. His method in these attacks is a clever mixture of fact, scandal and comic anecdotes. Philip Stubbs, whom he had already pilloried in the *Anatomy of Absurdity* and in the *Preface to 'Menaphon'*, is once again held up to ridicule as an ignoramus who cannot construe a bit of Latin. Yet in the strict sense of the term Stubbs, who was not opposed to the episcopacy, was not a Puritan at all and certainly had no connection with the Marprelate writings. Nashe, however, is flogging one of his favourite horses, namely that the Puritans are enemies of learning who begin preaching before they know anything. Thomas Cartwright, the most learned and courageous leader of the Puritan movement, is accused of ambition and of having attempted to become Vice-Chancellor of Cambridge; a charge for which there seems to have been no foundation in fact, but which had at the time an air of probability. And Nashe goes on to suggest that, having failed in this attempt, Cartwright, in no way discouraged, set on foot the Puritan agitation against the established church in the hope of establishing a church of his own, of which he would be the supreme head. It is all very unprincipled, but also very effective.

The same sweeping technique is applied to three other leading reformers of the day. Eusebius Paget is jeered at, because he was lame, and taken to task as a money-grubber. Yet there is nothing to connect him with the Martinists any more than there is in the case of Giles Wiggenton, the vicar of Sedbergh until 1586, when he was deprived of the living on account of his Calvinist views. Nevertheless, Nashe gibes at him and turns him into a comic figure, a pulpit-beater so put out by the entrance of the local whoremonger in the middle of his sermon

> that he could neyther goe forward nor backward, but stil repeated, Iohn a Borhead, Iohn a Borhead, that vild whooremaister Iohn a Borhead: to whom with the Father, the Sonne, and the holy Ghost, be al honor and praise both now and for euer.[46]

John Udall, vicar of Kingston until 1588, when he was deprived because of his opposition to bishops, and who really was connected with the Martinists, is held up to scorn for what Nashe describes as his affectation of holiness. No one could guess from

[46] III. 364.

Nashe's account of them that all three were men of learning and ability. The technique employed against them is that of the 'smear'.

These three violently partisan sketches form a fitting prelude to the later part of the *Almond*, which is devoted to the identification of John Penry (1559–93) as Martin himself. For Penry, a man of great courage and sincerity, who had certainly been involved in the setting up of the Martinist press and who was to perish on the gallows, Nashe reserves his harshest treatment. Penry is abused with ferocious invective and described in the 'unsavoury' terms that Nashe was to make peculiarly his own:

> For the constitution of his bodie, it was so cleane contrarie to all phisiognomie of fame, that a man wold haue iudged by his face, God and nature deuising our disgrace had enclosde a close stoole in skinne, and set a serpentine soule, like a counterfet diamond, more deepe in dong. Neither was this monster of Cracouia vnmarkt from his bastardisme to mischiefe: but as he was begotten in adultery and conceiued in the heate of lust, so was he brought into the world on a tempestuous daie, and borne in that houre when all planets wer opposite. Predestination, that foresaw how crooked he should proue in his waies, enioyned incest to spawne him splay-footed. Eternitie, that knew how aukward he should looke to all honesty, consulted with Conception to make him squint-eied, and the deuill, that discouered by the heauens disposition on his birth-day, how great a lim of his kingdom was comming into the world, prouided a rustie superficies wherein to wrap him as soone as euer he was separated from his mothers wombe: in euerie part whereof these words of blessing were most artificially engrauen *Crine ruber*, *niger ore*, *breuis pede*, *lumine lustus*.[47]

The whole thing is in the worst of taste, but the sheer nastiness of it all is palliated in some measure by the fantastic ingenuity of invention. The malicious invective is shot through with a kind of perverted poetry. The technique is that of allegorical verse transposed into another, and very much lower key. Brutality of image and attitude were nothing new at the time, but the ability to combine them with the play of fancy is something peculiar to Nashe.

This description of Penry's birth and appearance, carefully designed to present him as a monster, is followed by a long and fairly detailed account of his career at Cambridge, in the course of which he is taken to task for upholding Ramus against Aristotle, a

[47] III. 365–6.

charge, it will be remembered, that Nashe had already brought against the Puritans in general in the *Anatomy of Absurdity*. The account culminates in the accusation that Penry's main aim in writing against the bishops is the materialistic one of getting the bishoprics into his own hands and making a profit out of them. Finally, to round the tract off, Nashe relates a series of anecdotes to illustrate the ignorance and absurdity of the Puritan preachers and concludes with the adjuration to Martin to repent otherwise 'thou art like to heare of me by the next Carrier'.[48] The swash-buckling tone adopted at the beginning of the tract has been maintained to the very end.

As this summary of it indicates, the *Almond* is far more abuse and scandal than solid argument. Nashe's purpose is not to put a case, but to discredit and destroy an opponent. Like Martin himself, he has realized that, if his pamphlet is to have the effect he wants it to have, it must be readable. To make it so he adopts many of Martin's devices. That interest in the Puritan pamphleteer's style, which he had already shown in the *Preface to 'Menaphon'*, is much more in evidence here. Even in attacking Martin's fondness for invective he shows that he is fascinated by it. Writing of his opponent's 'rayling Epithites', he gives examples:

> A few of whose milder tearmes are of this making, wicked Priests, presumptuous Priests, proude Prelates, arrogant Bishops, horse-leeches, butchers, persecutors of the truth, Lamhethical whelps, Spanish Inquisitours . . . bounsing Priests, terrible Priests, venerable Maisters, proud and pontificall Patripolitians.[49]

Admiration is mingled with condemnation. Nashe clearly felt that Martin's manner was a challenge to his invention. Indeed, he says as much on more than one occasion, and deliberately calls attention to his own proficiency in the same kind of thing when, towards the end of his onslaught on Penry, he writes:

> Much good do it you, *M. Martin*, how like you my stile, am not I old *Ille ego qui quondam* at the besleeuing of a sicophant? Alas, poore idiot, thou thinkest no man can write but thy selfe, or frame his pen to delight except he straine curtesie with one of thy Northren figures; but if authority do not moderate the fiery feruence of my enflamed zeale [an interesting confirmation of the fact that Nashe was being employed by the bishops], ile assaile thee from terme to terme, with *Archilochus*, in such a compleat armour of

[48] III. 376. [49] III. 347–8. See also III. 346–7.

> Iambicks, as the very reflexcye of my fury shall make thee driue thy father before thee to the gallows, for begetting thee in such a bloody houre. O God, that we two might bee permitted but one quarter, to try it out by the teeth for the best benefice in England, then would I distill my wit into incke, and my soule into argumentes, but I would driue this *Danus* from his dunghill, and make him faune like a dog for fauour at the magistrates feete.[50]

That passage alone is enough to show that the author of the *Almond* was Thomas Nashe. He was to reproduce the same attitude and the same rhythms and diction some two years later, when, at the end of his attack on Richard Harvey in *Pierce Penilesse*, he wrote with considerable self-complacency:

> *Redeo ad vos, mei Auditores*, haue I not an indifferent prittye vayne in Spurgalling an Asse? if you knew how extemporall it were at this instant, and with what hast it is writ, you would say so.[51]

The *Almond* is to a large extent a piece of flyting. Nashe takes up the combative attitude and sustains it throughout, flinging himself into battle with a gusto that looks forward to his attacks on Gabriel Harvey in *Strange News* and *Have With You to Saffron-Walden*. Indeed, the very title of the latter work is anticipated in the *Almond* when he sets about his sketch of Giles Wiggenton with the words 'Haue with you, *Giles Wiggenton*, to Sidborough'.[52]

Nashe takes the opportunity the writing of this tract provided him with for practising and cultivating that 'extemporall veine in any humour', for which he had already praised Greene in the *Preface to 'Menaphon'* and which he also refers to in the *Almond* itself when he writes that Martin was 'not many moneths since most wittily scofte at by the extemporall endeuour of the pleasant author of Pap with a hatchet'.[53] In a sense this 'extemporall veine' is Nashe's version, as a writer, of that *sprezzatura* which Castiglione had seen as the mark of the true Renaissance courtier. Just as the courtier was expected to practise his various accomplishments with a negligent ease and grace and with no suggestion of labour or effort, so Nashe, though he lived by his pen, sought to cover up his professionalism by giving to his work the appearance of unpremeditated fluency. In his own eyes—and, I think, in ours also—it was precisely this quality that marked his work off

[50] III. 369. [51] I. 199. [52] III. 363.
[53] III. 347.

from the plodding pedestrianism of other professionals, such as Deloney, whom he despised. A would-be aristocrat among authors, Nashe found a suitable vehicle for the effect he wished to create in an artful assimilation of Martin's manner to the more elaborate style he had used in writing the *Anatomy of Absurdity*. The opening of the *Almond*, in which he refers to the final Martinist publication, *The Protestation of Martin Marprelate*, published in October 1589, and to some of the anti-Martinist plays that had been staged, will serve as an illustration:

> Welcome, Mayster *Martin*, from the dead, and much good ioy may you haue of your stage-like resurrection. It was told me by the vndanted purseuants of your sonnes, and credibly beleeued in regard of your sinnes, that your grout-headed holinesse had turnd vppe your heeles like a tired iade in a medow, and snorted out your scornefull soule, like a mesled hogge on a mucke-hill, which had it not beene false, as the deuill woulde haue it, that long tongd doctresse, Dame *Lawson*, muste haue been faine (in spite of insperation) to haue giuen ouer speaking in the congregation, and employ her Parrats tong in stead of a winde-clapper to scarre the crowes from thy carrion.[54]

The casual familiarity of tone, coupled with the use of colloquial phrases, serves to cover, though not to blunt, the effect of the clever alliterations and assonances that Nashe has carried over from his study of Lyly. The off-hand and the formal counterpoint one another. Like the poets of the time he makes much play with similes and compound words, but his similes are unsavoury and his compound words are low. There is a calculated indecorum about it all.

Nashe ridicules Martin's use of such phrases as 'So ho, brother *Bridges*. Wo ho ho, *Iohn* a London. Ha ha he, Doctor *Copecotes*',[55] but he is quite ready to use exactly the same devices himself. 'Tut, tut', he writes, and 'I, I, my maisters'. He inserts stage directions as he goes along, and slips easily from direct to indirect speech and back again to produce a dramatic effect. He sets his Puritans talking in an imaginary dialogue so that he may jeer at them:

> Our Ecclesiasticall gouernment and gouernours, say they, are wicked and vnlawfull. Why? because Sir *Peter* nor Sir *Paul* were neuer Archbishoppes of Canterbury, London, or Yorke. They were

[54] III. 344. [55] III. 354.

Fisher-men, and were not able. When *Caesars* Officers demaunded their tribute to make fiue groates amongst them, then what reason is it our Bishoppes should inioy their fiue hundreds, nay, that which is more their thousand and two thousands? They were none of these Cartercaps, Graduates, nor Doctors, therfore why should we tie our Ministrie to the prophane studies of the Vniuersitie? What is Logicke but the highe waie to wrangling, contayning in it a world of bibble-babble. Neede we anie of your Greeke, Latine, Hebrue, or anie such gibbrige, when wee haue the word of God in English? Go to, go to, you are a great company of vaine men, that stand vpon your degrees and tongues, with tittle tattle, I cannot tell what, when as (if you looke into the matter as you ought) the Apostles knew neare a Letter of the booke. Iwis it were not two pins hurt if your Colledges wer fired ouer your heades, and you turnde a begging forth your fellowshippes, like Fryers, and Monkes, vp and downe the Countrie. I, marie, sir, this is somewhat like, now *Martin* speakes like himselfe; I dare saie for him, good man, he could be contented there were nere a maister of Art, Bachelour of Diuinitie, Doctor, or Bishop in England, on that condition he prest Fishermen, scullers, Coopers, Stitchers, Weauers, and Coblers into theyr places.[56]

In such a passage as this Nashe has caught the accent of his opponents and guyed it, as well as carrying their arguments to an extreme which makes them look ridiculous. But, at the same time, he is involved in what he writes. Here, as in the *Anatomy of Absurdity*, it is the Puritan opposition to learning and the liberal arts that he goes for. There is seriousness of purpose mixed with the buffoonery, and on one occasion Nashe slips into another vein altogether by becoming 'pathetical' over the fate of the souls led astray by Martin and by trying the effect of melodramatic horrors on his adversary:

The humours of my eies are the habitations of fountaines, and the circumference of my heart the enclosure of tearefull contrition, when I thinke how many soules at that moment [the last judgment] shall carrie the name of *Martine* on their foreheads to the vale of confusion, in whose innocent bloude thou swimming to hell, shalt haue the tormentes of tenne thousande thousande sinners at once, inflicted vppon thee. There will enuie, mallice, and dissimulation bee euer calling for vengeance agaynst thee, and incite whole legions of deuilles to thy deathlesse lamentation.[57]

[56] III. 350–1. [57] III. 353.

There is an obvious striving for effect in this passage, but it does, nevertheless, leave an impression on the mind. Nashe has what has been described as the Gothic imagination, the kind of artistic sensibility that expressed itself in gargoyles and in the figures of Satan, Herod and Pontius Pilate in the miracle plays; a capacity for reconciling the horrible and the humorous in the grotesque, which makes itself felt in the account of Penry's birth and appearance that I quoted earlier. It is the most distinctive of his qualities; there is an element of nightmare about it; it belongs with the ferocious delight that the Elizabethans took in public executions, a delight Nashe seems to have shared if one can judge by the relish with which he writes of them. His account of the execution of Cutwolfe in *The Unfortunate Traveller* is anticipated in the *Almond* by a passage in which he prophesies Penry's death at the hands of Bull, the public executioner, of whom he writes:

> O, it is a hairebrande whooresonne, and well seene in Phlebotomie; if a but once take knife in hande, cha will as soone let out the seditious humours forth a Martinistes bodie, as the best he in England, that hath bin twentie yeeres practioners in Surgerie. Good munckie face Machiuell, shew but thy head once, and trie him at my request, and if he doe it not more handsomely then those whom thou callest Butchers and Horseleeches, then neuer trust an olde ladde whilest thou liuest.[58]

Nashe has for Bull the admiration of one public performer for another. The *Almond* is his execution of Martin, carried out with the same flourish and the same joy of the master in the exercise of his mystery that he attributes to Bull. To say that Nashe quelled Martin is to go too far. When the *Almond* came out the Martinist press had been captured and the last pamphlet to be issued from it, the *Protestation*, had appeared in October 1589. But one only has to read the *Almond* to see how Nashe's reputation as a Martin-queller was acquired. Of all the answers to Martin it is much the most effective. In it Martin's weapons have been borrowed and sharpened up and other weapons have been added to them. In the writing of it Nashe really found himself, discovered his gift for the luridly grotesque and established himself as 'yong *Iuuenall*, that byting Satyrist'. It is an example of the kind of 'savage farce' that T. S. Eliot observed in *The Jew of Malta*.[59]

[58] III. 348–9.

[59] T. S. Eliot, *Selected Essays*, London, 1951 (1st Edition 1932), p. 123.

# III

# THE MISERIES OF AUTHORSHIP

## and *Pierce Penilesse*

### I

THE *Almond* was probably published about the end of January 1590, and the *Anatomy of Absurdity* followed it in the February or March of the same year. Between this date and the appearance of *Pierce Penilesse* in September 1592, only one piece of work, and that a very minor one, from Nashe's pen made its way into print. This was the preface which he wrote for the first edition, now generally recognized as a pirated edition, of Sir Philip Sidney's *Astrophel and Stella*, published by Thomas Newman in 1591. The fact that Nashe became involved in this rather shady enterprise would seem to indicate that he was finding it hard to make a living and was ready to snatch at any opportunity that came his way to put something in his purse.

Labelled, not inappropriately, 'Somewhat to reade for them *that list*', the preface is an undistinguished bit of hack work. Nashe himself was obviously aware of its shortcomings. He accuses himself of presumption for daring to write it and concludes by apologizing for his own temerity. 'Gentlemen', he writes, 'I feare I haue too much presumed on your idle leysure, and beene too bold, to stand talking all this while in an other mans doore'.[1] The apology is, I think, quite genuine. Sidney was Nashe's hero. He had already praised him in the dedicatory epistle to the *Anatomy of Absurdity*, and he was to cite him frequently in his later

[1] III. 333.

works as the great example of what the courtier, poet and patron ought to be, and as a standing reproof to the niggardly attitude of the great towards men of letters. Moreover, with his usual acuteness of perception where contemporary writing was concerned, Nashe recognized at once the importance of the work he was introducing and the fact that its publication marked an era in the history of the English sonnet. He writes: 'Put out your rush candles, you Poets and Rimers, and bequeath your crazed quaterzayns to the Chaundlers; for loe, here he commeth that hath broken your legs'.[2] But, much as he admired Sidney and saw the true quality of *Astrophel and Stella* Nashe did not find that the writing of an encomium came easily to him. He admits his difficulties when he says: 'Indeede, to say the truth, my stile is somewhat heauie gated'.[3] It is so; the 'extemporall veyne' eludes him; throughout that part of the preface devoted to the praise of Sidney and of his sister, the Countess of Pembroke, there is a painful striving after a heightened effect through the use of ornate figures of speech and excessive alliteration. One admirably accurate and picturesque ray of literary criticism breaks through the clouds of rhetoric when he describes *Astrophel and Stella* as 'the tragicommody of loue . . . performed by starlight',[4] but, for the rest, the sky in which the lovers are set is murky with verbosity and with riddling hits, rather in the manner of the *Preface to 'Menaphon'*, at unspecified writers whose incompetence Nashe attacks as a foil to his praise of Sidney.

Much of the preface is quite frankly padding, and it is not surprising that when Newman, probably under pressure from the Countess of Pembroke, brought out a second and much improved edition of *Astrophel and Stella* late in 1591, Nashe's contribution was omitted from it.

How Nashe managed to live at all during this lean time is something of a puzzle, but, characteristically, he contrived, nevertheless, to make literary capital out of his hardships. The very title of *Pierce Penilesse*, pronounced 'Purse Peniless' in Elizabethan English, is both an indication of the straits to which he was reduced and of the spirit in which he faced his difficulties. Feeling himself undeservedly neglected, he grumbles, but without losing his sense of humour. The opening words of the pamphlet

[2] III. 330. [3] III. 332. [4] III. 329.

establish the dominant tone in which complaint and self-mockery are mingled. They run as follows:

> Hauing spent many yeeres in studying how to liue, and liu'de a long time without mony: hauing tired my youth with follie, and surfetted my minde with vanitie, I began at length to looke backe to repentaunce, and addresse my endeuors to prosperitie: But all in vaine, I sate vp late, and rose earely, contended with the colde, and conuersed with scarcitie: for all my labours turned to losse, my vulgar Muse was despised and neglected, my paines not regarded, or slightly rewarded, and I my selfe (in prime of my best wit) laid open to pouertie. Wherevpon (in a malecontent humor) I accused my fortune, raild on my patrones, bit my pen, rent my papers, and ragde in all points like a mad man.[5]

As well as setting the tone for what is to follow, this opening also raises something of a question. Allowing for the fact that Nashe is deliberately dramatizing his own situation, it would, nevertheless, appear from what he says that he had written a good deal more than is accounted for by the record of his published works up to this time. Further confirmation of this view is provided by a short passage in *Strange News*, published in January 1593, where he answers Gabriel Harvey's accusation, alleging that he is incapable of anything but railing, by writing:

> There is no kind of peaceable pleasure in poetrie, but I can drawe equally in the same yoke with the haughtiest of those foule-mouthd backbiters that say I can do nothing but raile.
>
> I haue written in all sorts of humors priuately, I am perswaded, more than any yoong man of my age in England.[6]

The self-vindication here is vigorous and confident, but, unfortunately, no specific works are mentioned. McKerrow's comment on the passage is to the point; he writes: 'his known work would not justify such a statement. Yet it is unlikely that anything published under his name has perished'.[7] There seems no reason to dissent from this verdict, though it ignores the fact that Nashe's play *Summer's Last Will and Testament*, although not published until 1600, had almost certainly been acted at the Archbishop of Canterbury's palace at Croydon in the autumn of 1592. The passage from *Strange News*, quoted above, clearly implies that a number of works are being referred to rather than a single play.

[5] I. 157. [6] I. 320. [7] V. 17.

What then is Nashe referring to? The clue to his statement lies in the word 'priuately', which, in this context, means, I would suggest, not merely 'unpublished', but 'not intended for publication'. Poverty could drive an Elizabethan author to strange shifts; and some indication of the kind of writing covered by the phrase 'in all sorts of humors priuately' is almost certainly to be found in the *Three Parnassus Plays* which were played at Cambridge between 1598–9 and 1601–2. These three anonymous plays, which are linked to each other and in effect form one whole, depict the careers of a number of students from their hopeful beginnings, when they first go up to the university, to their eventual frustrations when, having taken their degrees, they go out into a world which has no use for their learning and will only employ them on menial tasks. Both in attitude and in phraseology the plays clearly owe much to Nashe, and in the last of them he is mentioned by name as being now dead and an elegy is said over him. Moreover, as long ago as 1891, F. G. Fleay in his *Biographical Chronicle* stated, without adducing much evidence to support his claim, that the figure of Ingenioso, who appears in all three plays and is very prominent in the second, was intended for Thomas Nashe.[8] The evidence Fleay failed to provide has since been gathered together by J. B. Leishman in the introduction to his edition of the plays, and adds up to a most convincing identification.[9]

Now Ingenioso, like Nashe, after leaving Cambridge, goes to London and tries to support himself by his pen. For a time he follows 'a goutie patron', who does nothing for him, and eventually he decides to put his trust in the reading public. Despite this resolution, however, he continues to try his luck with potential patrons. In Act III of the *First Part of the Return from Parnassus* he is seen cultivating the acquaintance and, incidentally, exposing the pretensions of Gullio, a would-be gentleman, soldier and poet, whose speech is largely made up of plagiarisms from Shakespeare. In the upshot Gullio gives Ingenioso a commission, and the following dialogue takes place between them:

> *Gullio*. . . . new years day approcheth, and wheras other gallants bestowe Iewells vpon there Mistrisses (as I haue done whilome),

[8] F. G. Fleay, *Biographical Chronicle of the English Drama*, 1891, II. 348.

[9] *The Three Parnassus Plays*, ed. J. B. Leishman, London, 1949, pp. 71–9.

I now count it base to do as the common people doe; I will bestow vpon them the precious stons of my witt, a diamonde of Inuention, that shall be aboue all value and esteeme; therfore, sithens I am employed in some weightie affayrs of the courte, I will haue thee, Ingenioso, to make them, and when thou hast done, I will pervse, pollish, and correcte them.

*Ingenioso.* My pen is youre bounden vassall to commande, but what vayne woulde it please you to haue them in?

*Gullio.* Not in a vaine veine (prettie y faith); make mee them in two or three diuers vayns, in Chaucers, Gowers and Spencers and Mr. Shakspeares.[10]

Ingenioso goes away, does what is required of him and in IV. i. returns to Gullio with three poems, one in the manner of Chaucer, one in that of Spenser and one in that of Shakespeare. Gullio turns down the first two, but accepts the imitation of Shakespeare, telling Ingenioso:

> Well, Ile bestowe a Frenche crowne in the faire writinge of them out, and then Ile instructe thee about the deliuery of them. Meane while, Ile haue thee make an elegant description of my Mistris; liken the worste part of her to Cynthia, make also a familiar Dialogue betwixt her and my selfe. Ile now in, and correct these verses.

Ingenioso, left alone, expresses his indignation at Gullio's affectations, but adds that his poverty leaves him no choice but to do what he is asked:

> Well madame Pecunia, onc more for thy sake will I waite on this truncke, and with soothinge him vpp in time will leaue him a greater foole than I founde him.[11]

In the end, however, it is Ingenioso who is bitten. In V. i. he comes back to Gullio to report on the reception he has been given by Gullio's mistress, Lesbia. He has been unsuccessful. Lesbia has turned down Gullio's suit and rejected his letter. Gullio promptly takes his revenge on Ingenioso, turning him out of his service and refusing to pay him for his labour. The scene ends with

[10] *Ibid., The First Part of the Return*, ll. 1015–28.
[11] *Ibid.*, ll. 1205–17.

Ingenioso bitterly regretting the time he has wasted on this 'base carle' and deciding to turn satirist:

> My freer spirit did lie in tedious woe
> Whiles it applauded bragging Gullio,
> Applide my veyne to sottishe Gullio,
> Made wanton lines to please lewd Gullio.
> Attend hencforth on Gulls for mee who liste,
> For Gullios sake Ile proue a Satyrist.[12]

It would be foolish to regard these scenes from a university play as an exact picture of what happened to Nashe after he left Cambridge, but, since the author of them obviously knew Nashe's work very well and was deeply interested in him, it would be equally foolish to ignore them, especially as Nashe himself confirms some of the statements made in them and, above all, since one example of his facility in making 'wanton lines' has survived. In *Have With You to Saffron-Walden*, published in 1596, one of the characters, Senior Importuno, says that the public has had to wait so long for Nashe's answer to Gabriel Harvey's attack on him in *Pierce's Supererogation*, which had appeared three years before, that it has come to the conclusion that Nashe is incapable of meeting Harvey's charges. Importuno then continues:

> I, for mine owne part, know the contrarie, and will engage my oath for him (if need be) that the most of this time they thinke him houering ouer the neast, he hath sat hatching of nothing but toies for priuate Gentlemen, and neglected the peculiar busines of his reputation, that so deeply concerne him, to follow vaine hopes and had I wist humours about Court, that make him goe in a thred-bare cloake, and scarce pay for boate hire . . . he is idle and new fangled, beginning many things but soone wearie of them ere hee be halfe entred, and . . . hee hath too much acquaintance in London euer to doo any good, being like a Curtezan that can deny no man.[13]

Nashe's answer, made in his own person, comes very close to an admission of the truth of much that Importuno has said. He replies:

> As newfangled and idle, and prostituting my pen like a Curtizan, is the next *Item* that you taxe me with; well it may and it may not bee so, for neither will I deny it nor will I grant it; onely thus farre Ile goe with you, that twise or thrise in a month, when *res est angusta domi*, the bottome of my purse is turnd downeward, and my con-

[12] *Ibid.*, ll. 1463–8. [13] III. 26.

> duit of incke will no longer flowe for want of reparations, I am faine to let my Plow stand still in the midst of a furrow, and follow some of these newfangled *Galiardos* and *Senior Fantasticos*, to whose amorous *Villanellas* and *Quipassas* I prostitute my pen in hope of gaine; but otherwise there is no newfanglenes in mee but pouertie, which alone maketh mee so vnconstant to my determined studies.[14]

The precise nature of the poems referred to as *Villanellas* and *Quipassas* is not known; probably Nashe means no more than lyrics of a lively kind; but the general sense of the passage is clear enough; he acknowledges that he is able to pick up some ready money by acting as a ghost-writer and composing the verses that were one of the accomplishments expected of the complete gentleman, for those who were incapable of making them for themselves.[15] It is a confession that throws a rather disconcerting light on the Elizabethan literary scene, and that leaves one wondering just how many of the poems that Elizabethan gentlemen are supposed to have thrown off with such ease are in fact their own. It certainly explains the negligent ease and shows that even the much prized quality of *sprezzatura* could, like most other things for which there was a demand, be bought. Taken in conjunction with the passage from *The First Part of the Return*, quoted above, it looks very much as though we have here the explanation of how Nashe scratched a living together. It also provides an additional reason for his bitterness against patrons in general, and it helps one to understand how he came to develop that flair for parody and burlesque which is such a marked feature of his work.

The one example of Nashe's 'private' writings that has survived is a bawdy narrative poem called *The Choice of Valentines*. The first reference to it occurs in *Pierce's Supererogation* where Gabriel Harvey contemptuously tells Nashe:

> I will not heere decipher thy vnprinted packet of bawdye, and filthy Rymes, in the nastiest kind: there is a fitter place for that discouery of thy foulest shame, and the whole ruffianisme of thy brothell Muse, if she still prostitute her obscene ballats, and will needes be a young Curtisan of ould knauery.[16]

[14] III. 30–1.

[15] Similar charges are made by John Marston in his *Satires* (1598), but he may be borrowing from Nashe. See *The Works of John Marston*, ed. A. H. Bullen, London, 1887, vol. III, pp. 264–5 and 270–1.

[16] *The Works of Gabriel Harvey*, ed. Grosart, II. 91.

This is, of course, the accusation referred to by Importuno and, indeed, substantially repeated by him. That Nashe did not deny the attribution is not surprising. His authorship of the poem is beyond all doubt. Three manuscript copies of it have come down to us and two of them bear his name—in one case as a signature, in the other as part of the title. There are close verbal correspondences between it and some of his other writings, and further references to it—all emphasizing its bawdy nature and attributing it to Nashe—are to be found in *The Trimming of Thomas Nashe*,[17] in the poems of John Davies of Hereford and in the satires of Joseph Hall.[18]

The exact date of its composition is unknown, but, since *Pierce's Supererogation* was completed on 27 April 1593, it must have been in existence by then, and, since it was generally regarded as pornographic and clandestine, it seems reasonable to assume that a fair length of time must have elapsed between its composition and its coming to Harvey's notice. In other words it must be roughly contemporary with *Pierce Penilesse*. Two other facts support this theory. So far as we know, Nashe wrote only three sonnets, apart from some parodies of the form in *Strange News* and *The Unfortunate Traveller*; one occurs at the end of *Pierce Penilesse*, one serves as the dedication to *The Choice of Valentines* and one as the epilogue to it. All three were written under the influence of Spenser and derive from the dedicatory sonnets, addressed to great personages, which he appended to the first edition of *The Faerie Queene*, published in 1590. The sonnet at the end of *Pierce Penilesse* is an avowed imitation of Spenser in which Nashe regrets that his patron, Amyntas, was left out of the list of Spenser's dedicatees and does his best to remedy the omission. In the dedicatory sonnet to *The Choice of Valentines*, which is addressed 'To the right Honorable the Lord S.', there is an unmistakable echo of Spenser's sonnet 'To the right Honourable the Earle of Oxenforde'. Spenser opens his sonnet with the lines:

> Receiue most Noble Lord in gentle gree,
> The vnripe fruit of an vnready witt.

Nashe ends his sonnet with the lines:

> Accept of it Dear Lord in gentle gree,
> And better lynes ere long shall honor thee.

[17] *Ibid.*, III. 63.

[18] V. 153 and *A Supplement*, 78–9.

Like *Pierce Penilesse* then, *The Choice of Valentines* was written at a time when Nashe was under the influence of Spenser. It also seems to have been addressed to the same patron. McKerrow has provided good reasons for thinking that Amyntas and Lord S. are Ferdinando Stanley, Lord Strange.[19]

Running to over three hundred lines, *The Choice of Valentines*, or *Nashe's Dildo*, as it is variously entitled, is by far the longest poem of his that we have and his only attempt to write narrative verse. Viewed as a work of art it adds nothing to his literary stature. The story it tells has no real point and part of it is downright silly. Nor is the notoriety it so rapidly acquired easy to understand. Its bawdry is of the elementary, direct, indecent kind. Nashe's attitude to sexual matters is too normal and healthy to be anything but dull. Very briefly summarized, the poem, which is written in the first person, tells of a visit to a brothel on St. Valentine's day. The actual sexual encounter is described in considerable detail and some attempt is made to give it a poetic colouring. When it is over, the woman laments the short-lived ardours of the man and proclaims that henceforth she will put her trust in the dildo, or artificial phallus. Why a prostitute, of all people, should be driven to such extremes Nashe does not explain. It is merely an excuse for a satirical attack on the dildo, and it was probably this satirical element in the poem that gave it its notoriety.

Valueless as poetry, *The Choice of Valentines* is, nevertheless, of some interest as an example of Nashe's way of going to work. It is largely derivative. Most of the material comes from Ovid; there is a considerable debt to the *Ars Amatoria* and a whole section of it (ll. 123–42) is lifted from the seventh elegy in Book III of the *Amores*. Nashe makes no attempt to hide his borrowings, on the contrary he seeks to excuse himself by stating quite explicitly in the epilogue that Ovid 'is the fountaine whence my streames doe flowe'. The influence of Ovid extends to more than the matter of the poem, however, for there is also something of his exuberant wealth of conceit in the lines with which Nashe paints his mistress's provocative beauty:

> She faire as fairest Planet in the Skye
>   Hir puritie to no man doeth denye.
> The verie chamber, that enclowds hir shine,
>   Looke's lyke the pallace of that God deuine,

[19] IV. 150–1 and V. 141, Note 1.

Who leade's the daie about the zodiake,
  And euerie euen discends to th'Oceane lake:
So fierce and feruent is hir radiance,
  Such fyrie st[r]ake's she darts at euerie glance,
As might enflame the icie limmes of age,
  And make pale death his surquedrie aswage
To stand and gaze upon hir Orient lamps
  Where Cupid all his chiefest ioyes encamps,
And sitts, and playes with euerie atomie
  That in hir Sunne-beames swarme aboundantlie.[20]

The picturesque richness of this passage, coupled with the Ovidian material, might well suggest that *The Choice of Valentines* belongs to the same kind of Elizabethan narrative as Marlowe's *Hero and Leander* and Shakespeare's *Venus and Adonis*. In fact, however, it does not. The model Nashe had in mind when writing the poem was, I think, undoubtedly the Chaucer of the *fabliaux* and of the Wife of Bath's Prologue. There are several echoes of Chaucer in the poem and the diction, and even the manner, of the opening lines have a Chaucerian flavour about them, or rather a smack of Chaucer's manner as refracted through the medium of Spenser:

It was the merie moneth of Februarie
  When yong-men in their iollie roguerie
Rose earelie in the morne fore breake of daie
  To seeke them valentines so trimme and gaie.
With whom they maie consorte in summer sheene,
  And dance the heidegeies on our toune-greene.
As Ale's at Easter or at Pentecost
  Perambulate the fields that flourish most,
And goe to som village abbordring neere
  To taste the creame, and cakes and such good cheere,
Or see a playe of strange moralitie
  Shewen by Bachelrie of Maningtree.[21]

As pastiche the passage is not contemptible, but as the poem goes on the Chaucerian touch fades and disappears, its ultimate effect being to emphasize, by the comparison it suggests, Nashe's inferiority to Chaucer both as a story-teller and as a poet.

The author of the *Parnassus Plays* clearly knew what he was about when he depicted Ingenioso making poems in the style of

[20] III. 410. ll. 163–76.

[21] III. 403–4, ll. 1–12.

Chaucer and of Spenser. His accuracy on this score suggests that his account of Ingenioso's activities as a ghost-writer also deserves some credit. But, while work of this kind probably enabled Nashe to live, it did nothing positive for his reputation and, by its very nature, cramped his talents. The appearance of *Pierce Penilesse* in September 1592, marks his return to the high road of properly authorized publication—it was entered in the Stationers' Register on 8 August 1592—and of writing with some real content, submitted to the judgment of the public at large.

2

*Pierce Penilesse* enjoyed an immediate success. Three editions bear the date 1592, a further edition followed in 1593 and yet a fifth in 1595. Nashe himself recognized it as his most popular work and in *Have with You to Saffron-Walden* he accuses Gabriel Harvey of using the name of Pierce to increase the sales of his *Pierce's Supererogation.* He writes:

> he [Harvey] takes a new lesson out of *Plutarch*, in making benefit of his enemie, and borrows my name, and the name of *Piers Pennilesse* (one of my Bookes), which he knew to be most saleable, (passing at the least through the pikes of sixe Impressions,) to help his bedred stuffe to limpe out of *Powles Churchyard.*[22]

He also claims in the same work that by 1596 *Pierce Penilesse* had been translated into 'the *Macaronicall* tongue' and into French.[23] The first of these claims is, I think, merely a joke, and nothing is known of any translation into French. What we do know is that from the time of the pamphlet's appearance Nashe and his creation, Pierce, were completely identified with one another and continued to be so to the end of his life. He had now succeeded in that effort to build a distinct literary personality for himself with which he had been so concerned ever since he wrote the *Anatomy of Absurdity.*

A good pointer to some of the qualities in *Pierce Penilesse* which made it so attractive when it first came out is provided by the short address, entitled 'The Printer to the Gentlemen Readers', which appears only in the first edition. It runs as follows:

> In the Authours absence, I haue been bold to publish this pleasaunt and wittie Discourse of *Pierce Penilesse his Supplication to*

[22] III. 35. [23] III. 33.

> *the Diuell*: which Title though it may seeme strange and in it selfe somewhat preposterous, yet if you vouchsafe the Reading, you shall finde reason, aswell for the Authours vncouth nomination, as for his vnwonted beginning without Epistle, Proeme, or Dedication: al which he hath inserted conceitedly in the matter; but Ile be no blab to tell you in what place. Bestow the looking, and I doubt not but you shall finde Dedication, Epistle, and Proeme to your liking.[24]

This address is, of course, a piece of advertisement, but the features of the pamphlet that it picks out for mention—its originality of form, its cleverness and its 'pleasaunt and wittie' character—are really there. They struck others besides the printer. In 1606 an anonymous pamphlet was published under the title of *The Returne of the Knight of the Poste from Hell, with the Diuels aunswer to the Supplication of Pierce Penilesse, with some Relation of the last Treasons.* This work purports to be an attempt to supply that continuation of *Pierce Penilesse* which Nashe had half promised in his epistle to the printer, published in the second edition, where he had written:

> Indeed if my leysure were such as I could wish, I might haps (halfe a yeare hence) write the returne of the *Knight of the Post* from hel, with the *Deuils* answer to the *Supplication.*[25]

The anonymous pamphlet opens with an epistle in which the author recalls his familiarity with Nashe 'some tenne yeares agone', and then goes on to say that had Nashe written the promised sequel to *Pierce Penilesse* he would have bestowed on it 'great arte, witte and laborious studie', enriching the world 'with much wittinesse' in the process. He adds that he himself has 'neither the wittie pleasantnes of his [Nashe's] conceites, nor the gaulye bitternes of his pens sharpenes'.[26] The frequent recurrence of the words *wit*, *wittie* and *wittiness*, in this near-contemporary encomium of *Pierce Penilesse*, coupled with the printer's use of the same terms, is surely significant and so, I think, is the fact that the 'wittie pleasantnes' of the work is placed before its 'gaulye bitternes'. Its primary appeal to those who first read it lay in its cleverness. It was enjoyed as a brilliant display of ingenuity on a wide variety of topics, 'variation of humours', as the writer of the anonymous pamphlet puts it.

I stress this Elizabethan estimate of *Pierce Penilesse*, because much modern criticism of it seems to me to be misguided. Nashe

[24] I. 150 [25] I. 154. [26] IV. 84.

is taken to task for failing to do what he had no intention of doing. McKerrow, who in general refrains from critical comment in the introductory and explanatory matter of his edition, makes an exception to this practice in the case of *Pierce Penilesse*. He writes:

> We need not, however, suppose that the whole work was written at the same date: indeed I think that the utter want of unity and of definite plan, which is one of its most noticeable characteristics, strongly suggests that its composition extended over a considerable period. The original idea, that of a petition to the devil, is almost lost in a mass of scarcely relevant satire. The book was, I suspect, planned merely as an attack upon the niggardliness of the wealthy and the slight support accorded to men of wit, the groundwork being that *Pierce Penilesse*, recognizing that at the present day all the gold is imprisoned in the strong-boxes of the rich, petitions the devil that it may be released. Instead, however, of confining himself to reflections upon avarice, which would naturally flow from such an idea, Nashe proceeds to a general attack upon all the vices of the time, which is not even remotely connected with the supplication itself, winding up by a borrowed discussion of the nature of devils and spirits, which has nothing to do with either of the other sections. Even into this congeries he seems to have inserted oddments at the last moment. The attack upon Richard Harvey was almost certainly such an addition, while the abuse of the Danes, which from the hints of Robert Beal would seem to have had some political motive, was probably another. Altogether one is inclined to regard *Pierce Penilesse* as representing the gleanings of two or three years.[27]

McKerrow is almost certainly right when he says that the composition of *Pierce Penilesse* was spread over two or three years; there are passages in it which have a bearing on the Marprelate controversy and recall the *Almond*, as well as the last-minute insertions he refers to. But it does not follow that Nashe ever intended to write an ordered and coherent satire on avarice, as McKerrow, and others who have followed him,[28] suppose. What impressed the printer in 1592 was precisely the fact that the elements of which *Pierce Penilesse* is composed did not appear in the expected order, or in the expected places, but were 'inserted conceitedly in the matter'. To him the apparent disorder of it was

[27] V. 18.

[28] E.g. R. G. Howarth, *Two Elizabethan Writers of Fiction*, Cape Town, 1956, pp. 7–8.

one of its main attractions and he obviously thought it would please the reading public of the day, otherwise he would not have drawn attention to it.

The effcct Nashe aims at producing is one of casual, off-hand spontaneity, as he makes plain when he states: 'I write *Quicquid in buccam venerit*, as fast as my hand can trot'.[29] The absence of a logical, orderly exposition is deliberate. He even goes out of his way to draw attention to it. At the beginning of the work he describes it as 'this Paper-monster',[30] and later the Knight of the Post, after reading the Supplication, anticipates McKerrow by describing it as a rag-bag:

> A Supplication calst thou this? (quoth the Knight of the post) it is the maddest Supplication that euer I sawe; me thinks thou hast handled all the seuen deadly sinnes in it, and spared none that exceedes his limits in any of them. *It is well done to practise thy witte*, but (I beleeue) our Lord [the devil] will cun thee little thanks for it.[31] [My italics].

Nashe could hardly have been plainer about what it was that he was trying to do. Criticism of *Pierce Penilesse* on the score of its disorderly arrangement is clearly irrelevant.

*Wit* is not an easy word to define at any time, but one of the meanings it had for Nashe and his age implied, above everything else, agility of mind, the ability to see resemblances where the ordinary man sees none and to render them in striking similes, to catch an allusion, a pun, or the reversal of an idea in a flash, to make a quick transition from one idea to another. It meant, in fact, all that Falstaff means when he says:

> Men of all sorts take a pride to gird at me: the brain of this foolish-compounded clay, man, is not able to invent anything that tends to laughter, more than I invent or is invented on me: I am not only witty in myself, but the cause that wit is in other men.[32]

Like Falstaff, Nashe is inventive, never at a loss for an answer. 'Nowe you talke of a Bee, Ile tell you a tale of a Battle-dore',[33] says the Knight of the Post to Pierce, and he is as good as his word. It is, perhaps, not surprising that Shakespeare in writing *Henry IV* should have drawn extensively on Nashe.[34]

[29] I. 195. [30] I. 161.
[31] I. 217. [32] 2 *Henry IV*, I. ii. [33] I. 221.
[34] See 1 *Henry IV*, ed. J. Dover Wilson, Cambridge, 1946, pp. 191–6.

In its careful cultivation on the wayward and the unexpected *Pierce Penilesse* has some of the qualities of the medley poem and is more like Byron's *Don Juan* than almost anything written in the interval between them. In both works the author dramatizes his own personality in that of the hero and comments on his own times. In both he emphasizes the apparent disorder of his work and makes the same excuse. At the end of *Pierce Penilesse* Nashe says:

> Whilst I am thus talking, me thinks I heare one say, What a fop is this, he entitles his booke *A Supplication to the Diuell*, and doth nothing but raile on ideots, and tels a storie of the nature of Spirits. Haue patience, good sir, and weele come to you by and by. Is it my Title you find fault with? Why, haue you not seen a Towne surnamed by the principall house in the towne, or a nobleman derive his Baronrie from a little village where he hath least land? So fareth it by me in christning of my Booke.[35]

In effect he is claiming that *Pierce Penilesse* is all the closer to life, precisely because it is not schematized.

This excuse does not mean, however, that Nashe had no literary precedents in mind when he wrote it. Had he been pressed to account for its apparent formlessness, he would probably, I think, have pointed to the writings of the Roman satirists and especially to the example of Juvenal. He had announced his intention of being 'satyricall' in the *Anatomy of Absurdity*, and the fact that Greene in his *Groatsworth of Wit* actually addresses him as 'yong *Iuuenall*, that byting Satyrist' would seem to indicate that he saw some Juvenalian features in Nashe's work. Nor was he wrong to do so. Like Nashe, Juvenal has often been criticized for weak powers of construction. Moreover, some of the devices they use are similar; both are fond of the dramatic effect that can be derived from a sudden transition from indirect to direct speech and back again.[36] Now Juvenal in a well known passage in his First Satire describes his conception of the proper matter for satirical poetry as follows:

> quidquid agunt homines, votum timor ira voluptas
> gaudia discursus, nostri farrago libelli est. [ll. 85–6]

Such a definition, interpreted literally, makes satire a kind of hotch-potch, which is exactly how Nashe thinks of it. It had the

[35] I. 240.

[36] See Gilbert Highet, *Juvenal the Satirist*, Oxford, 1954, pp. 93–7 and 170–2.

further attraction for an Elizabethan writer of linking up rather conveniently with the mediaeval idea of satire as an attack on the Seven Deadly Sins (which included *ira* and *voluptas*) an idea still very much alive in Nashe's day. The choice of Pierce as the name of the protagonist was meant to remind the reader of Langland's Piers Plowman, a figure by no means forgotten.[37]

Inheriting the two traditions of satire, the classical and the mediaeval, Nashe marries them to each other. *Pierce Penilesse* is the fruit of their union, resembling both in some ways, yet fundamentally like neither. Two features in particular distinguish it from its literary parents: first, the deliberate infusion into it of a personality; secondly, the absence from it of that moral fervour which Juvenal and Langland have in common. For Nashe, by the time he comes to write *Pierce Penilesse*, satire is neither a vehicle for despairing protest, as it had been for Juvenal, nor an impassioned plea for reform, as it had been for Langland, but rather a stage, a convenient platform, on which he can exhibit his virtuosity as a writer. This is what I take C. S. Lewis to mean when he writes:

> Paradoxically, though Nashe's pamphlets are commercial literature, they come very close to being, in another way, 'pure' literature: literature which is, as nearly as possible, without a subject. In a certain sense of the verb 'say', if asked what Nashe 'says', we should have to reply, Nothing.[38]

The verdict is too sweeping; there are some subjects, notably learning and poetry, which really do matter to Nashe; but in the main it is true. In most of his writings he has no subject in the sense that he is not wholly absorbed in what he is saying, not concerned solely with conveying the nature and significance of something he is deeply interested in. Instead of his eye being fixed on a topic, it is fixed on himself writing about that topic, on the kind of figure he is cutting in the public eye, on the effect he is making. The way he says a thing counts for more with him than the thing said. It is for this reason that he is, and always has been, a minor writer.

*Pierce Penilesse* bears this view of him out. Lacking in plan or

[37] See Hallet Smith, *Elizabethan Poetry*, Cambridge, Mass., 1952, pp. 208–16.

[38] C. S. Lewis, *English Literature in the Sixteenth Century*, Oxford, 1954, p. 416.

order, when considered in terms of its exposition of a subject, it is anything but planless or shapeless, when looked at in terms of effect. Its structure is rhetorical, not logical. It falls into four clearly defined sections, nicely balanced against each other. In the first, which I shall call the Induction, Pierce speaks directly to the reader about his poverty and then describes the events leading up to his meeting with the Knight of the Post. In the second the Knight of the Post reads out what Pierce has written in the Supplication, which is really a satirical picture of English society in 1592. In return for his portrait of England and the behaviour of its inhabitants, Pierce very fairly asks the Knight of the Post, who is a minor devil in human shape, for a description of hell and a disquisition on its inhabitants. The request is granted, and the answer to it occupies the third section of the work. At the end of it the Knight of the Post goes off to attend to business. Pierce, left alone, turns to the reader once more; the fourth and last section opens with the words: 'Gentle Reader, *tandem aliquando* I am at leasure to talke to thee'. Thereupon he returns to his original theme, complains about the neglect of learning and the niggardliness of patrons, works in an epistle to his readers and a dedication to his patron, Amyntas, carefully placing them at the end, where no one would expect to find them, and then proceeds to 'breake off this endlesse argument of speech abruptlie'. The whole thing is rather like a little play in which the stage is occupied first by Pierce, then by Pierce and the Knight of the Post, each of whom has his say, and finally once again by Pierce alone. There is a marked symmetry about it all of the kind that the Elizabethans admired.

Of the four sections the least interesting to a modern reader is the third, which is given over to the Knight of the Post's discourse on hell and its devils and to some rather obscure political and religious satire. Its comparative failure is not due, however, to any faultiness of planning—on the contrary it is clearly designed to complement Pierce's discourse on men—but to the fact that Nashe, of necessity, can no longer draw on the personal experience which stands him in such good stead when he writes of London and of England, and is compelled, therefore, to fall back on his reading. Most of his account of hell is translated from a sixteenth-century work on demonology, *De Illorum Daemonum qui sub lunari collimitio versantur ortu . . . Isagoge*, by the German scholar Georgius Pictorius, published in 1563. Usually when Nashe translates a brief Latin passage, in the shape of a well-known tag or moral maxim, he contrives to give it a racy, idiomatic flavour and to add a touch of mockery to it, but in handling the passages he uses from the *Isagoge* he makes no attempt to do this. The result, as he himself recognized, was 'tedious'; writing of a flat and neutral kind which, though its matter may have been topical in 1592, has nothing to say to us now. Moreover, Nashe's great failing as a dramatist is already evident here. He can dramatize himself in the form of Pierce, but he cannot create characters distinct from himself. The Knight of the Post is a nullity with neither a personality nor an idiom of his own, and his description of hell is little more than a catalogue of names.

The rest of *Pierce Penilesse* is a very different matter. There is an infectious gaiety about it. Poor, neglected and, above all, quite unrespectable, Pierce, with a fine, cockney impudence dispenses moral advice to the nation at large and to the professional moralists in particular, and conducts a thorough-going campaign against the narrow-mindedness and materialism of the Puritans and the middle class, whom he tends to identify with one another. The whole situation is topsy-turvy and in itself favourable to wit, in the sense in which Nashe uses the term. Dissoluteness instructs self-righteousness.

His first task is to establish the identity of Pierce. He therefore opens with the autobiographical passage I have referred to already [p. 51] in which Pierce records his vain efforts to make a living by writing. The tone of the complaint is individual. There is nothing querulous about it; a vein of wry humour inhibits self-pity, and leads on to a direct attack on the main enemy when Pierce reflects in this fashion:

> Thereby I grew to consider how many base men that wanted those parts which I had, enioyed content at will, and had wealth at commaund: I cald to minde a Cobler, that was worth fiue hundred pound, an Hostler that had built a goodly Inne, and might dispende fortie pound yerely by his Land, a Carre-man in a lether pilche that had whipt out a thousand pound out of his horse taile: and haue I more wit than all these (thought I to my selfe)? am I better borne? am I better brought vp? yea and better fauored? and yet am I a begger? What is the cause? how am I crost? or whence is this curse? [39]

[39] I. 158.

It is the wealth of specific instances that gives the passage its reality, and the easy slide into direct speech with that volley of questions that makes it urgent. By the end of it Pierce already has a character and temper of his own. He is something more than the neglected scholar, and can now be used as the vehicle for an attack on patrons of literature for their inability to distinguish between work of merit and cheap journalism, for a lament over Sir Philip Sidney, the dead Mæcenas of the age, and for a verbal assault on wealthy upstarts who look on arts and learning as a waste of time and effort. The attitude that Mathew Arnold was to label Philistine is dramatized, set in a particular time and place and made concrete by an idiomatic turn of phrase when Nashe depicts the man of wealth shrugging off the scholar's criticism of him and his ways with the complacency begotten by material success:

> I, I, weele giue loosers leaue to talke: it is no matter what *Sic probo* and his pennilesse companions prate, whilest we haue the gold in our coffers: this is it that will make a knaue an honest man, and my neighbour *Cramptons* stripling a better Gentleman than this Grandsier.[40]

Faced with a world in which money is the only value and in which the rich will do nothing for the man of letters, Pierce decides to by-pass them, as it were, by appealing direct to their master, the devil, who, he has heard, is always ready to advance a loan on the security of a man's soul. Nashe is obviously trading on the interest created by Marlowe's *Dr. Faustus,* but he gives the familiar material a characteristic twist in the direction of the comic and the realistic. His devil, unlike Marlowe's, is closely related to the economic and social facts of the time. He is seen as an encloser and is 'so famous a Politician in purchasing, that Hel (which at the beginning was but an obscure Village) is now become a huge Cittie, whereunto all Countries are tributary'.[41] Hell, in fact, as Shelley was to remark some two hundred years later, is a city much like London, and Nashe's devil bears a close resemblance to the unscrupulous businessman of the day.

Pierce treats the devil as a potential patron and writes a supplication to him in proper form, but, having completed it, is then faced with the problem of finding a suitable postman to deliver it.

[40] I. 160. [41] I. 161.

This problem Nashe very ingeniously casts into the form of a dialogue between Pierce and the reader:

> But written and all, here lies the question; where shal I finde this olde Asse, that I may deliuer it? Masse, thats true: they say the Lawyers haue the Diuell and all; and it is like enough he is playing Ambodexter amongst them. Fie, fie, the Diuell a driuer in Westminster hall? it can neuer be.
>
> Now, I pray, what doe you imagine him to bee? Perhaps you thinke it is not possible he should bee so graue. Oh then you are in an errour, for hee is as formall as the best Scriuener of them all.[42]

The effect of this dialogue, deliberately unliterary in a manner Nashe had learnt from Martin and studiedly casual and informal in tone, is to create an intimacy between the writer and the reader, who is thus drawn into and takes part in the show that is being staged for his entertainment.

Pierce now goes to Westminster Hall to enquire among the lawyers 'if there were any such Sergeant, Bencher, Counsellor, Attorney, or Pettifogger, as *Signior Cornuto Diabolo*, with the good face'. He is met with true legal caution and the answer, No. Thereupon, he makes his way to the Exchange to consult the merchants. They also deny all knowledge of the devil. It is at this point that Nashe introduces the first of those humorous portraits of contemporary types which are the most impressive feature of *Pierce Penilesse*. He writes:

> At length (as Fortune serued) I lighted vpon an old, stradling Vsurer, clad in a damaske cassocke, edged with Fox fur, a paire of trunke slops, sagging down like a Shoomakers wallet, and a shorte thrid-bare gown on his backe, fac't with moatheaten budge; vpon his head he wore a filthy, course biggin, and next it a garnish of nightcaps, which a sage butten-cap, of the form of a cow-sheard, ouer spread very orderly: a fat chuffe it was, I remember, with a gray beard cut short to the stumps, as though it were grimde, and a huge woorme-eaten nose, like a cluster of grapes hanging downewardes.[43]

This word-picture is based on observation; but it is larger than life and more interesting. The carefully chosen adjectives, all

[42] I. 162. [43] I. 162–3.

emphasizing the squalor of the man's appearance, and the extravagant yet telling similes charge it with an imaginative vitality that no Elizabethan portrait painter can rival. It is a witty picture, expressing an attitude towards a social type in the process of describing him. Nashe's usurer, like his devil, is both comic and formidable at the same time.

Even the usurer, however, for all his promising appearance, can do little to help Pierce, beyond telling him that the devil is at home sick of the gout, and that it is a difficult and expensive business to obtain an audience with him. Depressed by this news, Pierce goes off to St. Paul's, at that time one of the great meeting places in London, in the hope of picking up an invitation to dinner from some acquaintance there. Here at last he is successful in his search. He is accosted by 'a neat pedanticall fellow, in forme of a Cittizen', who takes an immediate interest in his melancholy look and asks him what is wrong. Pierce tells him and the precise figure then reveals that he is 'a spirite in nature and essence', who has taken human shape in order to win souls for hell. The *métier* he has adopted for this purpose is that of a knight of the post, the cant term for a professional perjurer. He is, of course, in regular correspondence with his headquarters in the lower regions and offers to dispatch the Supplication by the soul of the next extortioner to die or next cutpurse to be hanged. Delighted with this fortunate solution to his difficulties, Pierce hands the Supplication over, telling the Knight of the Post that he may read it out if he so wishes. The offer is accepted.

I have described this Induction in detail, because the general effect produced by *Pierce Penilesse* is largely dependent on it. The autobiographical matter and the conversational tone not only establish Pierce himself as an individual, but also serve to root the whole fantastic episode firmly in the London of the times. Couched in these terms, the old complaint of the scholar, that the world has no use for the things of the spirit and will gladly leave its artists and thinkers to starve, takes on a new look. Satire has acquired some of the characteristics of a variety show in which the chief performer is also the producer, and the author of the script as well.

The Supplication itself, which forms the second part of *Pierce Penilesse* and is the real core of the whole work, is essentially a series of variations on the old formula of the Seven Deadly Sins.

Gabriel Harvey, in his *Four Letters*, accuses Nashe of plagiarizing it all from a play by Richard Tarlton. He says that it is

> not Dunstically botched-vp, but right formally conceiued, according to the stile, and tenour of Tarletons president, his famous play of the seauen Deadly sinnes.[44]

The charge was well calculated to annoy Nashe, who prided himself on his superiority to such popular writers as Tarlton, but, since nothing of the play in question has survived, except the stage-plot of its second part,[45] there is no means of knowing whether it is true or not. Nashe, as was to be expected, denied it with considerable force in his *Strange News*, seizing on Harvey's remarks as a golden opportunity for a display of violent, picturesque, personal abuse. He writes:

> Hang thee, hang thee, thou common coosener of curteous readers, thou grosse shifter for shitten tapsterly iests, haue I *imitated* Tarltons *play of the seauen deadly sinnes in my plot of Pierce Penilesse*? . . .
>
> Is it lawfull but for one preacher to preach of the ten commandements? hath none writ of the fiue senses but *Aristotle*? was sinne so vtterly abolished with *Tarltons* play of the seuen deadly sins, that ther could be nothing said *supra* of that argument?
>
> Canst thou exemplifie vnto mee (thou impotent moatecatching carper) one minnum of the particular deuice of his play that I purloind? There be manie men of one name that are nothing a kindred. Is there any further distribution of sins, not shadowed vnder these seuen large spreading branches of iniquity, on which a man may worke, and not tread on *Tarletons* heeles? If not, what blemish is it to *Pierce Penilesse* to begin where the Stage doth ende, to build vertue a Church on that foundation that the Deuill built his Chappell?[46]

The idea of the Supplication as a church for virtue is not one that is likely to occur to any reader of it; and I do not think it occurred to Nashe until he had to meet Harvey's criticism. The most striking features of his treatment of the old theme are that his approach to it is consistently comic and that he sees it in a social, not a religious, context. The comic tone is set by the

[44] *Harvey's Works*, ed. Grosart, I. 194.

[45] See W. W. Greg. *Dramatic Documents from the Elizabethan Playhouse*, Oxford, 1931.

[46] I. 304–5.

opening, which is a splendid piece of parody. Nashe takes the customary form of a petition to a great man and gives it a twist by the flamboyant mock titles he coins for the devil. The Supplication begins with the following address:

> To the high and mightie Prince of Darknesse, Donsell dell Lucifer, King of Acheron, Stix, and Phlegeton, Duke of Tartary, marquesse of Cocytus, and Lord High Regent of Lymbo: his distressed Orator, Pierce Penilesse, wisheth encrease of damnation, and malediction eternall, Per Iesum Christum Dominum nostrum.[47]

The prince of darkness is a gentleman; he is also, very topically, a Spaniard. There is a high-spirited ebullience of linguistic invention and a gay impudence of manner in this opening that is well sustained in what follows. Nashe never forgets that he is writing to the devil, and, during the course of the Supplication, addresses him by such titles as these: 'your sinfulnes', 'your graceles Maiestie', 'your helhood', 'noble Lants-graue of Lymbo', 'Master *Os foetidum*, Bedle of the Blacke-smithes' and 'Clim of the clough, thou that vsest to drinke nothing but scalding lead and sulpher in hell'.

Clearly Nashe's devil has nothing to do with the terrifying figure that haunted the imagination of the preachers and a great deal to do with the familiar figure of the morality plays. The same tilt away from the theological and terrifying and towards the social and ridiculous is to be seen in Nashe's treatment of the seven deadly sins. He is not interested in these sins as states of the soul, but as social phenomena, and, broadly speaking, he has two main objects: first, to attack the cult of money and material values in general; secondly, to expose affectation of every kind and to provide entertainment in the course of doing it. The main instrument he uses for both purposes is the character, the sketch of a social type, or, more rarely, of a social evil. It is, perhaps, significant of the value he sets on amusement that the second kind of sketch is used only at the outset. Pierce's first request to the devil is that he should give his servant, Avarice, orders to set gold free from the clutches of the wealthy, who hoard it, so that it may do its proper devil's work in the world at large. It is an ingenious plea made all the more effective by a lengthy description of the gaol in which gold is immured and of its two keepers, Greediness and his wife, Dame

[47] I. 165.

Niggardize. Greediness is basically that stock figure of so much Elizabethan and Jacobean satire, the usurer who employs all the instruments of the law in order to hook landed gentry into his clutches and to deprive them of their estates. We have already met a specimen of the class in the shape of the 'old, stradling Vsurer,' whom Pierce encounters at the Exchange [see p. 68 above], but in the figure of Greediness Nashe builds the type out into a larger allegorical being by contriving a most elaborate outfit for him which is, in effect, a lively, pictorial representation of his methods with the image of hooking recurring time after time. Greediness is presented in the inner part of the prison he has built for gold:

> prepared to deuoure all that enter, attyred in a Capouch of written parchment, buttond downe before with Labels of wax, and lined with sheepes fels for warmenes: his Cappe furd with cats skins, after the Muscouie fashion, and all to be tasseld with Angle-hookes, in stead of Aglets, ready to catch hold of all those to whom he shewes any humblenes: for his breeches, they were made of the lists of broad cloaths, which he had by letters pattents assured him and his heyres, to the vtter ouerthrowe of Bowcases and Cushin makers, and bumbasted they were, like Beere barrels, with statute Marchants and forfeitures. But of al, his shooes were the strangest, which, being nothing els but a couple of crab shels, were toothd at the tooes with two sharp sixpennie nailes, that digd vp euery dunghil they came by for gould, and snarld at the stones as he went in the street, because they were so common for men, women, and children to tread vpon, and he could not deuise how to wrest an odde fine out of any of them.
>
> Thus walkes hee vp and downe all his life time, with an yron crow in his hand in steed of a staffe, and a Sariants Mace in his mouth (which night and day he still gnaws vpon), and either busies himselfe in setting siluer lime twigs to entangle yoong Gentlemen, and casting foorth silken shraps to catch Woodcocks, or in syuing of Muckhils and shop-dust, whereof he will boult a whole cartload to gaine a bowd Pinne.[48]

The technique used to transform the social type into this allegorical being has much in common with that employed by Spenser, a poet for whom Nashe frequently expresses his admiration. From what he says at the end of *Pierce Penilesse*[49] it is evident that he had been reading the first three books of *The Faerie Queene*, published in 1590, with interest and pleasure and that they were

[48] I. 166–7. [49] I. 243–4.

fresh in his mind. I have no doubt that, like many readers since, he had been deeply impressed by such figures as Errour and Despair in Book I, Mammon in Book II and Malbecco in Book III, as well as by the Pageant of the Seven Deadly Sins, and that he learnt much from these examples about the art of translating human activities, such as those of the businessman, into concrete images that cohere to form a whole that is monstrous and fantastic yet at the same time significant and convincing.

Greediness, presented in this way and placed very much in the foreground, is the central and dominating figure in Nashe's picture of England in 1592. The rest of the canvas is filled in with figures of the other kind, portraits of social types that anticipate, and often in their vitality outdo, the Theophrastan characters that were to become so popular in the early seventeenth century. Compared with the characters of Overbury, or even of Earle, Nashe's are less studied, more spontaneous, closer to everyday life. The complaint of Pride, the sin to which he devotes most space, is largely made up of sketches of this kind and presents us with such types as the upstart, the counterfeit politician, the prodigal, 'Mistris Minx, a Marchants wife, that wil eate no Cherries, forsooth, but when they are at twenty shillings a pound,' and those regular butts of Elizabethan satire, the Spaniard, the Frenchman, the Italian and the Dane. The most effective of them—and some are very incisive indeed—are built on a close observation of manners and speech, geared to the same kind of healthy contempt for fashionable affectations that Shakespeare was to give to Faulconbridge, Mercutio and Hotspur a few years later. Nashe, in fact, like Fielding, sees affectation as the only source of the true Ridiculous, and through his attacks on it he is able to extend the range of his satire to cover other classes in society besides the business community. To demonstrate his way of going to work I quote his character of the upstart:

> All malcontent sits the greasie son of a Cloathier, and complaines (like a decaied Earle) of the ruine of ancient houses: whereas the Weauers loomes first framed the web of his honor, and the lockes of wool, that bushes and brambles haue tooke for toule of insolent sheep, that would needs striue for the wall of a fir bush, haue made him of the tenths of their tar, a Squier of low degree; and of the collections of their scatterings, a Justice, *Tam Marti quam Mercurio*, of Peace and of Coram. Hee will bee humorous,

forsoth, and haue a broode of fashions by himselfe. Sometimes (because Loue commonly weares the liuerey of Wit) hee will be an *Inamorato Poeta*, and sonnet a whole quire of paper in praise of Lady *Swin-snout*, his yeolow fac'd Mistres, and weare a feather of her rain-beaten fan for a fauor, like a fore-horse. Al *Italionato* is his talke, and his spade peake is as sharpe as if he had been a Pioner before the walls of *Roan*. Hee will despise the barbarisme of his own Countrey, and tel a whole Legend of lyes of his trauailes vnto *Constantinople*. If he be challenged to fight, for his delatorye excuse, hee obiects that it is not the custome of the Spaniard or the Germaine, to looke back to euery dog that barks. You shall see a dapper Iacke, that hath been but ouer at *Deepe*, wring his face round about, as a man would stir vp a mustard pot, and talke English through the teeth, like *Iaques Scabd-hams*, or *Monsieur Mingo de Moustrap*: when (poore slaue) he hath but dipt his bread in wilde Boares greace, and come home againe; or been bitten by the shins by a wolfe: and saith, he hath aduentured vpon the Barricadoes of *Gurney* or *Guingan*, and fought with the yong *Guise* hand to hand.[50]

The affectations pilloried in this sketch have been studied with care and, varied though the material is, it has all been given a particular slant. Even the sheep are described as 'insolent' and seen as though they were gallants standing upon their dignity, while the action of the man screwing up his face in order to talk English with a French accent is fixed for ever by the picturesque simile 'as a man would stir vp a mustard pot'. Observation and the imaginative use of language that gives it edge and bite work together to produce a portrait that looks forward to those which are to be found in some of Ben Jonson's comedies. Indeed, it looks as though Jonson learnt much from Nashe about the art of taking a social type and endowing it with individuality. *Every Man Out of His Humour* in particular is like a Nashe satire, provided with a few elements of plot and transferred to the stage. Moreover, it is highly probable that Carlo Buffone, one of the main figures in it is based on the same historical personage, Charles Chester, as Nashe describes in the section of *Pierce Penilesse* devoted to the sin of Wrath.[51] More striking still, the essential traits of Bobadil in *Every Man in His Humour* are already visible in Nashe's sketch of the counterfeit politician, as he calls him, who lives in misery for most of the year, so that he may make an occasional impressive

[50] I. 168–9. [51] I. 190–1.

appearance at 'the eighteene pence Ordenary', and who makes it his business to

> take vppe a scornfull melancholy in his gate and countenance, and talke as though our common welth were but a mockery of gouernment, and our Maiestrates fooles, who wronged him in not looking into his deserts, not imploying him in State matters, and that, if more regard were not had of him very shortly, the whole Realme should haue a misse of him, and he would go (I mary would he) where he should be more accounted of.[52]

This character is Bobadil in *decimo sexto* with attitude and idiom already complete.

These satirical characters are the staple of the Supplication and the best things in it. Through them Nashe succeeds in rendering the daily life of Elizabethan London with a peculiar combination of picturesqueness and incisiveness. Characters alone, however, were not enough for his purpose. By themselves they could be monotonous; and he was a commercial writer who had to please. He acknowledges as much in a passage which is part of an attack on his old foes, the 'dul-headed Diuines', who had shown themselves to be 'enemies of Poetrie' and who had described him as a 'babling Ballat-maker'. He retorts that his accusers have no vein of imagination in them, that they borrow the matter of their sermons from others, and then goes on to address them as follows:

> Should we (as you) borrowe all out of others, and gather nothing of our selues, our names should bee baffuld on euerie Booke-sellers Stall, and not a Chandlers Mustard-pot but would wipe his mouthe with our wast paper. Newe Herrings, new, wee must crye, euery time wee make our selues publique, or else we shall bee christened with a hundred newe tytles of Idiotisme.[53]

To meet the demand for variety, Nashe falls back on another traditional form of entertainment, the jest-book. He diversifies his descriptions of the various sins with comic anecdotes. These merry tales and rare witty jests, as he calls them, are in general much less interesting than the characters. They tend to smell of the lamp and are often too long-winded. Occasionally, however, one of them makes its point quickly and economically, as, for instance, does the following illustration of the sin of Wrath:

> Amongst other cholericke wise Iustices, he was one, that hauing a play presented before him and his Towneship by *Tarlton* and the

[52] I. 170. [53] I. 192.

> rest of his fellowes, her Maiesties seruants, and they were now entring into their first merriment (as they call it), the people began exceedingly to laugh, when *Tarlton* first peept out his head. Whereat the Iustice, not a little moued, and seeing with his beckes and nods hee could not make them cease, he went with his staffe, and beat them round about vnmercifully on the bare pates, in that they, being but Farmers and poore countrey Hyndes, would presume to laugh at the Queenes men, and make no more account of her cloath in his presence.[54]

Apocryphal or not, the tale has the appearance of truth, it belongs to the same order of things as Bully Bottom and his fellow mechanicals. But in general the inset stories compare poorly as narrative with the Induction where Nashe writes in the first person.

The actual topics Nashe handles in the Supplication, as distinct from the particular slant he gives to them, are not in general at all novel. He repeats the charges which preachers, poets and pamphleteers had been making since the fourteenth century. The lack of charity, the decay of 'housekeeping', the growth of luxury in food and dress, the prevalence of flattery, the maladministration of justice and the general spread of immorality were all well worn themes by the time he dealt with them. He reiterates the usual generalizations about foreigners and outdoes Ascham himself in his picture of Italy, which he describes as 'the Academie of manslaughter, the sporting place of murther, the Apothecary-shop of poyson for all Nations'.[55]

On the whole, however, minor abuses prove a more fruitful theme for stylistic fire-works than major ones. On subjects such as the use of cosmetics he can employ his eye for detail and his sense of the fantastic in a way that he cannot when he tries to deal with such general matters as wrath or envy. One remembers his 'curious Dames', whose 'lips are as lauishly red, as if they vsed to kisse an okerman euery morning',[56] and his ancient bawds, whom he describes as 'old hacksters . . . in the wrinckles of whose face ye may hide false dice, and play at cherry-pit in the dint of their cheekes'. Nashe is far more at home as a critic of manners than of morals; happier when abusing his personal enemy, Richard Harvey, than when attacking the national enemy, Philip of Spain. The real impulse behind his best writing is a delight in the multifarious variety of life, expressing itself in the form of comic exag-

[54] I. 188. [55] I. 186. [56] I. 180.

geration, not a passionate conviction about the nature of right and wrong, leading to moral censoriousness.

Nevertheless, there are two general complaints running through the Supplication which do matter deeply to Nashe, and they are closely connected with each other. The first, as I have already pointed out, is a protest against the growth of materialism and money power. Inevitably this protest tends to be an attack on the middle class, but it is by no means a blind or undiscriminating condemnation of them. The offence of this section of the community in his eyes is not that they 'get on'. On the contrary, he believes that ability should be rewarded and is proud of the fluid nature of English society. In his lengthy discourse on the pride of the Danes he contrasts their rigid social arrangements, in which 'none but the son of a Corporall must be a Corporall', very unfavourably with those existing in his own country, where merit is the criterion of social success and where it is possible for 'the common Lawyers (suppose in the beginning they are but husbandmens sons) [to] come in time to be chiefe Fathers of the land, and manie of them not the meanest of the Priuie Counsell'.[57] What Nashe disapproves of is, first, the use of illegitimate business methods, especially the practice of usury which he regards as iniquitous, and, secondly, the social irresponsibility of the successful. In his view far too many of the new rich fail to carry out the duties proper to the station in life they have won for themselves; they are uncharitable, they have no respect for valour or learning and, worst of all, they hate poetry.

To this last complaint Nashe reverts time and again and, although he was, of course, an interested party, he is very much in earnest about the importance of poetry. Some of his statements about it are conventional. Like his contemporaries, he regards it as a moral agent and justifies it on the grounds that it encourages virtue and discourages vice, but, unlike them, he does not see this as its only effect, or, indeed, even as its chief effect. Instead he tells us about the influence the poets were exerting on the speech of the nation at large. He writes:

> To them that demaund, what fruites the Poets of our time bring forth, or wherein they are able to proue themselues necessary to the state? Thus I answere. First and formost, they have cleansed our language from barbarisme and made the vulgar sort here in

[57] I. 178.

> *London* (which is the fountaine whose riuers flowe round about *England*) to aspire to a richer puritie of speach, than is communicated with the Comminaltie of any Nation vnder heauen.[58]

Now this statement is a really valuable piece of information of a kind all too rare in Elizabethan criticism. It tells us something about the interests, the speech habits and the general cultural level of the ordinary citizen of the day that we could only guess at without it, and that has a most significant bearing on his attitude to drama as well as to poetry. The notion that the much maligned groundling only tolerated splendid poetry in the theatre for the sake of the violent action and the clowning that went with it can hardly survive this piece of contemporary witness, which is all the more convincing because Nashe's appreciation of the influence that London English was having throughout the country at large shows that he really does know what he is talking about.

It is observations of this nature that make Nashe in some ways the most interesting and informative of all Elizabethan critics. The majority of them seem to have had no eyes at all for what was actually going on around them. Aristotle, Horace and their commentators mattered far more to them than the poems and plays that were appearing at the time. Nashe, however, did know what was going on, recognized its quality and voiced his pride in it. In the long drawn out and foggy battle[59] between the enemies of the drama and its apologists his contribution is distinguished by its spirit and its originality. Whereas most of those who sought to defend the theatre were far too apologetic and made the fatal mistake of meeting their opponents on the same moral and social grounds from which the attack had been launched, Nashe boldly turned the tables and conducted a counter-offensive. Two of the main charges levelled at the theatre were that it encouraged idleness and immorality, or, in theological terminology, the sin of Sloth and the sin of Luxury, which was looked on as a consequence of Sloth. What a shock of surprise, then, must the common reader of 1592 have had when on turning to Pierce's Complaint of Sloth (i.e. satire on Sloth) he found himself reading a defence of the theatre and an attack on its enemies! Here was wit in the true sense in

[58] I. 193.

[59] See E. K. Chambers, *The Elizabethan Stage*, Oxford, 1923, I. 236–68, and J. W. H. Atkins, *English Literary Criticism: The Renascence*, London, 1947, 216–61.

which he understood the word, the complete reversal of an expected idea.

The audacity of the general plan is matched by the gay *élan* with which the detailed argument is conducted. Nashe begins his defence of play-going by looking at the theatre from the political point of view. Working from the assumption that in any country 'there is a certaine waste of the people for whome there is no vse, but warre', he argues that it is essential these people be occupied in peacetime, otherwise they become troublesome and mutinous. He then continues thus:

> To this effect, the pollicie of Playes is very necessary, howsoeuer some shallow-braind censurers (not the deepest serchers into the secrets of gouernment) mightily oppugne them. For whereas the after-noone beeing the idlest time of the day; wherein men that are their owne masters (as Gentlemen of the Court, the Innes of the Courte, and the number of Captaines and Souldiers about *London*) do wholy bestow themselues vpon pleasure, and that pleasure they deuide (how vertuously it skils not) either into gameing, following of harlots, drinking, or seeing a Play: is it not then better (since of foure extreames all the world cannot keepe them but they will choose one) that they should betake them to the least, which is Playes?[60]

Here the Puritan argument that plays are incitements to immorality has been turned back on its authors with a vengeance by reference to the facts, by pointing to what actually happens. Not content with this victory, however, Nashe now goes on to show that plays are 'a rare exercise of vertue'. History plays in particular encourage patriotism and are a standing reproof to the degeneracy of the present in comparison with the glorious past they depict. And then with a fine flourish he accuses the enemies of the theatre, whom he cleverly identifies with the unscrupulous businessmen of the day, of being interested in nothing but money:

> I will defend it against any Collian, or clubfisted Vsurer of them all, there is no immortalitie can be giuen a man on earth like vnto Playes. What talke I to them of immortalitie, that are the onely vnderminers of Honour, and doe enuie any man that is not sprung vp by base Brokerie like themselues? They care not if all the auncient houses were rooted out, so that, like the Burgomasters of the Low-countries, they might share the gouernment amongst them

[60] I. 211–12.

> as States, and be quarter-maisters of our Monarchie. All Artes to them are vanitie: and, if you tell them what a glorious thing it is to haue *Henrie* the fifth represented on the Stage, leading the French King prisoner, and forcing both him and the Dolphin to sweare fealty, I, but (will they say) what do we get by it? Respecting neither the right of Fame that is due to true Nobilitie deceased, nor what hopes of eternitie are to be proposed to aduentrous mindes, to encourage them forward, but onely their execrable luker, and filthie vnquenchable auarice.[61]

At this point Nashe's two major concerns, his championing of poetry and the liberal arts and his firm opposition to Philistinism and materialism, coincide with one another. It is the centrepiece of his argument. Having stated it, he backs it up with the usual commonplaces about the function of the drama as a moral agent and as a vehicle for mass instruction, but he shows his independence of judgment once more when, with manifest pride, he contrasts English players and English theatres with those of other countries and of ancient Rome. It is a welcome change to find an Elizabethan critic who, far from considering it his job to apologize for actors, actually glories in their achievement. Yet this is what Nashe does when he writes:

> Our Players are not as the players beyond sea, a sort of squirting baudie Comedians, that haue whores and common Curtizens to playe womens partes, and forbeare no immodest speech or vnchast action that may procure laughter; but our Sceane is more statelye furnisht than euer it was in the time of *Roscius*, our representations honourable, and full of gallant resolution, not consisting, like theirs, of a Pantaloun, a Whore, and a Zanie, but of Emperours, Kings, and Princes; whose true Tragedies (*Sophocleo cothurno*) they do vaunt.
>
> Not *Roscius* nor *Aesope*, those admyred tragedians that haue liued euer since before Christ was borne, could euer performe more in action than famous *Ned Allen*.[62]

In his defence of plays and players, as in his portraits of London types, Nashe's strength lies in his powers of observation and in his respect for the facts observed. He follows no fashion, but looks at things as they are, makes up his own mind about them and records what he thinks without havering and without recourse to authority for support.

[61] I. 212–13. [62] I. 215.

In addition to the social satire and the literary criticism, which provide the two main strands of interest in *Pierce Penilesse*, Nashe also finds a place within the elastic confines of the pamphlet for religious, political and personal satire. Not only does he attack the Puritans on every occasion he can make, but he also expresses his strong opposition to those sceptical tendencies in religious thought which are associated with the name of Christopher Marlowe and with the so-called Raleigh circle. It is hard not to be reminded of the charges made against Marlowe by the informer, Richard Baines, [63] when Nashe writes:

> I heare say there be Mathematitions abroad that will prooue men before *Adam*; and they are harboured in high places, who will maintaine it to the death, that there are no diuels.[64]

Here, as throughout his work, Nashe's attitude to religious matters is thoroughly orthodox. A staunch adherent of the Church of England, he disapproves of sects and schisms; and the disquisition on hell and its devils that he puts into the mouth of the Knight of the Post is certainly intended to be, among other things, an answer to those 'phantasticall refyners of philosophie', as he calls them, who seek to persuade men that 'hell is nothing but error, and that none but fooles and Idiotes and Machanicall men, that haue no learning, shall be damned'.[65] It looks very much as though Nashe, when he wrote these words, was thinking of the lines in the Prologue to *The Jew of Malta* where the ghost of Machiavelli says:

> I count religion but a childish toy,
> And hold there is no sin but ignorance.

The marked similarity between the opposition to sects expressed in *Pierce Penilesse* and that expressed in the *Almond* is a further argument for Nashe's authorship of the latter work. Even closer resemblances to the *Almond* are found, however, in the political satire in *Pierce Penilesse*, which takes the form of two loosely connected fables, one about the Bear and the Ape, the other about the Fox and the Chameleon. The two tales are told by the Knight of the Post to illustrate the sin of hypocrisy. In the first he relates how the Bear, 'the chiefe Burgomaster of all the Beasts vnder the Lyon', begins to take advantage of his position and to prey on the

[63] *The Life of Marlowe and the Tragedy of Dido Queen of Carthage*, by C. F. Tucker Brooke, London, 1930, pp. 98–100.

[64] I. 172

[65] I. 218.

other animals until, surfeited with ordinary fare, he takes a fancy to a splendid horse which Nashe, for some reason that is quite obscure to me, refers to as a 'Cammell'. Not knowing how to overcome the horse, the Bear consults the Ape, who advises him to dig a pit. This the Bear does; the horse falls in; the Ape leaps on his back to bridle him and then the Bear seizes him. The Bear follows up this crime with others and eventually, growing weary of a meat diet, longs for honey. To secure it he makes use of the services of the Fox and the Chameleon, who go about the country persuading the husbandmen to give up keeping bees and to replace them with wasps. They manage to convince some of the 'light vnconstant multitude' to take this rash step, but in the end their plot is overheard and they are apprehended and imprisoned.

> But long ere this, the Beare, impatient of delaies, and consumed with an inward greife in himselfe, that hee might not haue his will of a fat Hind that outran him, he went into the woods all melancholie, and there died for pure anger.[66]

Gabriel Harvey in his *Four Letters* described these fables as 'parlous Tales',[67] implying that they had some allegorical meaning. Nashe in his *Strange News* denied the charge, but did so in a manner that makes it pretty clear that Harvey was right. He writes:

> The tale of the Beare and the Foxe, how euer it may set fooles heads a worke a farre off, yet I had no concealed ende in it but, in the one, to describe the right nature of a bloudthirsty tyrant, whose indefinite appetite all the pleasures in the earth haue no powre to bound in goodnes, but he must seeke a new felicitie in varietie of cruelty, and destroying all other mens prosperitie; for the other, to figure an hypocrite: Let it be *Martin*, if you will, or some old dog that bites sorer than hee, who secretlie goes and seduceth country Swaines.[68]

Following up the hint given here by Nashe himself, McKerrow came to the conclusion that 'the Fox is perhaps Cartwright or Martin, and the old Chamaeleon either Martin or Penry'.[69] He also made the suggestion that the Bear might be Robert, Earl of Leicester, whose cognizance was the bear and ragged staff. The whole matter has since been studied in considerable detail by

[66] I. 226. [67] *Harvey's Works*, I. 205. [68] I. 320–1.
[69] IV. 139–40.

Donald J. McGinn, who points to some close parallel passages in the *Almond* and decides that the Bear is Leicester, the Fox Cartwright and the Chameleon Penry, whom he identifies with Martin.[70] The two latter identifications are, I think, correct, but I am not convinced that the Bear is Leicester. In the first place, although Leicester had died in 1588, I cannot believe that Nashe would have taken the risk of offending so powerful a family. Secondly, Leicester does not seem to me to be nearly big enough to fill the skin of Nashe's Bear. There are a number of close resemblances, which neither McKerrow nor McGinn appear to have noticed, between Nashe's description of the Bear and its activities and his abuse of Philip of Spain earlier in *Pierce Penilesse* 'who', he says,

> not content to bee the God of gold, and chiefest commaunder of content that Europe affoords, but now he doth nothing but thirst after humane bloud, when his foot is on the thresholde of the graue: and as a Wolfe, beeing about to deuoure a horse, doth balist his belly with earth, that hee may hang the heauier vppon him, and then forcibly flyes in his face, neuer leauing his hold till he hath eaten him vp; so this woluish vnnatural vsurper, being about to deuoure all Christendom by inuasion, doth cram his treasures with Indian earth to make his malice more forcible, and then flyes in the bosome of *Fraunce* and *Belgia*, neuer withdrawing his forces (as the Wolfe his fastning) till he hath deuoured their welfare, and made the war-wasted carcases of both kingdomes a pray for his tyranny.[71]

I do not wish to suggest on the strength of this passage that the Bear is Philip of Spain, though the idea of Cartwright and Martin as his agents would have given no difficulty to the author of the *Almond*, but I do think it indicates that Nashe was telling the truth when he said in *Strange News* that in the figure of the Bear he sought 'to describe the right nature of a bloudthirsty tyrant'. The Bear represents a type, not a specific individual.

Some of his contemporaries, however, do not seem to have taken the view I have just put forward. Apparently the intelligencers set to work to interpret the fable, for some seven years later in his *Lenten Stuff* Nashe makes it pretty plain that he became involved in a lawsuit, as a consequence of the representations about it that

[70] Donald J. McGinn, 'The Allegory of the "Beare" and the "Foxe" in Nashe's *Pierce Penilesse*', *P.M.L.A.* LXI, 1946, pp. 431–53.

[71] I. 184–5.

they made to some great man or other.[72] He had made rather more of a stir than he had intended to make.

While the political satire was not, then, from Nashe's point of view an unqualified success, his violent yet comic abuse of Richard Harvey was. This piece of parson-baiting, which was probably added to *Pierce Penilesse* at the last minute, he wedged in with characteristic wit and effrontery at the end of the complaint of Wrath. It did all that he expected of it and probably more, since it provoked an answer, not from Richard, but from his more distinguished brother, Gabriel, and so initiated the quarrel that was to provide Nashe with the material for two further pamphlets and to keep him in the public eye for the next seven years. I shall discuss the whole quarrel in some detail later. All I want to say about Nashe's abuse of Richard here is that he was enormously delighted with his own performance, as his remarks on it (quoted at p. 45) amply show, and clearly regarded it as the tit-bit of the whole pamphlet. In fact, however, it was, I think, a danger point in his whole development. In *Pierce Penilesse* he had accomplished something. It has the virtue of vitality. It is not dull, it is not pedantic. In it prose has acquired wings; instead of crawling laboriously on the ground, it darts and swerves in a freer element, moving from subject to subject rapidly and easily, adapting itself now to one purpose now to another, yet retaining throughout the individuality of the personal voice. It was these qualities that made *Pierce Penilesse* so attractive to the reading public of the day and the most popular of all Nashe's works. It fixed him in the mind of the age as a wit, a satirist, a poor scholar, a gay dog and a formidable opponent. But it also left him with a problem. He could go on doing the same kind of thing, preserving a certain balance between observation of the world about him and comment on it on the one hand, and self display on the other; or he could concentrate on one or the other of these two latter activities. I think his success in goading Gabriel Harvey into print tipped the balance. To maintain and to exploit the personality of Pierce became increasingly his main endeavour. He turned aside from the firmer and more central areas of human experience into the easier, and ultimately less fertile, fields of literary showmanship and the meretricious cult of idiosyncrasy.

[72] III. 213–14.

# IV

## DRAMATIC INTERLUDE

FROM the outset of his literary career Nashe seems to have realized that prose was his medium and the pamphlet his form, if form it could be called when its most attractive feature for him was its accommodating shapelessness. Nevertheless, he had some pretensions as a poet and, as well as being deeply interested in the drama and very appreciative of what was being done in the theatre, he had shown himself possessed of some of the qualities of the playwright in both the *Almond* and *Pierce Penilesse*. Moreover, as a needy man of letters, he was almost bound to follow the example of other university men in a similar condition, such as Marlowe, Lyly, Greene and Peele, and to try his hand at writing a play. Indeed, there is good evidence that he had already done so before leaving Cambridge, where the tradition of topical student drama was a strong one. The author of *The Trimming of Thomas Nashe* says of him in a passage I have quoted already[1] that he 'had a hand in a Show called *Terminus et non terminus*'. The very use of the word 'Show' proves that the writer of *The Trimming* knew what he was talking about, for, according to Moore Smith, there was a distinction made at Cambridge between a show and a play in that ' "a show" represented the mediaeval tradition of a disguising . . . and probably relied for its success largely on its topical allusions and satire'.[2] A show is, in fact, exactly the kind of dramatic production that Nashe might be expected to have had a hand in; and we know that he was well aware of the distinction

[1] P. 8 *supra*.

[2] G. C. Moore Smith, *College Plays Performed in the University of Cambridge*, Cambridge, 1923, pp. 39–40.

between it and a play proper, because in his own *Summer's Last Will and Testament* he gives the clown, Will Summers, the comment 'nay, 'tis no Play neyther, but a shewe'.[3]

Nothing is known about *Terminus et non terminus* apart from the information contained in this one allusion, and in this respect it is a fitting prologue to Nashe's dramatic activities in general which are of the most tantalizing kind. His name is associated with five plays in all, yet we have only one dramatic text that is certainly his. The next reference to a play by him, or partly by him, occurs in that celebrated passage in *Greene's Groatsworth of Wit*, where, after referring to Marlowe, Greene goes on to say: 'With thee I ioyne yong *Iuuenall*, that byting Satyrist, that lastly with mee together writ a Comedie'.[4] It has never been finally established that the 'yong *Iuuenall*' concerned is Nashe, but he is much the strongest candidate for the title. He had been associated with Greene since 1589 and admired that writer's facility in 'plotting Plaies, wherein he was his crafts master'.[5] These words would seem to imply that Nashe had seen some of Greene's 'plots', as he would have done had he collaborated with him, but we do not know what the play was that they worked together on. Richard Simpson suggested that it was *A Knack to Know a Knave*, which he describes as being 'patched up by Nashe and Greene out of an older play as an attack on Martinism',[6] and C. M. Gayley considered the attribution as at least possible.[7] I can see no grounds whatever for it. *A Knack to Know a Knave* is a crude and primitive piece of work, utterly lacking the inventiveness and the wit that Nashe prided himself on, and without a trace of that linguistic vitality and originality which is the hall-mark of his writing.[8]

We seem to be on safer ground with *The Tragedy of Dido Queen of Carthage*, published in 1594, for the title page records that it was 'written by Christopher Marlowe, and *Thomas Nash. Gent.*', but an examination of the play leads to the conclusion that Nashe's share in it can have amounted to little or nothing. In conception and in execution alike *Dido* has the name 'Marlowe' written all over it. McKerrow's cautious verdict is 'that the

[3] III. 235. l. 75. [4] V. 143. [5] III. 132.

[6] R. Simpson, *The School of Shakespeare*, London, 1878, II. 382–3.

[7] C. M. Gayley, *Representative English Comedies*, New York and London, 1907, I. 422–6.

[8] For recent discussion on this matter see my Appendix pp. 254–5.

greater part of the work is Marlowe's, but what share, if any, Nashe had in it is very difficult to decide'.[9] Tucker Brooke finds the signs of Nashe's collaboration 'few and indefinite'.[10] It is also significant, I think, that Nashe, who had no shyness about advertising his wares, does not refer to the play in his other writings. It is quite possible that he contributed nothing at all to the play itself. His name may have been associated with Marlowe's by the printer either because he did something to prepare the tragedy for publication, or because he seems to have written for the first edition a prefatory elegy on Marlowe's death which has since disappeared and is not now to be found in any extant copy of it.[11]

After three false starts it is with a sense of relief and anticipation that one turns to *A Pleasant Comedy, Called Summer's Last Will and Testament*, published in 1600 and bearing on its title page the assurance that it was 'Written by *Thomas Nashe*'. Neither feeling is disappointed. Here, at last, is a complete play that is entirely Nashe's own work, that contains a good deal of evidence about when and where it was first produced and that is, above all, a work of art in its own right of a rather unusual kind, demonstrating that its author had abilities as a dramatic craftsman that his activities as a pamphleteer would hardly lead one to suspect.

The occasion for which *Summer's Last Will and Testament* was designed and the circumstances in which it was first produced are of such importance for the proper appreciation of it that they must be set out in some detail. We know that Nashe was in London a month or so before the death of Robert Greene, which took place on 3 September 1592, because he tells us so in *Strange News*, where he writes: 'I and one of my fellowes, *Will. Monox* . . . were in company with him [Greene] a month before he died, at that fatall banquet of Rhenish wine and pickled hearing'.[12] We know also that he was no longer in London when *Pierce Penilesse* came out early in September 1592, because in 'A private Epistle of the Author to *the Printer*,' published with the second edition of that work, he states that he was unable to supervise the printing of the first edition as 'the feare of infection detained mee with my Lord in the Countrey'.[13] A further reference to 'my Lord' occurs

[9] IV. 294.

[10] C. F. Tucker Brooke, *The Life of Marlowe and the Tragedy of Dido Queen of Carthage*, London, 1930, p. 115.

[11] II. 335–7. [12] I. 287–8. [13] I. 153.

in *Strange News*, which Nashe wrote in the winter of 1592-3. There, in reply to Gabriel Harvey's accusation that he had been leading a disorderly life in London, he writes:

> For the order of my life, it is as ciuil as a ciuil orenge; I lurke in no corners, but conuerse in a house of credit, as well gouerned as any Colledge, where there bee more rare quallified men and selected good Schollers than in any Noblemans house that I knowe in England.
>
> If I had committed such *abhominable villanies, or were a base shifting companion*, it stoode not with my Lords honour to keepe me.[14]

As McKerrow points out,[15] the house in question can hardly have been the home of Sir George Carey in the Isle of Wight, where Nashe was living when he wrote *Strange News*. Carey, although a generous patron of letters, was not, so far as we know, surrounded by scholars.

Who then was 'my Lord' and where was his house 'in the Countrey'? *Summer's Last Will and Testament* provides the answer. From references in the text we learn that it was written to be played in a 'lowe built house' [l. 1884] at Croydon in the presence of a 'Lord' who is also described as 'your Grace'. There is no need to give all the evidence, since it is set out in full by McKerrow[16] and by E. K. Chambers,[17] but it amounts to a complete proof that the play was written for presentation before Archbishop Whitgift on the 'tyle-stones' of the great hall in his palace at Croydon. At the time when it was first put on a very hot summer was drawing to a close, there was a bad outbreak of plague in the city and Queen Elizabeth was on progress. The year that satisfies all these conditions is 1592, and the original performance must have taken place not long before the royal progress came to an end on 10 October.

Moreover, Whitgift's household fits Nashe's description of the 'house of credit' he was staying in during the later summer of 1592 to a nicety, and would have provided exactly the right kind of audience for the play he wrote. The archbishop's first biographer, Sir George Paule, who was for many years 'Comptroller of his Grace's household', relates how Whitgift 'entertained in his house,

[14] I. 329. [15] V. 20. [16] IV. 416–19.

[17] E. K. Chambers, *The Elizabethan Stage*, Oxford, 1923, III. 451–3.

for many years together divers distressed ministers out of Germany and France',[18] and later he writes as follows:

> he [Whitgift] took into his house, besides his Chaplains, divers of quality to instruct them in the mathematics, and other lectures of sundry arts and languages. . . . And besides the many poor scholars, whom he kept in his house till he could provide for them, and prefer them (as he did sundry to good estates) he also maintained divers in the University at his own charge. . . . There were also divers others, that for learning, languages and qualities, were fit to be employed by any Prince in Christendom. Insomuch as his house, for the lectures and scholastical exercises therein performed, might justly be accounted a little academy.[19]

The one matter connected with the first production about which there is still some uncertainty is who the actors were. We know that the part of Will Summers was played by an actor called Toy, who was probably a professional. It is the others who give trouble. In the Prologue Will refers to them as 'nouices'—unless this word applies to the author rather than the players—later he calls them 'my good children' [l. 625] and at the end of the play he describes them as 'youths' [l. 1887] and remarks that now the play is over they are going off 'to the tauerne' [l. 1893]. On the basis of this evidence Chambers hovers between two different solutions. First he suggests that the play was given by 'members of Whitgift's household', but then modifies it to the idea that 'Whitgift might have entertained the Paul's boys during the plague and strengthened them for a performance with members of his own household'.[20] To this latter thesis there are two objections: first, as Chambers himself notes, the Paul's boys would have scarcely called themselves 'nouices', and, secondly, as McKerrow points out,[21] Whitgift would have been unlikely to take the risk involved in bringing players from London in time of plague.

Chambers's first solution is, I think, the correct one. The young men in the archbishop's house, waiting to be sent to the universities, could well be described as 'boys', 'youths' and 'nouices'. It seems improbable, however, that they would have been referred to as 'rude *Vulcans*, vnweldy speakers, hammer-headed clownes' [ll. 1935–6], yet these are the terms used in the Epilogue about

[18] Christopher Wordsworth, *Ecclesiastical Biography*, London, 1810, IV. 375.

[19] *Ibid.*, 383–4.

[20] *Op. cit.*, p. 453.

[21] IV. 419.

some of the actors. The words apply, I think, to genuine, homespun rustics from the archiepiscopal manor who, I believe, also had a part in the show. My reason for thinking so stems from the nature of the play itself, to which I would now like to turn.

*Summer's Last Will and Testament* is essentially an occasional play. Not merely was it written for particular actors and a particular audience, but also for a particular time of a particular year in a particular place. When it was put on summer was reaching its end, the harvest had been gathered and the time had come for the appropriate games and festivities, the death of the summer lord and the celebration of harvest-home. In Croydon, as elsewhere in Elizabethan England, the traditional merry-makings would have taken place in any case. What Nashe did was to seize on them and build his play around them. As C. L. Barber has so fully and ably demonstrated, *Summer's Last Will and Testament* is a holiday play.[22] Starting from the harvest-home festivities and the death of the summer lord, Nashe adds to them other festival occasions, May-day, Shrove-tide and Christmas. But at the time when he was writing these age-old activities, though still healthy and vital, were being attacked by the Puritans who saw them as survivals of paganism and incitements to immorality, loose-living and wasteful riot. His play, therefore, expands to take in wider aspects of the social scene. Within the general framework of the folk play a place is found for the manner and the matter of *Pierce Penilesse*. Simplicity and sophistication exist side by side. More important still, however, the death of summer, in Croydon, in the year 1592, took on a special significance and acquired an unwonted depth and poignancy from the proximity of the plague-ridden city. To Nashe and those for whom he wrote life itself appeared as a brief holiday from the terror of death. His play is pervaded by a sense of mutability, subdued to a pitch at which it does not conflict with the general lightness of tone, yet ever present as a kind of ground bass.

The broad design of the play is simple and turns, characteristically, on a pun. The action proper deals, as I have already stated, with the final activities of Summer, who is seen as a victim of the plague. It is introduced, however, by Will Summers, the court fool of Henry VIII, who had become a prominent figure in the popular imagination during the sixteenth century, and who

[22] See C. L. Barber, *Shakespeare's Festive Comedy*, Princeton, 1959, pp. 58–86.

was used, as such, not only by Nashe, but also by Thomas Deloney in his tale *Jack of Newbury*. Will is present throughout; he has the last word as well as the first and serves as a flouting, jeering chorus. As a professional actor, he adopts a mocking, patronizing attitude towards the efforts of the amateurs playing with him and towards the author, whose style and manner he regards as old-fashioned. As the common man, he finds the action slow and the learned debates it gives rise to tedious. He is, in fact, a combination of Toy, the professional actor, and of Tom Nashe, the wit and the critic, very thinly disguised. This arrangement of play and commentary, running side by side, is a neat and satisfactory one. It allows Nashe to write something that is in many ways rather naïve and conventional and that even has the unexpected charm of simplicity about it, without forfeiting his reputation for cleverness. Two of the most important aspects of the late sixteenth century, the old traditional ways of the countryside and the new brilliance of court and town, are mirrored in the interplay between the Summer and Summers parts of the show. Indeed, they may well have been present in the body of the hall, if the spectators included workers from the archbishop's manor as well as the bright young men of his little academy.

The marked contrast between the main action and the commentary on it must not be allowed to obscure the fact that this main action itself is both more interesting and more complex than Miss Bradbrook admits when she sums it up as a pageant and describes it as 'more like Spenser's procession of the months than it is like a full-fledged play'.[23] It certainly owes much to the pageant, but, as I have indicated, it owes even more to the folk play and to rural merry-makings, from which it draws much of its vitality, and it contains pronounced elements of the learned debate as well. In these respects it looks back to the past. But Nashe the satirist, the critic of manners and the author of *Pierce Penilesse* also contributed to it, and in this respect, as Miss Bradbrook shows, it foreshadows the new comedy of Ben Jonson.

It is certainly not a 'full-fledged play'. The action is altogether too slight to warrant that title, as Nashe himself recognized in making Will Summers forestall any criticism on these grounds with his comment in the Prologue, ''tis no play neyther, but a

[23] M. C. Bradbrook, *The Growth and Structure of Elizabethan Comedy*, London, 1955, p. 72.

shewe' [l. 75]. The main lines of its construction are simple, taking the shape of a linear progression, complicated by a single reversal of direction. At the opening Summer enters as an aged king, sick and weary, leaning on the shoulders of his successors, Autumn and Winter, and attended by a train of satyrs and wood-nymphs who sing the song 'Fayre Summer droops, droope men and beasts therefore' and so set the elegiac tone that is present in the background for the rest of the play. He is followed by Vertumnus, the god of seasonal change, who serves as his messenger. Realizing that he is about to die, Summer recognizes Autumn and Winter as his heirs and decides to make his will. As a preliminary to doing so, he summons his various officers before him and asks each of them to give an account of his stewardship. The roll-call-cum-inspection that ensues provides the pattern for the greater part of the action. One by one, Ver, Solstitium, Sol, Orion, Harvest and Bacchus are summoned to the presence. Each enters with music and pageantry and is then submitted to an examination in which he is usually found wanting. When Bacchus, the last of them, has made his exit, the direction changes. Summer laments the way they have wasted their resources and appoints Autumn as his heir. Hitherto Summer, though failing, has been recognized as undisputed king; Autumn and Winter, who have been present from the beginning, have done nothing beyond expressing their disapproval of the behaviour of his officers. Now, however, they begin to dispute with one another about the succession and Autumn accuses Winter of having two sons, Christmas and Back-winter, who are more churlish than their father. They also are summoned and give threatening accounts of their tyrannical intentions. Summer then makes his will—a witty piece of work in which the legacies are given to those who already have more than enough of what is bestowed on them—and bids farewell to the world. There follows the stage-direction: 'Heere the Satyres and Wood-nimphes carry him out, singing as he came in', and the song they sing is 'Autumne hath all the Summers fruitefull treasure' with its refrain, taken from the Litany, 'From winter, plague and pestilence, good Lord, deliuer vs.' A complete pattern, in which all the seasons have had their place, has been evolved; the formal similarity of the various scenes has served to emphasize the regular passage of time; and the elegiac note, announced at Summer's first entrance, has been reinforced by the final song accompanying his exit.

Slight though the action is, it draws a certain strength from its obvious connection with the age-old ceremonies representing the death of the year, and it provides an adequate frame-work for the exhibition of the seasons and for debate. Nashe's treatment of the seasons is particularly effective. They could so easily have become mere allegorical ghosts, distinguishable from one another only by their names and, perhaps, their costumes; but in fact each is endowed with distinct attributes and a personality of his own, because Nashe can think and imagine in more than one set of terms at the same time. His sense of, and feeling for, the weather is as keen and accurate as his eye for social follies. Ver, for instance, is three different things that have been fused into one. First and foremost he is spring incarnate. He enters 'with his trayne, ouerlayd with suites of greene mosse, representing short grasse, singing'. Their song is the delightful lyric 'Spring, the sweete spring, is the yeres pleasant King', which anthologists innumerable have recognized as the very breath of Elizabethan England. In it Nashe has subdued his habitual cleverness entirely to the needs of the occasion. He is content to make a song out of a simple, artless enumeration of the pleasures of the time, its sights, its sounds and its smells. But, having conjured up the season in this way, he then proceeds to extend Ver's significance. The hint contained in the phrase 'then maydes daunce in a ring' is developed into a full-scale picture of the human activities, the May-day revels, proper to the occasion. When Summer asks Ver how he has spent his time, he leaves the stage for a moment to return with 'the Hobby horse and the morris daunce, who daunce about', and, not content with this, he also brings in three clowns and three maids who dance and sing a May song. It is, incidentally, passages like this that lead me to think that Nashe may have used some of the workers on the Archbishop's manor as actors. The morris dancing and the May song would merely have required them to do what they probably did in any case every May-day.

After the show is over, Ver sums up his stewardship as follows:

> in these sports you haue seene, which are proper to the Spring, and others of like sort (as giuing wenches greene gownes, making garlands for Fencers, and tricking vp children gay) haue I bestowde all my flowry treasure, and flowre of my youth [ll. 227–31.]

These words serve to effect an easy transition from the natural to the human world. So far Ver has been the season indicated by his name, now he becomes a social type, assuming the characteristics of that popular figure in the drama of the day, the prodigal son, or, as Nashe describes him in *Pierce Penilesse*, 'the prodigall yoong Master'. Will Summers seizes on the parallel at once and, as a commentary on Ver's carefree improvidence, he says:

> A small matter. I knowe one spent, in lesse then a yere, eyght and fifty pounds in mustard, and an other that ranne in det, in the space of foure or fiue yeere, aboue foureteene thousand pound in lute strings and gray paper. [ll. 232–6.]

The behaviour described here is that of the young man who came up to London and fell into the hands of the usurer. Summer himself endorses the identification by addressing Ver as 'monstrous vnthrift'. In the course of some seventy lines or so the allegorical pageant has been transformed into a piece of social comedy, yet no violence has been done to Ver's character. Nor does his development stop at this point. As a final flourish to his insouciance, Nashe endows him with wit and ingenuity. Accused by Summer of having no sense of moderation and of being incapable of living within his means, Ver retorts with a skilful piece of sophistry in defence of improvidence, well sprinkled with learned citations in the style of a scholar, and, to crown the jest, sounding suspiciously like a sermon. The passage, a mock encomium of the kind Nashe was to develop at greater length in *Lenten Stuff*, is too long to quote in full, but a short excerpt from the beginning of it will serve to make the point about the parsonic mode of utterance, and one from the end will illustrate the learning and gusto with which it is all done. Ver begins his defence thus:

> This world is transitory; it was made of nothing, and it must to nothing: wherefore, if wee will doe the will of our high Creatour (whose will it is, that it passe to nothing), wee must help to consume it to nothing. Gold is more vile then men: Men dye in thousands, and ten thousands, yea, many times in hundreth thousands, in one battaile. If then the best husband bee so liberall of his best handyworke, to what end should we make much of a glittering excrement, or doubt to spend at a banket as many pounds as he spends men at a battaile? [ll. 256–65.]

And he ends his apologia with this fine flourish:

> All the Poets were beggers: all Alcumists and all Philosophers are beggers: *Omnia mea mecum porto*, quoth Bias, when he had nothing but bread and cheese in a letherne bagge, and two or three bookes

in his bosome. Saint Frauncis, a holy Saint, and neuer had any money. It is madnes to dote vpon mucke. That young man of Athens (Aelianus makes mention of) may be an example to vs, who doted so extremely on the image of Fortune that, when hee might not injoy it, he dyed for sorrow. The earth yelds all her fruites together, and why should not we spend them together? I thanke heauens on my knees, that haue made mee an vnthrift. [ll. 310–21.]

This is learned fooling indeed in its logical 'proof' of an improbable argument, and it takes on an extra spice of impudent gaiety and appropriateness when it is recalled that the original audience included an archbishop and, probably, a fair sprinkling of divines and intending clergy as well. Yet, while the mockery of the sermon manner is there, and is even emphasized by Will Summers who says, 'I promise you truely, I was almost asleep; I thought I had bene at a Sermon' [ll. 337–8], nevertheless, in its concern with the transitory nature of life the speech does link up with the awareness of mutability that runs all through the play and, in its defiance of prudential morality, with the anti-Puritan bent of it.

In his treatment of Ver Nashe sets himself a model which he follows, more or less, in his handling of the other figures who are called before Summer, or, at least, in his handling of the more vigorous and indecorous of them. Sol is the fervent sunshine of 1592 that dried up the bed of the Thames, but he is also the upstart promoted to be a royal favourite, whom Nashe attacks so vigorously in *Pierce Penilesse*, and Apollo, the god of music and poetry, ready to defend those arts against the attacks of his enemies, Autumn and Winter. But, while Ver uses the kind of prose one expects from Nashe, Sol, like all the more exalted figures in the play speaks blank verse, and blank verse of some quality too. The lines are largely end-stopped, but, when one considers the date of it, much that he says surprises by its lyrical grace and easy flow. Accused by Autumn of having wronged Daphne and of leading a wanton life with Thetis, Sol defends himself as follows:

For *Daphnes* wrongs, and scapes in *Thetis* lap,
All Gods are subiect to the like mishap.
Starres daily fall (t'is vse is all in all)
And men account the fall but natures course:
Vaunting my iewels, hasting to the West,
Or rising early from the gray ei'de morne,
What do I vaunt but your large bountihood,
And shew how liberall a Lord I serue? [ll. 516–23.]

The argumentativeness comes as no surprise, but the Marlovian accent of the line, 'Or rising early from the gray ei'de morne', does.

It is by variations of style as well as attitude that Nashe manages to give individuality to the allegorical figures who appear before Summer, but it must be admitted that the more indecorous they are, the happier he is with them. It is the holiday characters who have the most vitality and significance, Ver, Orion, who enters 'like a hunter, with a horne about his necke, all his men after the same sort hallowing and blowing their hornes', Harvest and Bacchus, who is at one and the same time the classical deity, the Elizabethan toper using the appropriate drinking jargon and, as C. L. Barber suggests,[24] the round-bellied carnival king of the Shrove Tuesday games. The release from normality and restraint associated with May-day, with hunting and with drinking is conveyed by the noise and the jollity with which Ver, Orion and Bacchus make their entries. It is also present in what they say. All three of them are Lords of Misrule who delight in turning things topsy-turvy and in exercising their wit in the defence of unlikely positions. I have pointed out already how cleverly Ver goes to work to justify prodigality and riot as part of the divine order of things; Orion is equally ingenious in the long apologia, borrowed from Sextus Empiricus, that he makes for the dog. It is, perhaps, too long since it runs to some eighty unbroken lines but it is worth while, nevertheless, for such happy comments as, 'They barke as good old Saxon as may be' [l. 677], and for the verdict it draws from Will Summers, who says of it:

> Faith, this Sceane of *Orion* is right *prandium caninum*, a dogs dinner, which as it is without wine, so here's a coyle about dogges without wit. [ll. 776–8.]

Bacchus goes even further. He is the spirit of learned Folly incarnate, ready to quote Plato and Aristotle in justification of drink, to argue syllogistically for its health-giving properties and to establish his kinship with the jester, Will Summers, and even get the better of him by forcing him to drink—no difficult task—and dubbing him knight with a blackjack.

Nashe tries to keep a certain balance and to find a place in his play for the moralizing that was regarded as part of the poet's task by having Summer condemn these holiday figures for the crime

[24] *Op. cit.*, p. 72.

of excess, but the life goes out of his writing when he does so. There is something wooden about Summer's judgment on Ver:

> O vanitie it selfe! O wit ill spent!
> So studie thousands not to mend their liues,
> But to maintayne the sinne they most affect,
> To be hels aduocates gainst their owne soules.
> *Ver*, since thou giu'st such prayse to beggery,
> And hast defended it so valiantly,
> This be thy penance; Thou shalt ne're appeare,
> Or come abroad, but Lent shall wayte on thee:
> His scarsity may counteruayle thy waste.
> Ryot may flourish, but findes want at last. [ll. 322–31.]

Nor is Nashe any more successful in his attempt to present a positive ideal of moderation in the figure of Solstitium, the exponent of the middle way, who meets with Summer's unqualified approval, but, significantly, never escapes from the allegorical terms in which he is conceived to link up with, and become part of, the social life of the times. Nashe pays lip-service to the moral ideals of his day, but he does not really believe in them. He is on the side of folly, wit and excess, not on that of moderation.

As the play develops certain general conflicts and problems begin to emerge from it. The broad line of division is that between Summer and Winter, so long established as a topic of mediaeval debate and soon to be employed by Shakespeare at the end of his *Love's Labour's Lost*. But for Nashe this basic seasonal opposition serves as a focus for those characteristic preoccupations of his which I have already referred to in my discussion of *Pierce Penilesse*. Summer's officers belong to the old order of things, to the world of traditional ways, of seasonal festivities; like Feste and Sir Toby in *Twelfth Night*, they are on the side of cakes and ale. The identification, marked though it is in the figures of Ver, Orion and Bacchus, is most obvious in that of Harvest. Dressed in straw, he is the embodiment of the harvest-home feast. He makes his entry 'with a sythe on his neck, and all his reapers with siccles, and a great black bowle with a posset in it borne before him: they come in singing'. Their song, with its refrain

> Hooky, hooky, we haue shorne,
> And we haue bound,
> And we haue brought Haruest
> Home to towne.

is a traditional hock-cart song of Norfolk and the Eastern Counties;[25] and, when their share in the entertainment ends, Harvest and his followers, like all rural performers, call for a largesse. Harvest is addressed by Summer as 'the Bayly of my husbandry' [l. 812] and the part could well have been played by the bailiff of Croydon manor. But, as well as being harvest-home, Harvest is also a social type and a social ideal. He is the yeoman farmer, as the age liked to imagine him. Summer, on hearsay, accuses him of the crimes that delinquent members of his class were generally suspected of practising, hoarding of grain and uncharitableness. His answer, given in a down-to-earth prose that is admirably sustained, amounts to a complete self-vindication and equates him with the virtue of liberality and the much admired practice of housekeeping, or hospitality. In the end he receives unstinted praise from Summer, who tells him:

> Haruest, when all is done, thou art the man,
> Thou doest me the best seruice of them all:
> Rest from thy labours till the yeere renues,
> And let the husbandmen sing of thy prayse. [ll. 920–3.]

Even Will Summers cannot withhold a certain measure of admiration. He comments: 'Well, go thy waies, thou bundle of straw; Ile giue thee this gift, thou shalt be a Clowne while thou liu'st . . . this stripling *Haruest* hath done reasonable well' [ll. 941–52].

Harvest, then, more than any other figure in the play represents the positive ideal of work well done, social obligations properly carried out and holiday as a fitting reward. His antithesis in Winter's train is to be seen in the person of Christmas. Even before he appears he has been characterized by Autumn, who describes him as

> a pinch-back, cut-throate churle,
> That keepes no open house, as he should do,
> Delighteth in no game or fellowship,
> Loues no good deeds, and hateth [friendly ?] talke,
> But sitteth in a corner turning Crabbes,
> Or coughing o're a warmed pot of Ale. [ll. 1511–16.]

His entry is in character. He appears unaccompanied by music or

[25] See Collier's note, quoted by McKerrow at IV. 432. *Hookey* or *Hockey* was an East Anglian word.

attendants. Summer at once draws attention to this fact by asking him:

> Christmas, how chaunce thou com'st not as the rest,
> Accompanied with some musique, or some song?
> A merry Carroll would haue grac't thee well;
> Thy ancestors haue vs'd it heretofore. [ll. 1623–6.]

The answer that this appeal to traditional pieties and usages receives is truculent and has all that contempt for the past which was so typical of Puritanism and, indeed, of humanism, at their worst, 'I, antiquity was the mother of ignorance', says Christmas. He goes on to reject hospitality as an old-fashioned god and the enemy of good husbandry, and proceeds to 'prove' that it is a mere incitement to gluttony and that banqueting is a pagan institution. He ends his defence with a diatribe against the cost of labour. In him the Puritan opposition to such festivals as Christmas, and the ethics of the business community—he is a citizen, not a countryman—have been fused. His whole attitude bears out completely C. S. Lewis's view of the Puritans as a group who drew much of their dynamism from their sense of being up-to-date.[26] Summer condemns him out of hand, and undoubtedly speaks for Nashe when he tells him:

> Christmas, I tell thee plaine, thou art a snudge,
> And wert not that we loue thy father well,
> Thou shouldst haue felt what longs to Auarice.
> It is the honor of Nobility
> To keepe high dayes and solemne festiuals:
> Then, to set their magnificence to view,
> To frolick open with their fauorites,
> And vse their neighbours with all curtesie;
> When thou in huggar mugger spend'st thy wealth.
> Amend thy maners, breathe thy rusty gold:
> Bounty will win thee loue, when thou art old.
> [ll. 1722–32.]

Closely associated in Nashe's mind with the issues of old ways versus new and of traditional relaxation versus Puritan austerity was the conflict between the arts and the utilitarian spirit. This matter also has its place in the play. All Summer's officers enter to the sound of music, none of Winter's does so, nor have they any

[26] *Op. cit.*, pp. 42–3.

use for songs. Moreover, when Sol comes in, Autumn accuses him of patronizing poetry and of setting 'wanton songs vnto the Lute' [l. 497]. Sol defends both arts, as 'exercises of delight' [l. 525], but the debate is not concluded at this point. It is taken up once more towards the end of the play after Summer has appointed Autumn to be his successor. Winter at once objects, saying that he is far worthier to take the crown than Autumn, because Autumn, like Spring, is a shilly-shally creature. He then continues:

> He and the spring are schollers fauourites.
> What schollers are, what thriftles kind of men,
> Your selfe be iudge, and iudge of him by them.
> [ll. 1252–4.]

The words usher in the wittiest piece of writing in the play, a sustained and sweeping diatribe against scholars and learning generally, that runs to over two hundred lines of sheer virtuosity. It must have had a special piquancy for the original audience, but even today it extorts admiration for the vigour and gusto with which it is carried through, and for the way in which the blank verse is handled to express and contain a veritable torrent of abuse and misrepresentation. Having invented a mythological origin for ink, Winter continues in this fashion:

> After eche nation got these toyes in vse,
> There grew vp certaine drunken parasites,
> Term'd Poets, which, for a meales meat or two,
> Would promise monarchs immortalitie:
> They vomited in verse all that they knew,
> Found causes and beginnings of the world,
> Fetcht pedegrees of mountaines and of flouds
> From men and women whom the Gods transform'd:
> If any towne or citie they pass'd by
> Had in compassion (thinking them mad men)
> Forborne to whip them, or imprison them,
> That citie was not built by humane hands,
> T'was raisde by musique, like Megara walles;
> Apollo, poets patron, founded it,
> Because they found one fitting fauour there:
> Musæus, Lynus, Homer, Orpheus,
> Were of this trade, and thereby wonne their fame.
> [ll. 1267–83.]

The insistent use of hammering alliteration to convey scorn and contempt is extremely effective, and so is the way in which all the detail is integrated into a long verse paragraph, building up to the climax in which four poets are huddled into a one-line catalogue and poetry itself is dismissed as a mere trade. And these lines are only the prologue; in the one hundred and eighty lines that follow, broken only by two short approving interruptions from Will Summers, Winter makes a comprehensive onslaught on every kind of learning, ending with a fine admonitory flourish which must have found its perfect audience in the members of Whitgift's 'little academy':

> Young men, yong boyes, beware of Schoolemasters,
> They will infect you, marre you, bleare your eyes:
> They seeke to lay the curse of God on you,
> Namely, confusion of languages,
> Wherewith those that the towre of *Babel* built
> Accursed were in the worldes infancie.
> Latin, it was the speech of Infidels.
> Logique hath nought to say in a true cause.
> Philosophie is curiositie:
> And *Socrates* was therefore put to death,
> Onely for he was a Philosopher:
> Abhorre, contemne, despise these damned snares.
> [ll. 1450–61.]

The argument works in reverse, of course. It is discredited before it is begun by being placed in the mouth of Winter, but, as a witty display of misapplied learning and of scholarship used for the praise of ignorance, it is the climax of the whole play and a fitting culmination to the pageant of Misrule which is its main theme. It looks back to Erasmus's *Praise of Folly* and forward to the logical and verbal pyrotechnics of Shakespeare's Berowne in *Love's Labour's Lost*, of whom the King says: 'How well he's read, to reason against reasoning'.

*Summer's Last Will and Testament* springs, it seems to me, from two conflicting impulses, an affection for the past and an impulse to laugh at it. It is both naïve and sophisticated. The two attitudes and manners are reconciled in the process of presentation, and by the activities of Will Summers, the presenter. He belongs to a different order of created being from the other figures in the play, in the sense that there is nothing allegorical about him, but, like them, he has two faces. On the one side, as Henry VIII's jester, he belongs to the past and to the popular tradition, on the other, as professional player and as Tom Nashe, wit, buffoon, satirist and literary critic, he belongs to London in the last decade of the sixteenth century. His main *rôle* is to mediate between the audience and the play, to anticipate their criticisms and voice their reactions. He has much of the old Vice about him and speaks directly to audience and players alike. Occasionally he applauds, but more frequently he scoffs and jeers, deliberately breaking in on, and breaking up, any dramatic illusion that may have been created. He is indecorum incarnate. At the very opening of the play he emphasizes its occasional nature by coming in with 'his fooles coate but halfe on' and by remarking that he has only just had his things 'brought me out of the *Lawndry*'. He actually borrows a chain and a fiddle from 'my cousin Ned', who was, presumably, the archbishop's own jester. He then proceeds to announce himself as Will Summers's ghost in what looks suspiciously like a hit at the Induction to *The Spanish Tragedy*, and describes the author of the play as an idiot, a fop and an ass. His casual informality is set against the artificiality of the show he presents. He reveals his qualities as a literary critic at once by dismissing the Prologue, before it has been spoken, as a scurvy thing, written 'in an old vayne of similitudes'. The description is apt, and it directs the attention of the audience to that feature of the Prologue that Nashe wished them to notice, its clever parody of the Euphuistic manner. When the Prologue is over he turns his attention to the play and, at one and the same time, forestalls any criticism of it on the grounds that it lacks action, and tells the audience what to expect, by describing it as a 'shew' and then continuing thus:

> What can be made of Summers last will and Testament? Such another thing as *Gyllian* of *Braynfords* will, where shee bequeathed a score of farts amongst her friends. Forsooth, because the plague raignes in most places in this latter end of summer, Summer must come in sicke: he must call his officers to account, yeeld his throne to Autumne, make Winter his Executour, with tittle tattle Tom boy: God giue you good night in Watling Street. [ll. 77–84.]

Having made it clear what kind of interest the play will have, Will finally turns his attention to the actors and gives them advice on what to do and what not to do.

By the time Summer enters and the play proper opens all the essential functions of Will's *rôle* have been established and for the rest of the play he exercises them. To a large extent he is the ordinary playgoer of the day. He has no use whatever for moralizing. After the scene in which Solstitium, who represents moderation, appears he expresses his disapproval with the words:

> Fye, fye, of honesty, fye: Solstitium is an asse, perdy; this play is a gally-maufrey: fetch mee some drinke, some body. What cheere, what cheere, my hearts? are not you thirsty with listening to this dry sport? [ll. 421–4.]

Like Polonius, he is all for a jig; he points time after time to the play's lack of action, and his contempt for the author is unbounded. The effect he has on the play is to give it an extra dimension, as it were, by emphasizing the fact that it is a work of art and, as such, something distinct from everyday reality though related to it.

The individuality that Will takes on comes mainly from the lively colloquial idiom that Nashe endows him with. It is not going too far, I think, to say that when one considers the date of the play, his prose is some of the most vigorous and natural that had been heard on the English stage up to that time. Its only competitor would be that used by Shakespeare in the Cade scenes of *2 Henry VI*. His comment on Winter's diatribe against scholars and learning will serve to give a taste of its quality:

> Out vpon it, who would be a Scholler? not I, I promise you: my minde alwayes gaue me this learning was such a filthy thing, which made me hate it so as I did: when I shuld haue beene at schoole, construing *Batte, mi fili, mi fili, mi Batte*, I was close vnder a hedge, or vnder a barne wall, playing at spanne Counter, or Iacke in a boxe: my master beat me, my father beat me, my mother gaue me bread and butter, yet all this would not make me a squitter-booke. It was my destinie; I thanke her as a most courteous goddesse, that shee hath not cast me away vpon gibridge. O, in what a mightie vaine am I now against Horne-bookes! Here, before all this companie, I professe my selfe an open enemy to Inke and paper. Ile make it good vpon the Accidence body, that In speech is the diuels Pater noster: Nownes and Pronounes, I pronounce you as traitors to boyes buttockes: Syntaxis and Prosodia, you are tormentors of wit, and good for nothing but to get a schoole-master two pence a weeke. Hang copies; flye out, phrase books; let pennes

> be turnd to picktooths: bowles, cards, and dice, you are the true liberal sciences; Ile ne're be Goosequil, gentlemen, while I liue.
> [ll. 1462–83.]

The effect of this prose depends, it seems to me, on its very skilful combination of two different things. By and large the constructions and vocabulary are those of ordinary conversational speech, but playing across them and giving them a spice and tang are words and ideas that are stamped with Nashe's own personality. In the words 'my master beat me, my father beat me, my mother gaue me bread and butter, yet all this would not make me a squitter-booke', everything is perfectly normal and natural until one reaches the last word, which, in this context, is right and yet startling. On investigation it turns out to be one of Nashe's coinages—at least the N.E.D. gives him as the first employer of it. In a rather similar fashion the use of grammatical terms and the pun on *Nownes*, *Pronounes* and *pronounce* add a peculiar individual flavour to the otherwise colloquial and down-to-earth sentence in which they appear. This style fits the speaker like a glove, for Will, as I have said already, is a combination of the ordinary playgoer on the one hand and Tom Nashe on the other.

The total effect that Will Summers has on the play is great. He alters its whole character, jazzing it up, making it sophisticated and self-critical, turning it into something rather like a revue. Yet even he does not dominate it. The thing one remembers, when all else about it has faded, is that element in it which is the antithesis of Will and of all that he stands for, the lyrics with which it is studded and, above all, the great dirge 'Adieu, farewell earths blisse' that is sung towards the end while Vertumnus is summoning Christmas and Backwinter to appear before Summer. Here the reality of the plague, and the awareness of mortality and mutability that its presence engendered and reinforced, are given a powerful and haunting utterance. Suppressing completely the flamboyance, the fooling and the idiosyncrasy that have gone into the creation of Will Summers, abandoning his self-chosen *rôle* of wit and jester, Nashe is content in these songs to be the voice of the age, to sing of the great elementary experiences—spring, love, decay and death—that belong to all men at all times. Taking up the *ubi sunt* motive of mediaeval poetry, he furbishes it anew and becomes an English Villon as he writes:

Beauty is but a flowre,
Which wrinckles will deuoure,
Brightnesse falls from the ayre,
Queenes haue died yong and ſaire,
Dust hath closde *Helens* eye.
I am sick, I must dye:
Lord, haue mercy on vs. [ll. 1588–94.]

The plangent note of this song echoes through the play, giving it an unexpected weight and resonance. The fleeting procession of the seasons becomes an image of human life and takes on a universality from Nashe's full appreciation of the nature of the occasion he was writing for.

In the history of Elizabethan drama *Summer's Last Will and Testament* can never occupy any but a minor place. It lies outside the main stream of development, because it was not written for the popular stage and because its lack of plot and of story interest would have been an insuperable barrier in the way of its presentation at a public theatre. Yet in its own kind, as an occasional entertainment, it is a work of distinction in its clever counterpointing of the formal and the artificial on the one hand and the casual and simple on the other, in its blending of the naïve and the sophisticated, in its combination of folk play and learned fooling and in the delicate balance that it achieves between surface gaiety and the deeper undertone inspired by the plague. Moreover, it extended the potentialities of comedy enormously. No earlier English comedy has anything like the intellectual content or the social relevance that it has. Seen in the context of Nashe's own work, it is remarkable for its homogeneity, its artistic unity and its restraint. In it he avoids, for once, the irrelevance that stems from exuberance of manner coupled with a paucity of matter. The discipline imposed by the very nature of drama was exactly what he needed.

Unfortunately, having written *Summer's Last Will and Testament*, Nashe chose to have no more dealings with the theatre for the next five years. His return to it with *The Isle of Dogs* in 1597 was ill-starred. The play got him into serious trouble with the authorities, no text of it is extant and its interest now is wholly biographical. I therefore propose to say no more of it here, but to deal with it, as an event in Nashe's life, at the appropriate time.

# V

# 'THE TERRORS OF THE NIGHT'

## and *Christ's Tears Over Jerusalem*

### I

WHY Nashe left the archbishop's house at Croydon we do not know. It may have been for reasons of health. He appears not to have been very strong and Whitgift's palace was regarded as an unhealthy place, because of its low situation. At any rate, leave it he did and not long after the first performance of *Summer's Last Will and Testament*, for in *Have With You to Saffron-Walden* he states quite explicitly that at Christmas, 1592, 'I was in the *Ile of Wight* then and a great while after'.[1] He had found a new patron in Sir George Carey, who had been Captain-general of the island since 1582 and whose home at Carisbrooke Castle enjoyed a high reputation for hospitality. Even more important, perhaps, for Nashe than Carey himself were his wife and daughter. Lady Elizabeth Carey, whom Sir George had married in 1574, was the second daughter of Sir John Spencer of Althorpe and a distant relation of the poet, Edmund Spenser, who dedicated his *Muiopotmos* to her and also addressed one of the dedicatory sonnets of *The Faerie Queene* to her. A poet herself and the translator of Petrarch, if Nashe is to be believed—he writes of her 'Into the Muses societie her selfe she hath lately adopted, and purchast diuine *Petrarch* another monument in *England*'[2]—Lady Elizabeth was friendly and bountiful to poets. So also, apparently, was her only daughter, Elizabeth. McKerrow suggests that Nashe may either

[1] III. 96. [2] I. 342.

have been invited to Carisbrooke by Sir George, or that Whitgift may have sent him there 'on some business the transaction of which required more than an ordinary messenger'.[3] Is it not quite likely, however, that Nashe could have been employed as a tutor to the daughter—I have not found the date of her birth, but she can hardly have been more than seventeen or eighteen in 1592—and as a kind of literary adviser and assistant to her and her mother? Some relationship of this kind would seem to be indicated by a passage in the dedication of *The Terrors of the Night*, which is addressed to the daughter, for there Nashe writes: 'giue me leaue (though contemptible and abiect) once more to sacrifice my worthles wit to your glorie'.[4] The words can only mean either that he had previously dedicated a work to her—and of this there is no record—or that he had helped her in some way.

Whatever Nashe's reason for going to the Isle of Wight may have been, his stay there appears to have been happy and productive. He refers repeatedly to the generosity of all three Careys, and in *The Terrors of the Night* he describes his journey to the island as the one good voyage he made in his life.[5] The context in which this statement occurs is a typical piece of complaint about the misery of 'long depending hope frivolously defeated', and the phrase refers, I think, not so much to the actual crossing from the mainland, as to the fact that only in the Careys did Nashe find patrons who were really prepared to do something for him. Apart from anything else, they must have given him a home for some considerable time, if the words 'a great while after' mean anything at all. While he was there he wrote *Strange News*, *The Terrors of the Night*, part, if not all, of *The Unfortunate Traveller* and, probably, most of *Christ's Tears over Jerusalem* as well. The two latter works were entered in the Stationers' Register on 17 and 8 September 1593, respectively, as though their author had newly arrived in London with the two manuscripts ready for the printer in his pocket. McKerrow doubts whether *Christ's Tears* can have been written while Nashe was at Carisbrooke, because there is 'a tone about the whole piece which is hardly consistent with prosperity or with a happy outlook on life',[6] but the verdict ignores the fact that in composing this work Nashe was writing in a particular 'kind', where gloom was expected, and it ignores also the

[3] V. 22. [4] I. 341. [5] I. 374.
[6] V. 24.

constant straining for effect which is such a marked quality of *Christ's Tears*, and which suggests to me that it was written with a different audience from Nashe's usual one in mind. In any case, there was every reason why Nashe should stay out of London for as long as possible in 1593, since the plague, which had begun in the summer of 1592, did not come to an end in the autumn of that year, as it normally did, but continued through the winter and gathered fresh strength in the spring and summer of 1593.

Of the four works that he produced in less than twelve months I propose to discuss two, *The Terrors of the Night* and *Christ's Tears*, in this chapter, because they provide a striking contrast with one another. *Strange News* belongs to the story of Nashe's quarrel with Gabriel Harvey, and *The Unfortunate Traveller* is so different from the rest of his work as to demand separate treatment.

The date of the composition of *The Terrors of the Night* can be fixed fairly accurately. It must have been in existence by 30 June 1593, because on that date it was entered in the Stationers' Register by John Danter. Moreover, during the course of it Nashe relates an incident which, he says, took place when 'It was my chance in Februarie last to be in the Countrey some threescore myle off from London'.[7] But in February 1593 he was in the Isle of Wight and he must, therefore, have written the pamphlet before that date, the February referred to being that of 1592. No publication seems to have followed the entry in the Stationers' Register in 1593, but it was entered for a second time by Danter, a most unusual procedure, on 25 October 1594. The earliest and only extant edition is dated the same year.

The reason for the same work's being entered twice is obscure, but there may be some indication of what it was in the dedication to Mistress Elizabeth Carey, where Nashe writes as follows:

> A long time since hath it line suppressed by mee; vntill the vrgent importunitie of a kinde frend of mine (to whom I was sundrie waies beholding) wrested a Coppie from me. That Coppie progressed from one scriueners shop to another, and at length grew so common, that it was readie to bee hung out for one of their signes, like a paire of indentures. Wherevppon I thought it as good for mee to reape the frute of my owne labours, as to let some vnskilfull pen-man or Nouerint-maker startch his ruffe and new spade his beard with the benefite he made of them.[8]

[7] I. 378.  [8] I. 341.

Allowing for the fact that Nashe may be doing his best here to excuse the appearance in print of a work written for his patroness and her family, there may still be some truth in his account of how copies of it were multiplied in manuscript. One can well imagine how a copy may have come into the hands of Danter, who entered it in the Stationers' Register and was about to publish it, when Nashe discovered what was going on and somehow or other managed to get the printing held up until he had established his claim and come to some sort of arrangement with Danter, who had already published his *Strange News*. The second entry in the Register could then have been made after thc arrangement had been come to and when Danter's ownership of the work was no longer questionable. The theory gains some weight from the fact that the dedication was almost certainly written in 1594, immediately before the pamphlet was published, and did not exist when it was first entered in June, 1593. It seems most unlikely that a needy author like Nashe would, at this stage in his career, have handed a manuscript over to a printer without doing his best to obtain the extra remuneration that a dedication brought, or, at any rate, was supposed to bring.

The other possibility is that Nashe sent the manuscript off to Danter before 30 June 1593, and, having done so, then discovered that its publication might give offence to the Careys, or, alternatively, realized that he might have flattered them more than he had done. He, therefore, got the work back from Danter before it could be printed, added the dedication and the passage in praise of the Isle of Wight and its Captain-general that I have referred to already, part of which, as McKerrow shows,[9] cannot have been written until 1594, and cooked up the story about many copies circulating in manuscript in order to provide an excuse for publication. The explanation is a tortuous one, but so was the route by which some works of the day eventually made their way into print.

To an even greater extent than *Summer's Last Will and Testament*, *The Terrors of the Night* is an occasional work. At the very beginning Nashe states what led to its composition. The first words are:

> A Litle to beguile time idlely discontented, and satisfie some of my solitary friends heere in the Countrey, I haue hastily vndertooke to

[9] IV. 197.

> write of the wearie fancies of the Night, wherein if I weary none with my weak fancies, I will herafter leane harder on my penne and fetch the petegree of my praise from the vtmost of paines.[10]

Further evidence of its occasional nature comes from the dedicatory epistle, where Nashe tells Mistress Elizabeth Carey:

> As touching this short glose or annotation on the foolish Terrors of the Night, you partly are acquainted from whose motiue imposition it first proceeded, as also what strange sodaine cause necessarily produced that motion.[11]

There seems to be a bit of deliberate mystification about this latter statement, but, taken in conjunction with the previous one, it would indicate that either Mistress Elizabeth herself, or some other member of the family, set Nashe the task of writing something to interest and amuse them during the winter of 1592–3.

The rightness of this deduction is endorsed by the whole nature of the pamphlet itself. Here, for the first time in Nashe's work, the didactic moralizing, which the age regarded as the true *raison d'être* of literature, though not entirely dropped, becomes the most transparent of pretences and is clearly intended to be seen as such. *The Terrors of the Night, or a Discourse of Apparitions*, to give it its full title, grew out of an incident in real life, the visions which appeared 'to a Gentleman of good worship and credit' during the course of an illness from which he eventually died. But, while he vouches for the truth of the story, Nashe has no hesitation in saying that he thought the incident itself rather commonplace and, therefore, did his best to brighten it up in the telling, even though he was not very satisfied with the results. He writes, having brought the story to a close with the death of the gentleman concerned:

> God is my witnesse, in all this relation, I borrowe no essential part from stretcht out inuention, nor haue I one iot abusde my informations; *onely for the recreation of my Readers*, whom loath to tyre with a course home-spunne tale, that should dull them woorse than Holland cheese, *heere and there I welt and garde it with allusiue exornations and comparisons*: and yet me thinks it comes off too goutie and lumbring.[12] [My italics.]

'Welt and garde' are, of course, tailor's terms, used to describe the process of adorning a suit by sewing decorative material on to

[10] I. 345. [11] I. 341. [12] I. 382.

it, and to see exactly what Nashe means by them in a literary context it is worth taking a look at part of the passage he is referring to. The visions that appeared to the sick man were a series of temptations. Here is Nashe's description of one of them:

> Then did ther, for the third pageant, present themselues vnto him, an inueigling troupe of naked Virgins, thrice more amiable and beautifull than the bright Vestals, that brought in *Augustus* Testament to the Senate, after hys decease: but no Vestall-like Ornament had they about them; for from top to toe bare despoyled they were, except for some one or two of them that ware maskes before their faces, and had transparent azur'd lawne veyles before the chiefe iewell houses of their honors.
>
> Such goodly lustfull Bonarobaes they were (by his report) as if anie sharpe eyd Painter had been there to peruse them, he might haue learned to exceed diuine *Michel Angelo* in the true boske of a naked, or curious *Tuns* in quicke life, whom the great masters of that Art do terme the sprightly old man.
>
> Their haire they ware loose vnrowled about their shoulders, whose dangling amber trammells reaching downe beneath their knees, seemed to drop baulme on their delicious bodies; and euer as they moou'd too and fro, with their light windye wauings, wantonly to correct their exquisite mistresses.
>
> Their daintie feete in their tender birdlike trippings, enameld (as it were) the dustie ground; and their odoriferous breath more perfumed the aire, than Ordinance would, that is charged with Amomum, Muske, Cyuet, and Amber-greece.
>
> But to leaue amplications and proceed: those sweet bewitching naked maides, hauing maiestically paced about the chamber, to the end their naturall vnshelled shining mother pearle proportions might be more imprintingly apprehended, close to his bed-side modestly blushing they approched, and made impudent profer vnto him of theyr lasciuious embraces. He, obstinatly bent to withstand these their sinfull allurements no lesse than the former, bad them goe seek entertainment of hotter bloods, for he had not to satisfie them. A cold comfort was this to poore wenches no better cloathed, yet they hearing what to trust too, verie sorrowfully retyred, and shrunk away.[13]

Now, in this passage Nashe is doing a good deal more than 'welt and garde' the narrative with 'allusiue exornations and comparisons'. The original material has almost disappeared under the froth of decoration that has been stitched on to it. The story

[13] I. 380–1.

element is confined to the first two lines of the first paragraph and a few phrases in the last. All else, as Nashe self-consciously emphasizes, is 'amplifications', elaborate descriptions and comparisons in the manner of the Ovidian narrative poems of the day, works such as Marlowe's *Hero and Leander* and Shakespeare's *Venus and Adonis*, in which the story is largely an excuse for displays of descriptive and rhetorical brilliance. But, even while he ministers to the Elizabethan love of the 'brave' and the ornate, Nashe also criticizes it. His descriptions are deliberately over-written to a point at which they become parodies of the style they imitate. When he writes, 'those sweet bewitching naked maides, hauing maiestically paced about the chamber, to the end their naturall vnshelled shining mother pearle proportions might be more imprintingly apprehended', the insistent and excessive alliteration, coupled with the over-charged sensuousness, carry their own criticism with them. And, to settle any lingering doubts on this score, the whole descriptive balloon is pricked and goes off with a bang at the end when Nashe drops slap in to the colloquial and the commonplace with the words, 'A cold comfort was this to poore wenches no better cloathed'.

This combination of over-wrought description on the one hand, and mocking scepticism on the other, is the outstanding characteristic of the whole pamphlet and the real unifying factor in it, for *The Terrors of the Night* is essentially a *jeu d'esprit*, a piece of deliberate book-making and a demonstration of literary skill in overcoming obvious difficulties. With his habitual self-depreciatory swagger Nashe says as much, when, having concluded the story of the apparitions that appeared to the gentleman, he writes:

> Vpon the accidentall occasion of this dreame or apparition (call or miscall it what you will, for it is yours as freely as anie wast paper that euer you had in your liues) was this Pamphlet (no bigger than an old Praeface) speedily botcht vp and compyled.[14]

It is clear from this statement that he regarded the task of swelling an incident into a pamphlet—even though a short one—as something of a challenge to his virtuosity, and that he was rather proud of the way he had met it. The problem becomes the occasion for a display of literary artifice. Keeping the actual incident up his sleeve for the climax, he makes it part of a general disquisition on

[14] I. 382.

the interpretation of dreams and other related topics, carried out in an apparently rambling and casual fashion in which one digression leads to another, and even digression itself, in anticipation of Swift, becomes the theme of further digression. Above all, he relies on 'exornations and comparisons' to clothe the skeleton of ideas and observation with flesh and blood. Never was a prose work so loaded and bombasted out with similes. Like some self-generating organism they multiply and proliferate from page to page. The boundary line between prose and poetry, never very definite for the Elizabethans, disappears, and analogy takes over from argument.

Nevertheless, this display of literary artifice is geared to a certain purpose and idea. Nashe's general intention, as he informs Mistress Carey in the dedicatory epistle, is to show that the terrors of the night are foolish and idle fears. The work is meant as an attack on superstition and credulity. But the nature of the attack changes. At the beginning it is serious and even religious in tone. Night is pictured as the time when a man's conscience assaults him, and the idea is developed through a series of elaborate, detailed, formal similes of the kind that one associates with Spenser, or with the Shakespeare of *Richard III*. There is even a rhythmical regularity and formality about the prose Nashe uses for this purpose, as the following passage will demonstrate:

> As touching the terrors of the night, they are as many as our sinnes. The Night is the Diuells Blacke booke, wherein hee recordeth all our transgressions. Euen as when a condemned man is put into a darke dungeon, secluded from all comfort of light or companie, he doth nothing but despairfully call to minde his gracelesse former life, and the brutish outrages and misdemeanours that haue throwne him into that desolate horrour; so when Night in her rustie dungeon hath imprisoned our ey-sight, and that we are shut seperatly in our chambers from resort, the diuell keepeth his audit in our sin-guilty consciences, no sense but surrenders to our memorie a true bill of parcels of his detestable impieties. The table of our hart is turned to an index of iniquities, and all our thoughts are nothing but texts to condemne vs.
>
> The reste we take in our beds is such another kinde of rest as the wearie traueller taketh in the coole soft grasse in summer, who thinking there to lye at ease, and refresh his tyred limmes, layeth his fainting head vnawares on a loathsome neast of snakes.[15]

[15] I. 345.

Nashe thinks in images, but the thought, such as it is, is quite serious and orthodox. It does not remain so. Having made a gesture towards moral didacticism in the first couple of pages, he then feels free to enjoy himself at the expense of popular superstitions and to amuse his readers in the process.

For the author of *Pierce Penilesse* the devil provides the transition. Even in the passage I have quoted the reference to his 'Blacke booke', with its allusion to Robert Greene, has a contemporary touch and potentially comic undertones. These are soon developed as Nashe turns to English folk-lore and to the activities of 'the Robbin-good-fellowes, Elfes, Fairies, Hobgoblins of our latter age, which idolatrous former daies and the fantasticall world of Greece ycleaped *Fawnes*, *Satyres*, *Dryades* and *Hamadryades*'.[16] For a short time the solemn, admonitory note, to the effect that dreams and apparitions are devices of the devil, is still to be heard, but it is finally overwhelmed by the grotesque, slapstick fooling that becomes dominant when Nashe switches to the subject of devils and their infinite variety:

> What do we talke of one diuel? . . . for no place (bee it no bigger than a pockhole in a mans face) but is close thronged with them. Infinite millions of them wil hang swarming about a worm-eaten nose.
>
> Don *Lucifer* himselfe, their grand *Capitano*, asketh no better throne than a bleare eye to set vp his state in. Vpon a haire they will sit like a nit, and ouer-dredge a bald pate like a white scurffe. The wrinkles in old witches visages, they eate out to entrench themselues in.[17]

Needing to 'botch up' something in a hurry Nashe has reverted to the manner and the matter of *Pierce Penilesse*. And he continues in it. Dreams and apparitions, the ostensible subject, are laid on one side for the time being. 'From this generall discourse of spirits', he writes, 'let vs digresse, and talke another while of their seperate natures and properties'.[18] 'Talk' is the operative word. For him there is no line drawn between the literary language and that of common speech. Formal similes, both savoury and unsavoury, seem to come as naturally to him and to be as much a part of his 'talk' as colloquial words and phrases are part of his writing. He rambles on describing the various spirits of fire, water, earth and air, reworking the material he had already used in *Pierce*

[16] I. 347. [17] I. 349. [18] I. 350.

*Penilesse*, and fitting in a certain amount of casual social satire by the way. Ultimately spirits lead to melancholy and melancholy back to dreams. But, having returned to his subject, Nashe does not stay with it. Instead he sets off after witches, who eventually lure him to Iceland, and, when he has exhausted his notes on this topic, he finds a new one in his own tendency to digress:

> A poyson light on it, how come I to digresse to such a dull, Lenten, Northren Clyme, where there is nothing but stock-fish, whetstones, and cods-heads? Yet now I remember me, I haue not lost my way so much as I thoght, for my theame is The terrors of the Night, and *Island* is one of the chiefe kingdomes of the night; they hauing scarce so much day there, as will serue a childe to ask his father blessing. Marry, with one commoditie they are blest, they haue Ale that they carry in their pockets lyke glue, and euer when they would drinke, they set it on the fire and melt it.[19]

The very process of justifying one digression has provided the occasion for another. It is all very disarming and very gay.

Moreover, in its own way it works. The rambling, desultory, inconsequential fashion in which Nashe treats the various forms of credulity that he deals with conveys, far better than any carefully worked out discourse on them could, his mocking contempt for them. By the manner in which he handles them he creates the impression that they are silly and hardly merit serious consideration. Nevertheless, he continues on his way, drawing on reading and observation for his material and mingling social satire with his exposure of superstitions and with the medical and psychological explanations that he finds for the phenomena he writes about. Dreams and auguries raise the subject of mock-astrologers, and they, in turn, bring him back to the devil once more. Thereupon he pulls himself up with the words:

> I haue rid a false gallop these three or foure pages: now I care not if I breathe mee, and walke soberly and demurely halfe a dozen turnes, like a graue Citizen going about to take the ayre.[20]

The image of the runaway horse is an apt one to describe his progress up to this point. For a few pages he settles down, at last, to dismiss the interpretation of dreams as nonsense and dreams themselves as the results of indigestion, but he is soon off on another tack, complaining of the stinginess of patrons, praising Sir

[19] I. 360. [20] I. 368.

George Carey and the Isle of Wight, and eventually coming back to dreams and the story of the apparitions that appeared to the 'Gentleman of good worship and credit'. When the tale is over he seeks for some natural explanation for it, but abandons the search in the end with a sigh of exhaustion:

> Fie, fie, was euer poore fellow so farre benighted in an old wiues tale of diuells and vrchins. Out vpon it, I am wearie of it.[21]

And even now he manages to spin his pamphlet out for another three pages with a long 'good night' to the reader, advising him how to order his diet and his way of living so as to avoid bad dreams.

The most impressive single item in this latter part of *The Terrors of the Night* is a self-contained and easily detachable sketch of the process by which a conjurer establishes himself and makes a reputation. In a sense this is a new departure for Nashe. There are numerous sketches of social types in *Pierce Penilesse*, but there Nashe does not spend much time or space on the way a particular type has evolved. His interest is in the 'character' as a social phenomenon, not in narrative. With the conjurer in *The Terrors of the Night*, however, the 'character' comes much closer to the kind of thing that Greene writes in his coney-catching pamphlets. The sketch begins as something generalized. Nashe relates how men (the plural is significant) with some grammar school education, waste their substance among harlots and then look round for some profitable occupation. With a few bits of rubbish they set themselves up in the far north, remote from London, and soon earn a name as conjurers. Gradually they make their way south and establish themselves in the suburbs. At length news of their skill reaches the ears of

> some dappert Mounsier Diego, who liues by telling of newes, and false dice, and it may be hath a pretie insight into the cardes also, together with a little skill in his Iacobs staffe and hys Compasse; being able at all times to discouer a new passage to *Virginia*.[22]

This individual spreads the story of the conjurer's (at this point, as the narrative interest develops, the plural is dropped and the singular takes its place) skill and miraculous cures at some nobleman's house, and does it so well that the great man expresses a desire to have the conjurer brought to him. Thereupon, the inter-

[21] I. 384. [22] I. 365.

mediary goes to the conjurer and offers, for a half share in any profits that may arise, to introduce him to the nobleman. The bargain is struck and the conjurer becomes a force in the land for a time until, 'when he wexeth stale, and all his pispots are crackt and wil no longer hold water, he sets vp a coniuring schoole, and vndertakes to play the baud to Ladie Fortune'.[23] The whole process is described in the most vigorous and lively fashion; the tricks of speech and manner are caught and rendered with Nashe's usual blend of realism and fantasy; and, as with some of the sketches in *Pierce Penilesse*, one's mind goes to Ben Jonson, but to a play, *The Alchemist*, rather than to a single figure. In this sketch, as it seems to me, are to be found the first hints of the imaginary biography or autobiography, as Nashe was to use it in *Christ's Tears*, in *Have With You to Saffron-Walden* and, above all, in *The Unfortunate Traveller*.

The most realistic thing in the whole pamphlet, the account of the conjurer is, nevertheless, part of the total performance, and in the end it is the performance that counts. Subject, in the proper sense of the word, Nashe has none. Everything that can be related, no matter in how tenuous a fashion, to dreams and to human credulity is grist to his mill. The pamphlet rambles and meanders, turns back on its course, loses itself and almost founders, but always the author sets it on its feet again. The only unifying factor in it is the personality of the performer, and it is sufficient for the purpose. Showmanship and style carry the day in what is, surely, one of the most sophisticated prose-works of the age. Indeed, it seems to have been too sophisticated for Nashe's contemporaries; only one edition of it appeared during his life-time and it was never reprinted until 1883. Essentially it is a trifle; but it compels a certain admiration by the very fact that it exists at all, which is, perhaps, as much justification as any trifle needs.

McKerrow is very cagey about *The Terrors of the Night*; he writes of it:

> It is a slight production, which has been viewed very differently by different critics. To me it seems to be a hasty piece of work, almost certainly composed for the most part of a mere stringing together of matter taken from elsewhere, and on the whole of very little importance either as regards Nashe's biography or the history of letters in his time.[24]

[23] I. 366. [24] V. 23.

That it is slight, that it was put together hastily and that it was composed of matter taken from elsewhere, I would agree; but the final verdict is much too harsh. McKerrow views it as though it were a contribution to *The Review of English Studies*, looking to it for carefully considered conclusions and a reasoned argument. Quite plainly it is nothing of the sort. Nor are there any grounds for complaining because it throws little light on Nashe's life. It was not intended to. What it does illuminate is his cast of mind and the age he was living in. The incident out of which it arose had something in common with that which Defoe utilized for *The Apparition of Mrs. Veal*, but there all similarity between the two works ends. Defoe, living in a sceptical age, deploys all his skill as a realist to make the miraculous credible; Nashe, living in a credulous age, uses his gift for the fantastic, for the comic and for parody to undermine and sap the significance of the all too credible and too readily credited. It seems to me, further, that *The Terrors of the Night*, although it had no influence on anything written after it, does have its place in the history of letters in Nashe's time and in his own development as a literary artist. It is one of the first, if not the first, prose works in English that exists for no other end than to give the pleasure a discriminating reader can find in a difficulty overcome, the difficulty in this particular case being that of making something out of nothing by sheer literary artifice, by a display of stylistic ingenuity that carries with it the impress of a personality. The pleasure, admittedly, is of a minor order, but none the less real for that. In essence *The Terrors of the Night* is a piece of literary clowning, and good clowning in writing, no less than in the theatre or the circus, is neither a common nor a contemptible thing.

A very different view of the pamphlet from that which I have put forward and, indeed, from that set out by McKerrow, is taken by those who seek to connect Nashe with *Love's Labour's Lost*. For them *The Terrors of the Night* is an important link in an involved chain of evidence that throws a rather confused light on the history of letters at the time when it was written. Miss M. C. Bradbrook, for instance, sees it as an attack on George Chapman and, through him, on the School of Night generally, the circle of writers, scientists and sceptics, who were, she thinks, connected in some way or another with Sir Walter Raleigh.[25] She points

[25] M. C. Bradbrook, *The School of Night*, Cambridge, 1936, pp. 171–8.

out that *The Terrors of the Night* appeared shortly after the publication of Chapman's obscure and difficult poem *The Shadow of Night* (1594), and not long before his *Ovid's Banquet of Sense* (1595). In the first of these poems Chapman praises the night as the time of illumination for the man of true learning, while the second is even more paradoxical, for in it he describes how Ovid comes upon Julia bathing, satisfies each of the five senses in turn and so comes to an understanding of the true nature of spiritual love which is beyond the reach of sense. Miss Bradbrook's thesis is that Nashe, the 'villanist' and realist, could not take Chapman's Platonic paradoxes seriously and found *Ovid's Banquet of Sense* in particular 'a tempting subject for ribaldry'. *The Terrors of the Night* is intended, as its title indicates, as a tilt at the School and its doctrines, and the central incident in it, the account of the visions that appeared to the Gentleman, is a deliberate parody of Ovid's encounter with Julia. The Gentleman himself, whose house, according to Nashe, 'stood in a low marish ground, almost as rotten a Clymate as the Low Countreyes',[26] is identified with Chapman, whose home 'was about 30 miles from London, in the fen country, at Hitchin'.[27]

I do not think this thesis will hold water. In the first place Miss Bradbrook has failed to notice that when Nashe introduces the story of the Gentleman he is more explicit about the situation of his house than he is later: it was, he says, 'in the Countrey some threescore myle off from London.'[28] The Elizabethans were not very exact about figures, but Nashe would hardly have said threescore if he meant thirty. Secondly, Nashe relates that after seeing the visions the Gentleman 'grewe to trifling dotage, and rauing dyde within two daies following'.[29] The remark could be meant as a joke, of course, but it seems worth recording, nevertheless, that Chapman showed no signs of dying in 1594 and in fact went on living for another forty years. Thirdly, and more to the point, the correspondences between the poem and the pamphlet are of a very loose and general kind; there is no agreement between them in any point of detail. It is true that the poem falls into five sections, one for each sense, and the temptations the Gentleman is exposed to into five acts, but these acts are not related to the five senses. Verbal parallels and echoes there are none. This is not Nashe's

[26] I. 382. [27] *Op. cit.*, p. 177. [28] I. 378.
[29] I. 382.

way of writing burlesque. When he makes fun of Gabriel Harvey he quotes extensively, though not always accurately, giving chapter and verse, when he parodies Marlowe's *Hero and Leander* in *Lenten Stuff* he refers to its author by name. There is never any doubt about the object of his attack. Fourthly, there are insuperable difficulties of dating. *The Terrors of the Night*, which, Nashe tells us, was written round the incident of the Gentleman and his visions, was composed late in 1592 or early in 1593. How, when he wrote it, could Nashe possibly have seen *The Shadow of Night*, still less *Ovid's Banquet of Sense* which, Miss Bradbrook admits, must have still been in MS. when *The Terrors of the Night* was published? And, finally, why in any case should Nashe have wished to attack Chapman? The two men, different though they were in some ways, shared certain common interests and values. Like Nashe, Chapman was a poor scholar who found life hard, yet who constantly championed the cause of poetry and the liberal arts and never wavered in his opposition to Ignorance, Avarice and Barbarism.

I do not think, then, that *The Terrors of the Night* has any connection with Chapman and his poems and I am very sceptical about the existence of the School of Night. The arguments against it, as set out by E. A. Strathmann,[30] seem to me unanswerable, and there is no point in repeating them here. Nor, tempting though it is to assume that one's subject has a place in the work of Shakespeare, am I convinced that the figure of Moth in *Love's Labour's Lost* is intended for Nashe. That the play glances here and there at the Harvey-Nashe quarrel seems likely. It is hard to see how a work as concerned as *Love's Labour's Lost* is with words and language could fail to do so around 1594. But the identification of Moth with Nashe is another matter.[31] It rests mainly on two pieces of evidence: Armado's calling Moth 'my tender Iuuenall' [I. ii. 8] and the subsequent elaborations of this phrase, and on the puns about purses and pennies which centre on Moth. The first of these is taken by those who hold the theory to be a pointed reference by Shakespeare to Greene's description of Nashe in his *Groatsworth of Wit* as 'yong *Iuuenall*, that byting Satyrist'. Yet the

[30] See E. A. Strathmann, *Sir Walter Raleigh*, New York, 1951, pp. 262–71 and 'The Textual Evidence for "The School of Night",' *Modern Language Notes*, LVI (1941), pp. 176–86.

[31] For a recent summary of the evidence in favour see *Love's Labour's Lost*, ed. Richard David, London, 1951, pp. xxxvii–l.

fact remains that Shakespeare also uses the word 'juvenal' at two other places in his work [*A Midsummer Night's Dream*, III. i. 97 and *2 Henry IV*, I. ii. 22] with no reference whatever to Greene or Nashe, but with the meaning 'juvenile' or 'youth'. Nor do I see why the punning on pennies and purses, which may well owe something to *Pierce Penilesse*, necessarily implies that Moth is Nashe. After all, Shakespeare makes far more use of Nashe's writings in the two parts of *Henry IV* than he does in *Love's Labour's Lost*, yet no one has suggested, so far as I know, that Falstaff is Nashe. The most characteristic and easily identifiable feature of Nashe's writing is his highly individual style, yet only once in the entire play of *Love's Labour's Lost* does Moth speak in a manner reminiscent of Nashe's characteristic mode of utterance. It happens at the opening of III. i. [ll. 9–24] when Moth guys the poses of the fashionable lover and resorts to low similes when explaining to Armado how he ought to behave: 'with your hat penthouse-like o'er the shop of your eyes; with your arms crossed on your thin-belly doublet like a rabbit on a spit, etc.' But, if his use on one occasion of this kind of speech means that Moth is Nashe, Biondello, in *The Taming of the Shrew*, must also be Nashe on the strength of his description of Petruchio's garments and horse in III. ii. Evidence of this kind seems to me altogether too slight and uncertain. Leishman, in his edition of the *Parnassus Plays*, provides a mass of solid arguments for identifying Ingenioso with Nashe. Their careers, their activities, their interests and their attitudes are substantially the same. But Moth has had no career. He is a page, not a writer, and he shows no marks of Nashe's anti-Puritanism, of his opposition to the middle class and to money values, or of his defence of the humanistic spirit. I can see no real parallel between Shakespeare's light, tricksy creation and the truculent pamphleteer who had made such a stir at the time. Nor, I believe, did Nashe see any resemblance. Had he done so, he would almost certainly have made some kind of literary capital out of it somewhere.

Doubtful as I am about all these hypotheses, I am also unconvinced by the theory—conveniently summarized by Mr. David—that Nashe began as an adherent of the Raleigh group and then moved over, with the publication of *The Terrors of the Night*, to the rival group of Essex and Southampton. This notion rests on the fact that *Pierce Penilesse* and *The Choice of Valentines* were dedicated in all probability to Lord Strange, who is supposed to have been a member of the Raleigh group, *The Terrors of the Night* to Elizabeth Carey, whose father was connected with both groups, and *The Unfortunate Traveller* to Southampton. The objections to all this are two: first, those who make play with Nashe's attack on Atheism and Atheists in *The Terrors of the Night*, interpreting it as evidence of a turning away from the Raleigh group, have failed to notice that it is merely a re-hash, of a less forceful kind, of what he says in *Pierce Penilesse*, which was dedicated to Lord Strange. Either, therefore, Strange was not a sceptic, or Nashe did not know that he was. In either case the idea of the group and of Nashe's adherence to it suffers. Secondly, it is assumed that Nashe received patronage from Strange—it is admitted that Southampton seems to have made no response to Nashe's overtures—an assumption for which no evidence can be adduced. My reading of the whole business of Nashe's dedications is that they were kites which he flew with no consideration of groups or parties, but in the hope of obtaining favour of some kind, a hope that was disappointed except by the Careys.

## 2

*Christ's Tears over Jerusalem*, which was probably published about the end of September 1593, has exactly those qualities that McKerrow desiderates in *The Terrors of the Night*. It is of considerable importance both for Nashe's biography and for the history of letters in his time; far from attracting little attention when it first came out,[32] it attracted altogether too much for its author's comfort and safety; and it is not only the longest and most serious of all his productions, but also the most carefully planned and orderly. All of which merely goes to show the inadequacy of such considerations as criteria for any kind of literary judgment, because *Christ's Tears* is, it seems to me, far and away the worst thing Nashe ever wrote. Neither trivial nor dull, it has about it all the fascination of the positively and thoroughly bad. It could have been written at no other time and by no other writer. Those features of Nashe's work which are most characteristic and typical of him and of his age are here carried to lengths of excess that render them either ridiculous or revolting, and some-

[32] IV. 198.

times both at once. *Christ's Tears* is a monument of bad taste, literary tactlessness and unremitting over-elaboration for which it is not easy to find a parallel; a kind of gigantic oxymoron in which style and content, tone and intention are consistently at odds.

Nevertheless, it appealed to readers of the day more than *The Terrors of the Night* did. The unsold sheets of the 1593 edition were reissued the following year with a fresh Epistle to the Reader and a cancel leaf, and a further edition followed in 1613. It was, in fact, the only major work by Nashe that was republished in the seventeenth century. For this comparative success several reasons, not all of them strictly literary, can be adduced. First, *Christ's Tears* has its place in the story of the controversy between Nashe and Gabriel Harvey. On this matter it is sufficient to say at this point that in the Epistle to the Reader that appeared with the issue of 1593 Nashe begged Harvey's pardon and sought for a reconciliation with him. Finding, however, that Harvey did not respond to his overtures, he withdrew this Epistle from the issue of 1594 and replaced it with a fresh one, containing a new attack and threatening revenge on a large and exemplary scale for the future. Secondly, the pamphlet seems to have had a scandalous and topical appeal. A passage in it,[33] attacking the citizens and merchants of London as usurers and accusing them of making illegal private profits out of moneys entrusted to them for charitable purposes, aroused such resentment that Nashe, according to what he says in a private letter of 1596, was 'piteously persecuted by the Lord Maior and the aldermen'.[34] Exactly what form their persecution took we do not know, but it was strong enough to cause him to write a cancel leaf for the issue of 1594, softening the tone of the whole attack, making it far less specific and removing it from the sphere of the actual to that of the hypothetical by the addition of the words: 'I speake not this for I know any such, but if there be anie such, to forewarne and reforme them'.

Neither of these reasons will account, however, for the publication of a second edition in 1613, when the Harvey-Nashe quarrel and Nashe's charges against the citizens were both things of the past. *Christ's Tears* was brought out again at this late date, because it was topical once more—London in 1613, like London in 1593, was in the grip of the plague—and because it was different in kind from Nashe's other works and belonged to a tradition of

[33] II. 158–9. [34] V. 194.

writing that appealed to a wider and, I think one may guess, a more respectable audience than that which he usually had in view. From the time of Boccaccio's *De Casibus Virorum Illustrium* the use of history for moral and didactic purposes had been a well established literary mode, and in this country it developed a fresh impetus with the publication of *The Mirror for Magistrates* in 1559. The 'mirror' became the accepted convention in poetry, in prose and in the drama for all who sought to warn their age against the consequences that would, as they loved to assert, inevitably follow wrong-doing of any kind. The whole of human history, near or remote, was seen as a gigantic admonition to the present. When Antwerp fell in 1576 George Gascoigne, who had already utilized the mirror idea in his play, *The Glass of Government* (1575) and in his satire, *The Steel Glass* (1576), and who had actually been in Antwerp when the Spaniards overwhelmed it, promptly produced an account of what had happened there, entitled *The Spoil of Antwerp*, with the express intention of warning England in general, and London in particular, of the dangers of arousing God's wrath and of not being in a state of military preparedness. At the other end of the time scale, Greene and Lodge in their play, *A Looking Glass for London and England*, produced about 1590, had used Jonah's mission to Nineveh as the fable for a dramatic homily on the sins of the time.

Within this broad tradition a special place was occupied, as Dr. E. D. Mackerness has shown,[35] by the fall of Jerusalem, the example *par excellence* of the frightful results of not heeding Christ's word. Among the works on this subject that Nashe could have used for models, the one that seems to have supplied the ground plan for *Christ's Tears* was a sermon by the popular preacher, John Stockwood, published in 1584 under the following title, which is worth giving in full, since it well indicates both the content and the attitude:

> *A very fruitfull and necessarye Sermon of the moste lamentable destruction of Ierusalem, and the heauy iudgementes of God, executed vppon that people for their sinne and disobedience: published at this time to the wakening and stirring vp of all such, as bee lulled a sleepe in the cradle of securitie or carelesnesse, that they maye at length repente them of their harde hartednes, and contempt of God his word, least*

[35] E. D. Mackerness, '"Christs Teares" and the Literature of Warning', *English Studies*, XXXIII, 1952.

*they taste of the like plagues for their rebellion and vnrepentance, not knowing with the wilfull inhabitants of Ierusalem, the daye of their visitation. By Iohn Stockwood, Schoolemaister of Tunbridge. Luke* 13. 3. *Vnlesse yee repent, yee shall all perish in like manner.*

Taking as his text Luke 19. 41–4, which contains an account of how Christ came near to Jerusalem, wept over it and prophesied its forthcoming destruction, Stockwood first describes why Christ wept on this occasion, then gives a shortened version of Joseph Ben Gorion's narrative of the siege and capture of the city, and concludes by urging men to buy his work and to read it as a warning. I agree with McKerrow when he says that there are no close verbal parallels between Stockwood's work and *Christ's Tears*,[36] but the style of the sermon is lively and of a kind that would have excited Nashe's interest. Already in 1584 Stockwood makes use of the trick of deliberately mistaking words that both Marprelate and Nashe were to exploit, writing of 'our holy monster, master I shoulde saye, the Pope',[37] and he is quite ready to lapse into the colloquial, as when he describes the emperor, Vitellius, as 'a foole, a soufer and a blowbole drunkard'.[38]

The full title of Nashe's pamphlet is *Christs Teares Over Jerusalem. Whereunto is annexed, a comparatiue admonition to London*, and, as it indicates, the work falls into two distinct halves, the first being devoted to the fall of Jerusalem, seen as a divine punishment inflicted on the Jews for their sins, and the second to a description of the sins of Elizabethan London and a warning to its citizens that unless they repent their city will suffer the same fate as Jerusalem. It is in the first half that Nashe makes Stockwood his model. It falls into three sections; an account of the stubbornness of the Jews in their refusal to listen to God in spite of his mercies towards them; a 'Collachrimate oration' delivered by Christ, reproaching the Jews for their treatment of the prophets; and, finally, the story, drawn from Joseph Ben Gorion, of the siege and fall of Jerusalem. In the second half Nashe goes his own way, reverting to the same kind of pattern for describing the sins of London that he had used in *Pierce Penilesse*, and ending with a prayer to God to be merciful to London, to free her from the plague and not to overwhelm her as he overwhelmed Jerusalem.

The way in which the whole thing falls into clearly defined sections and sub-sections argues that Nashe took an unusual

[36] IV. 213. [37] *Op. cit.*, B2 [38] *Ibid.*, B5

amount of trouble over the planning of it and meant it quite seriously. There was every reason why he should have done. Thoroughly orthodox and conventional where religion was concerned, he had found a place even in *Pierce Penilesse* for an attack on sectarianism and scepticism,[39] and for singing the praises of 'siluer tongu'd Smith', one of the most popular preachers of the day.[40] Moreover, *Summer's Last Will and Testament* shows how deeply moved he was by the plague and how he regarded it in terms of the Litany as a visitation on London for its sins. The continuance of the plague through the winter of 1592–3, an unusual occurrence, would have endorsed and reinforced that view by the time he came to write *Christ's Tears* in the late spring or early summer of 1593. At the same time religious conviction may well have coincided with other motives. The space he devotes to Atheism in his account of the sins of London looks suspiciously like an attempt to stand well with Whitgift and Bancroft, who seem to have conducted something of a campaign against religious scepticism in the years 1593–4, while in bidding farewell to 'fantasticall Satirisme', as he does in the Epistle to the Reader,[41] he could have been trying to mollify those who had apparently been annoyed by the fable of the Bear and the Fox in *Pierce Penilesse*. It would also appear from what he says to Lady Elizabeth Carey in the Dedication that she, perhaps, had some influence in causing him to adopt a new manner. He writes:

> Pardon my presumption, lend patience to my prolixitie, and if any thing in all please, thinke it was compiled to please you. This I auouche, no line of it was layde downe without awfull looking backe to your frowne. To write in Diuinitie I would not haue aduentured, if ought els might haue consorted with the regenerate grauitie of your iudgement.[42]

It is not beyond the bounds of conjecture that the patroness of Spenser may have had something to do with Nashe's retraction of his attack on Spenser's friend, Gabriel Harvey.

Religious ardour, however, is by itself no guarantee of good writing, especially when, like Nashe's, it appears to have been of only temporary duration. He may well have thought that he had something of importance to say to his countrymen and yet have been mistaken, for he never shows any real imaginative grasp of his

[39] I. 171–2. [40] I. 192–3. [41] II. 12.
[42] II. 11.

subject. His whole nature, the literary personality he had created for himself and the manner of writing he had developed were all inimical to the success of this new departure. Essentially a clown and an exhibitionist, he could not turn preacher merely by removing his red nose; in any case it was irremovable. His love of the witty, the flamboyant and the grotesque was too deep to be eradicated by a pious impulse. What happened when he wrote the first half of *Christ's Tears* was that he sought to put it to a pathetic purpose for which it was completely unfitted. Nor could he draw in this part of the work on that feeling for, and grasp of, the everyday life of his own times which is the life-blood of his best writing. Cut off from it, he substitutes words for experience and tries to make linguistic invention do the work that only thought and feeling can do.

From the very beginning there is a marked element of the strained and the factitious about *Christ's Tears*. The Dedicatory Epistle is unusually elaborate and high flown, even for an age in which dedicatory adulation habitually walked on tip-toes. Lady Elizabeth Carey, anticipating Ophelia, is addressed as 'the most honored, and vertuous beautified ladie', and as 'Excellent accomplisht Court-glorifying Lady'. Euphuistic cross-alliteration abounds. Nashe laments his abortive efforts to pay her a fitting compliment and then continues thus:

> My woe-infirmed witte conspired against me with my fortune. My impotent care-crazed stile cast of his light wings and betooke him to wodden stilts.[43]

Meant as a bit of self-depreciatory posing not to be taken too literally, these words are in fact a very accurate description of Nashe's writing in the first half of the pamphlet. It is stilted in the extreme. Setting out 'to vtter some-thing that may mooue secure *England* to true sorrow and contrition', he clearly intended, among other things, to give the average preacher, whose inability to exercise the art of rhetoric for this purpose he had already deplored on several occasions in the past, an object lesson in method. Indeed, he almost says as much when, in the course of his attack on Atheism, he writes:

> It is onely ridiculous dul Preachers (who leape out of a Library of Catechismes, into the loftiest Pulpits) that haue reuiued thys scornefull Secte of Atheists.

[43] II. 10.

> They boldly will vsurpe *Moyses* chayre, without anie study or preparation. They would haue theyr mouthes reuerenced as the mouthes of the *Sybils*, who spoke nothing but was registred; Yet nothing comes from theyr mouthes but grosse full-stomackt tautology. They sweat, they blunder, they bounce and plunge in the Pulpit, but all is voyce and no substance: they deafe mens eares, but not edifie. Scripture peraduenture they come of thicke and three-folde with, but it is so vgly daubed, plaistred and patcht on, so peeuishly speckt and applyde, as if a Botcher (with a number of Satten and Veluette shreddes) should cloute and mend Leather-doublets and Cloth-breeches.
>
> Gette you some witte in your great heades, my hotte-spurd Diuines, discredite not the Gospell: if you haue none, damme vp the Ouen of your vttrance, make not such a bigge sound with your empty vessels. At least, loue men of witte, and not hate them so as you doe, for they haue what you want. By louing them and accompanying with them, you shall both doe them good and your selues good; They of you shall learne sobriety and good life, you of them shal learne to vtter your learning, and speake mouinglie.[44]

And, speaking as a man of wit, Nashe goes on to recommend to the preacher that he should 'art-enamel' his speech, make it 'sweete and honny-some . . . in the mouth, and . . . musicall and melodious in the eare', and enrich and adorn it with 'similitudes and comparisons'.

Nashe certainly has the courage of his critical convictions and follows his own prescription, but the results do not justify the claims made for the method. The business of 'welting and garding' a narrative, which had worked so well in the case of the story of the sick gentleman in *The Terrors of the Night*, where it is part of a game, could not be automatically switched over to another and very different purpose. At the opening of *Christ's Tears* he tries to turn himself into one of the twelve apostles and prays for divine inspiration and assistance. He writes:

> Mine owne witte I cleane disinherite: thy fiery Clouen-tongued inspiration be my Muse. Lende my wordes the forcible wings of the Lightnings, that they may peirce vnawares into the marrow and reynes of my Readers. Newe mynt my minde to the likenes of thy lowlines: file away the superfluous affectation of my prophane puft vp phrase, that I may be thy pure simple Orator.[45]

[44] II. 123–4. [45] II. 15–16.

The request and the terms in which it is made contradict each other; literary artifice is apparent in every word of this prayer for simplicity, which, in any case, runs counter to Nashe's whole theory of preaching. He did not mean it and, fittingly, the Holy Ghost did not listen to it. In spite of what he says here about simplicity, he seems to have had no understanding of how much the Gospel owes to the nakedness and directness of its prose, and to have worked on the assumption that it was altogether too austere for the ordinary reader and needed to be adorned with poetical figures and enlivened with sensational illustrations to make it effective. His treatment of the parable of the two houses, the one built on rock and the other on sand, will illustrate both his incomprehension and his perversity. In the course of the oration that he puts into Christ's mouth he takes up the final words of the parable and expands them into a 'poetical' reproof to Jerusalem. In Tyndale's version of Matthew they run thus: 'and the fluddes cam and the wyndes blewe and beat vppon that housse and it was over throwen and great was the fall of it'. Here is what Nashe does with them:

> With the foolish builder, you haue founded your Pallaces on the sands of your owne shalow conceits: had you rested them on the true Rocke, they had beene ruine-proofe; but now the raine wil rough-enter through the crannies of theyr wayuering, the Windes will blow and batter ope wide passages for the pashing shoures: With roring and buffetting lullabies, in stead of singing and dandling by-os, they will rocke them cleane ouer and ouer. The onely commodity they shal tithe to their owners will be (by their ouer-turning) to affoord them Tombes vnaskt. Great shall bee the fall of thy foolish building (oh *Jerusalem*): like a Tower ouertopt, it shal fal flatte, and be layd low and *desolate*.[46]

This 'improvement' on the original, in which prophetic denunciation fights a losing battle against nursery-rhyme, stems from a misguided search for the picturesque in place of the plain, from a rooted distrust of the monosyllabic and from a total inability to resist the temptations of word-play and alliteration. Determined to get in his pun on the word *rocke*, Nashe is quite blind to the absurdity of depicting the palaces of Jerusalem as a child in the cradle and the winds that blow them over as lullabies. On the contrary, the difficulty he gets himself into by using *lullabies* for

[46] II. 47.

rough winds merely stimulates his wayward ingenuity and leads him to coin the nonce-word *by-o* for the noise made by a gentle breeze. And throughout there is a constant striving for the sound effects produced by clever but unrelenting alliteration. The technique draws so much attention to itself that the sense, which makes such a direct and immediate impact in the Gospel, is almost lost in the welter of noise and imagery.

Nashe's handling of this brief parable is a fair specimen of what he does all through the 'continued Oration' that he gives to Christ. It is really an elaborate sermon. Christ is transformed into an Elizabethan preacher—or, rather, into an unintentional parody of an Elizabethan preacher—newly down from the university, with all his learning fresh in his head and filled with the determination to impress his hearers at all costs and at every word. He takes his text from Matthew, 23. 37–8, which, in the version Nashe used, ran thus:

> O Ierusalem, Ierusalem, which killest the Prophets, and stonest them that are sent vnto thee: How often would I haue gathered thy Chyldren together, as the Henne gathereth her Chickins together vnder her wings, and ye would not! Therefore your habitation shall be left desolate.[47]

On the peg provided by this text is hung an extended discourse that shows the Elizabethan cult of eloquence and 'copie' at its worst. Words beget words in an incessant, bubbling stream. Nashe picks up a phrase, or, on occasions, even a single word from the text and works it to death. His concern is not to squeeze every possible significance out of it in the manner of a Lancelot Andrewes, but rather to pump significances into it, to inflate it into a balloon, by giving free rein to his own love of word-play and his fecund sense of association.

In his attack on Atheism in the second part of *Christ's Tears* he writes for the benefit of parsons:

> No knowledge but is of God. Vnworthy are wee of heauenly knowledge, if we keepe from her any one of her hand-maydes. Logique, Rhetorique, History, Phylosophy, Musique, Poetry, all are the handmaides of Diuinitie. Shee can neuer be curiously drest or exquisitely accomplisht, if any one of these be wanting.[48]

The two arts from the mediaeval hierarchy of learning that Nashe draws on most to adorn his own essay in divinity are those of music

[47] II. 21. [48] II. 126.

and poetry. Describing the way the oration is put together, C. S. Lewis remarks:

> In the speech given to the Saviour he uses a strange artifice of which I do not know the history (the 119th Psalm might be the ultimate model). A series of keywords (*stones*, *gather*, *echo*, *would not*, and *desolate*) are used in turn like *leitmotifs*.[49]

I can see little resemblance to the Psalm in question; but Lewis's use of the word *leitmotif* shows that he also finds an analogy between the construction of the oration and the process of musical composition. To me the oration reads like an attempt to make prose reproduce something of the effect of a complex part-song. A theme is stated, a maximum number of variations on it are evolved, and then another theme is taken up and treated in the same manner. Eventually the various themes are woven together. The themes are, of course, drawn from the text, while the variations are the product of an uninhibited verbal imagination. The use of a word in one context reminds Nashe of its use in another, or of a different word that resembles it in some way or other. Nor does he restrict himself to the Bible; his Christ is as familiar with Ovid and Horace and with English ways of life in the sixteenth century as he is with Holy Writ. He is, in fact, Tom Nashe in a surplice, and not very comfortable in it.

The first theme is announced thus:

> *O Ierusalem, Ierusalem, that stonest*, and astoniest thy Prophets with thy peruersnesse, that lendest stonie eares to thy Teachers, and with thyne yron breast drawest vnto thee nothing but the Adamant of GODS anger: what shall I doe to mollifie thee? The rayne mollifieth harde stones; oh that the stormie tempest of my Teares might soften thy stony hart! Were it not harder then stone, sure ere this I had broken and brused it, with the often beating of my exhortations vpon it.
>
> *Moyses* strooke the Rocke and water gusht out of it; I (that am greater then *Moyses*) haue strooken you with threates, and you haue not mourned. O ye heauens, be amazed at this, be afraide and vtterly confounded: my people haue drunke out of a Rocke in the Wildernesse, and euer-since had rockie harts. Yet wil the Rocks tremble when my Thunder fals vpon them. The Mason with his Axe hewes and carues then at his pleasure. All the thunder of iudgements which I spend on this stony *Ierusalem*, cannot make her

[49] *Op. cit.*, p. 414.

to tremble, or refraine *from stoning my Prophets*. Should I raine stones vpon her, with them shee would arme her-selfe against my holy ones.[50]

The evolution of this passage is determined by verbal association and the desire for a witty conclusion rather than by any development of sense or argument. The verb *to stone* has suggested the unrelated but similar word *astoniest* and the adjective *stonie* applied to *eares*. It has also suggested the word *loadstone*, which appears disguised in the learned form *adamant*, and which, in its turn, dictates the use of *yron* to describe the hearts of the Jews, instead of the *stonie* that one would expect. Another property of *stone* leads on to the figure of *teares* as a *stormie Tempest*, and the association of *rocks*, *water* and *striking* brings in Moses.

Once launched in this fashion, Nashe ranges over the Bible bringing in every allusion to *stones* and *stoning* that he can think of. There is no logical progress. The keywords act as a kind of focus for a miscellaneous collection of references. Promising the Jews a fitting punishment for their treatment of the prophets, Christ says:

For this shalt thou grinde the *stones* in the Myll with *Sampson*, and whet thy teeth vpon the *stones* for hunger; and if thou askest anie man Bread he shall gyue thee *stones* to eate. The dogges shall licke thy blood on the *stones* lyke *Iezabels*, and not a *stone* be found to couer thee when thou art deade. One *stone* of thy Temple shall not be left vppon another that shall not be throwne downe. The *stone* which thy foolish Builders refused shall be made the head *stone* of the corner. Your harts (which are Temples of *stone*) I will for-sweare for euer to dwell in. There shall be no *Dauid* any more amongst you, that with a *stone* sent out of a sling, shall strike the chiefe Champion of the *Philistines* in the for-head: And finally, you shall worship stockes and *stones*, for I will be no longer your God.[51]

At this point, having defied proverbial wisdom by wringing an unconscionable amount of blood, not to mention tears, out of the *stone*, Nashe drops it (for the time being) and finds another *leitmotif* in the word *gather*, which he submits to the same kind of elegant variation, but at considerably greater length. By the time he has worked his way through the entire text in this fashion, it has supplied him with the ground-work on which to elaborate

[50] II. 23. [51] II. 25.

some thirty-two pages of extravagant, decorated prose. And even then he has not done with it; having brought the sermon to its climax with a prophecy of the desolation to ensue, he takes care to round it off with a recapitulation of the various themes that have gone into its making; and the same keywords are still used as a kind of echo in the account of the fall of Jerusalem. The analogy with music seems to me unmistakable, but, while Nashe shows enterprise in undertaking such a form of composition and considerable ingenuity and artifice in working it out, it is hard to see what he gains by it. The constant repetition of a few keywords, far from making what he has to say more 'penetrating', has the reverse effect. The reader is bludgeoned until his ears become as stony as those of the Jews.

The other art that Nashe sought to enlist under the banner of divinity was that of poetry, or, more specifically, that of dramatic poetry. Alive, as he shows himself to be in *Pierce Penilesse*, to the fact that the popular dramatists of the day were succeeding in moving men, he attempted to use some of their devices for his own purpose, and clearly thought of the first part of *Christ's Tears*, including the account of the fall of Jerusalem as well as Christ's sermon, as a kind of prose tragedy, the sermon being a tragical prologue to the tragical fact of the city's destruction. He practically says so when, turning from the one to the other, he invites the reader to consider the magnitude of the task:

> Heere doe I confine our Sauiours collachrimate Oration, and putting off his borrowed person, restore him to the tryumphancie of his Passion. Now priuately (as mortall men) let vs consider howe his threats were after verified in *Ierusalems* ouer-turne.
>
> Should I write it to the proofe, weeping would leaue me no eyes: like tragick *Seneca*, I shoulde tragedize my selfe, by bleeding to death in the depth of passion. Admirable Italian teare-eternizers, *Ariosto*, *Tasso*, and the rest, nere had you such a subiect to roialize your Muses with.[52]

The reference to Seneca is no accident. The account of the fall of Jerusalem that Nashe used provided him with an abundance of the kind of sensational material that is to be found in Seneca's plays, and he set out to heighten its effect by the use of every rhetorical trick he knew. Even before the oration opens he already has the notion of Christ as a kind of tragic hero in mind. He

[52] II. 60.

begins his pamphlet by retelling in his own words the parable of the vineyard and the story of Christ's ministry and during the course of it, gives way to a 'bright idea' and draws a singularly tactless parallel between Christ and Marlowe's Tamburlaine. He writes of the Jews' refusal to listen to Christ's teaching:

> As I said before, no remedy, or signe of any breath of hope, was left in their Common-wealths sinne-surfetted body, but the maladie of their incredulity ouer-maistred heauenly phisick. To desperate diseases must desperate Medicines be applyde. When neither the White-flag or the Red which *Tamburlaine* aduanced at the siedge of any Citty, would be accepted of, the Blacke-flag was sette vp, which signified there was no mercy to be looked for; and that the miserie marching towardes them was so great, that their enemy himselfe (which was to execute it) mournd for it. Christ, hauing offered the Iewes the White-flagge of forgiuenesse and remission, and the Red-flag of shedding his Blood for them, when these two might not take effect nor work any yeelding remorse in them, the Black-flagge of confusion and desolation was to suceede for the obiect of their obduration.[53]

The incongruous nature of the comparison does not strike Nashe, because he seems to have conceived of tragedy as violent and sensational action tricked out in extravagantly passionate speech. He therefore fills Christ's mouth with 'high astounding terms' and makes him dramatize his emotions in the manner of Kyd's Hieronimo or Shakespeare's Titus Andronicus. Hyperboles, long-drawn-out similes and conventional *exempla* crowd on one another's heels with results that are often most inappropriate to the occasion and at times lapse into the sheerest bathos. For instance, when Christ laments Jerusalem's rejection of him, he resorts to a variant on a well worn fable illustrating the sin of ingratitude and says:

> Ouer thy principall gates and the doores of thy Temple, let therefore this for an Emprese be engrauen: A kinde compassionate man, who, grieuing to see a serpentine Salamander fry in the fire (so pittiouslie as it seem'd), cast water on the raging flames to quench them, and was by him stung to death for his labour. The mott or word thereto, AT NOLVISTI, *but thou woldst not*. As who should say, thank thy selfe though thou stil burnest: I wold haue ridde thee out of the fire, *but thou wouldst not*. By stinging mee (mortally) thou disturbest mee.[54]

[53] II. 20. [54] II. 46.

Even allowing for the fact that the word *disturb* had, perhaps, for Nashe a stronger sense than it has for us, the final sentence still remains a fine example of the fatuous anti-climax. It is, unfortunately, all too typical of what is constantly happening in the first half of the work.

The difficulties that the dramatists of the time were having in developing a tragic idiom that would be passionate and heightened, and yet avoid the pitfalls of the grotesque on the one hand and the pretty on the other, are high-lighted to such an extent in Nashe's prose that they are almost burlesqued, because, keen though his eye was for tricks of technique, he had no real sense of the tragic. Seeking to express extreme emotion, he combines physical with figurative imagery, as the dramatists so often did, but he loses control of both and produces this kind of nonsense in attempting to render Christ's feelings as he recalls his unavailing efforts to bring Jerusalem to repentance:

> My leane withered hands (consisting of nought but bones) are all to shiuerd and splinterd in their wide cases of skinne, with often beating on the Anuile of my bared breast. So penetrating and eleuatedly haue I prayd for you, that mine eyes woulde fayne haue broke from theyr anchors to haue flowne vp to Heauen, and myne armes stretcht more then the length of my body to reach at the Starres. My heart ranne full-butt against my breast to haue broken it open, and my soule flutterd and beate with her ayrie-winges on euery side for passage. My knees crackt and the ground fledde back. Then (oh *Ierusalem*) would I haue rent my body in the midst (lyke a graue) so I might haue buried thy sinnes in my bowels.[55]

Straining after pathos, Nashe writes turgid bombast. He employs images without visualizing them. He does not seem to realize that by fixing the eyes with anchors he has turned them into boats, and that boats do not fly. Had these words been written in the age of balloons, they might have meant something. As it is, they merely betray a habit of mind in which the idea of fastening brings the image of the anchor with it, just as the action of beating something has to be represented by an anvil. In discussing *The Terrors of the Night* I said that Nashe thinks in images, but in *Christ's Tears* images are all too frequently not instruments of thought but substitutes for thinking. Nashe seems to look on the poetry, and particularly the dramatic poetry, of the day as a kind of second-

[55] II. 37.

hand shop, where suits of ready-made imagery may be had for the asking, and to rely on their striking appearance to cover any mistakes in the fitting.

Two images in particular recur time after time in Christ's oration and are carried on into the story of the fall of Jerusalem, those of tears and of blood. Nashe's recourse to them is obviously deliberate and must be one of the first thorough-going exploitations of a device Shakespeare was to make so much use of. But the strain of tricking them out in fresh colours again and again proves too much for him and leads him into some of his wildest flights of absurdity. The words he gives to Christ as a prophecy of the state of Jerusalem after its sack by the Romans are a collector's piece of Elizabethan excess:

> *Ierusalem*, euer after thy bloody hecatombe or buriall, the Sunne (rising and setting) shal enrobe himselfe in scarlette, and the mayden-Moone (in the ascention of her perfection) shal haue her crimson cheekes (as they wold burst) round balled out with bloode. Those ruddy inuesturings and scarlet habilements, from the clowde-climing slaughter-stack of thy dead carkases, shall they exhalingly quintessence, to the end thou maist not onelie bee culpable of gorging the Earth, but of goring the Heauens with blood: and in witnes against thee, weare them they shall to the worlds end, as the lyueries of thy wayning.[56]

It is one thing for Marlowe, in a witty, fanciful love poem, such as *Hero and Leander*, to play with the idea of metamorphosis and to suggest that his heroine used up so much of Nature's stock of beauty that 'Since Hero's time hath half the world been black'; it is quite another for Nashe, in what is intended as a tragical and moving sermon, to put forward the notion that only since the fall of Jerusalem have the sun and moon had a reddish tinge at their rising and setting, and to imagine that he has made his fancy all the more pathetic by picturing the moon as a girl with her mouth so full of blood that her cheeks look like the sides of a football.

In the passage I have considered Nashe's addiction to 'mythologizing' results in writing that is absurd and silly. Very often, however, it leads to a mixture of the pretty and the gruesome not unlike that which frequently occurs in *Titus Andronicus*. For his brief account of the siege and fall of Jerusalem he drew on Peter Morwyn's translation, published in 1558, of Joseph Ben Gorion's

[56] II. 49.

*History of the Latter Times of the Jews' Commonweal*, and there he found a passage, describing the consequences of the rule of Eleazar and Jehochanan in the beleaguered city, in which it is stated that their massacres were so numerous

> that the chanel of Iordane was so stuffed and stopt with dead bodyes, that the waters rose and ranne ouer the bankes here and there into the fieldes and playnes. Yet at the length the waters encreased, and bare the carkases downe the riuer, as farre as the Sea of *Sedom*, which is the Sea of pitche, otherwyse called the salt Sea.[57]

Morwyn's prose has at least the virtue of forcefulness, but it was not pathetical enough or picturesque enough for Nashe, who plays with it to the following effect:

> The channell of *Iordan* was so ouer-burdened and charged wyth dead carkasses, that the waters contended to wash theyr hands of them, and lightly leapt ouer theyr banckes, as shunning to mixe themselues with so many millions of murders: but after many dayes abstinence from theyr propper entercourse, (obseruing they must liue for euer banisht from theyr bounds, except they made some riddance of them,) they recollected theyr liquid forces, and, putting all theyr wauy shoulders together, bare the whole shole of them before them, as farre as the Sea of *Sodom*.[58]

In this display of exuberance the grisly fact of the dead bodies, which is a fact in Morwyn's version, is almost entirely submerged by the wealth of poetic colouring in which it is set. The reader's attention is distracted from the carnage and focused on the waters and their all-too-human behaviour. Like Ophelia, Nashe turns 'Thought and affliction, passion, hell itself to favour and to prettiness;' but Ophelia had the excuse of being mad, whereas Nashe does it of set purpose in order to show his wit and to overgo Morwyn.

As well as overworking, abusing and misapplying the figurative element in his writing, Nashe also does some very odd things with the actual vocabulary of the English language in his efforts to evolve a lofty and passionate style in keeping with his subject matter. The coining of new words from the classical tongues, a readiness to make old words do new things by treating nouns as verbs or adjectives as verbs and, above all, by linking two words together to form a new compound—all these things were common-

[57] IV. 223. [58] II. 68.

place at the time when Nashe was writing and had been for many years. Indeed the battle over 'inkhorn terms' between those who wished to experiment and the more conservative-minded had been going on for half a century, and Nashe himself had taken part in it—on the conservative side—in his *Strange News*, where he shows no hesitation in taking Gabriel Harvey to task for what he describes as that author's 'ouer-rackt absonisme', and even goes so far as to draw up a list of offending words and phrases used by his opponent. But even in a time of linguistic experiment the bizarre vocabulary of *Christ's Tears* drew attention to itself. In the new Address to the Reader, which he wrote for the reissue of *Christ's Tears* in 1594, Nashe tells us something about the criticism that the style of his work had already met with and puts forward his own defence of it. He writes:

> What talke I so longe of *Iacke Wilton*? I may tell you he hath but a sleight wringing by the eares, in comparison of the heauie penance my poore Teares here haue endured, to turn them cleane vnto tares: there be that haue laboured, and haue got salt Catars in their throats with vehement railing vpon it. The ploddinger sort of vnlearned Zoilists about London exclaim that it is a puft-vp stile, and full of prophane eloquence: others obiect vnto me the multitude of my boystrous compound wordes, and the often coyning of Italionate verbes which end all in Ize, as mummianize, tympanize, tirannize. To the first array of my clumperton Antigonists this I answer, that my stile is no otherwise puft up, then any mans should be which writes with any Spirite; and whom would not such a deuine subiect put a high rauishte Spirite into? For the prophanesse of my eloquence, so they may tearme the eloquence of Sainct *Austen*, *Ierome*, *Chrysostome*, prophane, since none of them but takes vnto him farre more liberty of Tropes, Figures, and Metaphors, and alleadging Heathen examples and Histories.
>
> To the second rancke of reprehenders that complain of my boystrous compound wordes, and ending my Italionate coyned verbes all in Ize, thus I replie: That no winde that blowes strong but is boystrous, no speech or wordes of any power or force to confute or perswade but must bee swelling and boystrous. For the compounding of my wordes, therein I imitate rich men who, hauing gathered store of white single money together, conuert a number of those small little scutes into great peeces of gold, such as double Pistols and Portugues. Our English tongue of all languages most swarmeth with the single money of monasillables, which are the onely scandall of it. Bookes written in them and no other seeme

> like Shop-keepers boxes, that containe nothing else saue halfe-pence, three-farthings, and two-pences. Therefore what did me I, but hauing a huge heape of those worthlesse shreds of small English in my *Pia maters* purse, to make the royaller shew with them to mens eyes, had them to the compounders immediately, and exchanged them foure into one, and others into more, according to the Greek, French, Spanish, and Italian?[59]

The terms in which the excuse is couched tell their own tale. Nashe admits that it came more naturally to him to write in simple English, but that on this occasion he deliberately altered his normal manner in order 'to make the royaller shew to mens eyes', and chose to use an outlandish vocabulary in deference to a theory that the only impressive words are those which are 'swelling and boystrous'. It all amounts to an admission that in this particular work he really has nothing to say and, consequently, seeks to make verbal eccentricity supply the place of any kind of felt experience, valuing words for their sound and fury rather than for their meaning. His conviction that he was called on to undertake a work of moral suasion, however sincere he may have felt it to be, was at bottom factitious. Entertainment, not instruction, was his real vocation. The only parts of the first half of *Christ's Tears* that really come alive are those in which he throws off the surplice for a moment, and allows his sense of contemporary life and his delight in villainy to get the better of his preaching, as in his description of the Jewish leaders, especially Schimeon, of whom he writes: 'hee might well haue beene Schoole-maister to *Cayne* or *Iudas*, hee was such a grand *Keysar* of cut-throates'.[60]

Flashes of this kind are, however, rare and merely serve to underline the artificiality of the context in which they appear by burlesquing it. The final effect of the first part of the pamphlet is endorsed by the Miriam story, which was plainly intended to serve as the climax to it and which has the doubtful distinction of being the most tasteless piece of writing that Nashe ever produced. It fitted in neatly with his ideas of tragedy, of course, since it was the Jewish equivalent of the bloody banquet in Seneca's *Thyestes*. He therefore took great pains over it. In the pages of Ben Gorion it is already in bad taste, but by the time that Nashe has finished with it, this story of the woman who killed and ate her own child can only be described as silly and revolting in its laboured efforts

[59] II. 183–4. [60] II. 63.

to mix pathos with horror and bloody actions with moving oratory. The one word that will cover it is his own 'horrorsome'. He decorates and prettifies the unspeakable. When some of the starving inhabitants of Jerusalem, smelling roast meat, rush into Miriam's house, she sets the remains of the child's flesh before them and says:

> Eate, I pray you, heere is good meate, be not afrayd, it is flesh of my flesh, I bare it, I nurst it, I suckled it. Loe, heere is the head, the handes, and the feete. It was myne owne onely sonne, I tell you. Sweet was he to mee in his life, but neuer so sweet as in his death. Beholde his pale perboyld visage, how pretie-pitteous it lookes. His pure snow-moulded soft fleshe will melt of it selfe in your mouthes: who can abstaine from these two round teat-like cheeks? Be not dainty to cut them vp; the rest of his body haue I cutte vp to your hands.[61]

This speech and the whole context in which it appears raise in an acute form the problem, that is never long out of sight in the first half of *Christ's Tears*, of the whole nature and quality of Nashe's sensibility. The great gulf between the words and the facts, between the horror he tries to convey and the impression of callous sadism that he creates, leaves one wondering just what kind of man he was. He seems to have been singularly lacking in human feeling, to have had no real understanding of the events he describes, no imaginative insight into the nature of suffering and to have looked on human experience as so much raw material, interesting only for the fact that it could, as he thought, be turned into an artefact by 'endeauors of arte', by the exercise on it of style, conceived of in a wholly external manner as the application of 'art-enamel'. As a consequence at every turn his method defeats his intention; trying to horrify he becomes comic, trying to be impressive he becomes absurd and trying to be moving he writes what looks all too like burlesque.

As might be expected, there is far less of the kind of falsity I have just discussed in the second half of the pamphlet, where Nashe turns his attention to London. Moving on more familiar ground here, he no longer relies to the same extent on eccentricities of imagery and vocabulary; instead he degenerates into dullness. By the time he came to write it he had clearly grown bored with the whole task. Even in his account of the fall of Jerusalem he had

[61] II. 75–6.

complained more than once of weariness and had found it necessary to spur his jaded invention with such encouragements as this: 'Plucke vppe a good courage, mine infant pen, and wearily struggle (as well as thou maist) thorow thys huge word-dearthing taske'.[62] In the second part there are more complaints of the same kind. After describing some of the tricks of bawds and whores, for instance, he abandons the topic with the words 'I am weary of recapitulating theyr rogery';[63] and, when he deals with the sin of gluttony, he cuts his denunciation of it off in the middle, saying: 'Very largely haue I inueighed against this vice elsewhere, wherefore heere I will trusse it vp more surcinct'.[64] 'Elsewhere' in this passage refers, of course, to *Pierce Penilesse*, and the extent to which Nashe draws on his own earlier work fully endorses the impression of a flagging invention that one gets from this part of the pamphlet.

The debt to *Pierce Penilesse* is at its clearest in the way that the London section of *Christ's Tears* is planned and set out. Once again the Seven Deadly Sins provide the design, though Nashe attempts to produce a variant on the old motif by giving them new names and making a kind of family-tree for them with Pride as the father, Ambition, Vaine-glory, Atheisme, Discontent and Contention as his sons and Disdaine, Gorgeous-attyre and Delicacie as his daughters. The appearance of novelty thus created is, however, quite superficial. In essence Nashe's attack on the sins of London is far more traditional, and much closer to what John Peter has called the literature of complaint,[65] than the corresponding section of *Pierce Penilesse*. There Nashe had substantially transformed the old material by treating it all from a personal point of view, by transposing it into the individual idiom of Pierce, by substituting mockery and humour for denunciation and the concrete and particular, especially in the form of lively character sketches, for the abstract and the general. In *Christ's Tears* he reverts to the time-honoured formula. In fact, a pretty adequate summary of what he has to say is provided by John Peter when he writes:

> The themes of medieval Complaint tend to fall naturally into four rough categories. In the first place there are direct attacks upon

[62] II. 69. [63] II. 153. [64] II. 147.

[65] See John Peter, *Complaint and Satire in Early English Literature*, Oxford, 1956.

> various professional or business classes which seem to the poet corrupt: lawyers, usurers, and so forth. Secondly, there are similar attacks upon other less definite classes, groups that are thought of in relation not to trades or professions but to some specific abuse or abuses with which they are associated. Examples are backbiters, atheists, misers, and so on. Thirdly, there are attacks directed against certain abuses like swearing and the use of cosmetics. This sort of attack is often indistinguishable from the category just mentioned, since it is not always possible to declare which is the immediate target, the abuse itself or the type of delinquent who is guilty of it. Lastly, and most difficult of all to describe in a few words, there are a number of general themes which are not attacks at all but rather the fundamental ideas and beliefs from which the whole attitude of Complaint may be said to grow.[66]

Among the general themes mentioned in the last sentence the fear of death and a proneness to insist on the decay of the body occupy an important place in Mr. Peter's account and in *Christ's Tears*.

The exactness with which a modern definition of a whole body of mediaeval literature fits Nashe's assault on the sins of London emphasizes very neatly the traditional nature of that assault. Doing his best to wear the mantle of an Old Testament prophet, Nashe goes, as the writers of mediaeval Complaint had done, to the Fathers of the Church, and especially to St. Augustine, for his material. He grumbles, he rails, he denounces, he remonstrates and he admonishes, exemplifying the various sins by long lists of instances drawn from the Bible, from the Classics and from Ancient History. Writing of Ambition, he begins thus:

> *Dauid* was ambitious when hee caused the people to be numbred. *Nabuchadnezer* eate grass for hys ambition. *Herod* was ambitious when in angelicall apparraile he spoke to the people. The truest image of thys kind of ambition was *Absolom*. *Iulius Caesar* amongst the *Ethnicks* surmounted . . . [67]

It is all stale and repetitive and has no connection with London until an image drawn from a familiar scene suddenly lights the whole thing up and reminds one that Nashe can write after all. This is what happens when, in the course of drawing a general moral from the examples of ambition he has mentioned, he says:

> Let the ambitious man stretch out his lymbes neuer so, he taketh vp no more ground (being dead) then the Begger. *London*, of many

[66] *Op. cit.*, p. 60. [67] II. 82.

> ambitious busie heades [the string of instances has not included a single one] hast thou beheld the rysing and downe falling. In thy stately Schoole are they first tutord in theyr Arte. With example thou first exaltest them, and still still liftes them vp, till thou hast lifted vp theyr heads on thy gates.[68]

The witty allusion to the rotting heads above Traitors' Gate has an immediacy of impact that underlines the flatness and lack of urgency in the trite moralizing that has gone before it.

There are other flashes of a similar kind, including a caricature, almost Burns-like in its bounce and vigour, of the contemporary preacher in his pulpit,[69] a brilliant satirical sketch of merchants' wives dressed in the height of fashion[70] and an imaginary account of the whole process of going bankrupt in order to become rich. In all these Nashe writes with his eye on the object, but also allows his fancy freedom to expand into the comic mode. The beginning of the last passage I have referred to gives some idea of the quality of them all:

> This is the course now-a-dayes euery one taketh to be ritch: beeing a young Trader, and hauing of olde Mumpsimus (his auaritious Maister) learnd to bee hys Craftsmaister, for a yeere or two he is very thrifty, and husbandly he payes and takes as dulie as the Clock strikes, he seemeth very sober and precise, and bringeth all men in loue with him. When he thinketh he hath thorowlie wrunge himselfe into the Worlds good opinion, and that his credite is as much as hee will demaund, hee goes and tryes it, and on the Tenter-hookes stretches it. No man he knoweth but he will scrape a little Booke curtesie of, two or three thousand pound (perhaps) makes vp his mouth. When hee hath it all in his handes, for a month or two he reuels it, and cuts it out in the whole cloth.[71]

Here there is a continuous thread of events, the narrative moves forward all the time, while the events themselves are enlivened by the play of simile and metaphor, which also serve to convey Nashe's own attitude of amused contempt. There is a world of difference between this kind of thing and the dreary catalogue of ambitious men that I quoted above, or the flat denunciation of usury that precedes it. It is the work of an artist as distinct from a mouth-piece.

In the main, however, it is the mouthpiece that dominates in

[68] II. 82–3. [69] II. 123. [70] II. 137–8.
[71] II. 93–4.

the second part of *Christ's Tears* and, as a result, such interest as it has lies not in what it is, but in the record it provides of the traditional attitude towards such things as religious scepticism, usury, fine clothes and so forth, but there is little to distinguish Nashe's treatment of these topics from that of other moralists of the day. He shows no originality of thought and, as I have emphasized already, only makes use occasionally of his faculty for keen observation and striking expression. Moreover, there is no proper connection between the London part of the pamphlet and the Jerusalem section. The sins of London are almost entirely social; they seem rather small beer compared with the sins attributed to Jerusalem and a rather inadequate reason for London's suffering a similar fate.

It is hard to escape the conclusion that whatever Nashe's motives may have been when he began *Christ's Tears*, his enthusiasm for the subject declined rapidly as he proceeded with it and that long before he reached the end of it he had realized that prophecy and moral admonition were not his field. Significantly he made no further expeditions into it.

# VI

# 'THE UNFORTUNATE TRAVELLER'

> All that in this phantasticall Treatise I can promise, is some reasonable conueyance of historie, and varietie of mirth. By diuers of my good frends haue I been dealt with to employ my dul pen in this kinde, it being a cleane different vaine from other my former courses of writing.[1]

SUCH is the description of *The Unfortunate Traveller, Or, The Life of Jack Wilton* that Nashe gives in the Dedicatory Epistle, prefixed to the first edition of that work and addressed to the Earl of Southampton. On the face of it the statement, that the book is entirely different from anything he had written before it, seems completely justified, for in it he tells a story, of some length and full of incident, through the mouth of the hero. Moreover, the imaginary events the story recounts are set in a time before the writer was born and are given a certain air of verisimilitude by being mingled with genuine historical facts and personages. It looks as though Nashe had stumbled on the historical novel long before anyone else, and historians of the novel have been ready to take up the idea. Some seventy years ago J. J. Jusserand had no hesitation in suggesting that Nashe got the idea for this new 'kind' from Spain and was consciously imitating the picaresque novel as it had emerged in that country during the sixteenth century, and that he had particularly in mind *Lazarillo de Tormes*, of which an English translation by David Rowland was published in 1576.[2]

[1] II. 201.

[2] J. J. Jusserand, *The English Novel in the Time of Shakespeare*, London, 1890, pp. 287–327.

This idea of the story's origin was taken up and repeated by Sir Walter Raleigh,[3] but was then effectively disposed of, or so one would have thought, by McKerrow, who points out that Nashe's hero is not a *picaro* at all and that there is 'practically nothing in the work which can have been suggested by the picaresque type of romance, such as *Lazarillo de Tormes*'.[4] He might have added that the two works are written in entirely different spirits. *Lazarillo* is essentially realistic; it draws its strength and significance from the truth with which it portrays the life of poor people in a poor country. Lazarillo becomes a rogue because he has to; no other way of obtaining a living is open to him. The story is factual, unemphatic, makes no attempt to be sensational and does not moralize. Rowland gave to his translation of it the sub-title of *The Spaniard's Life*, and that sub-title is fully justified; *Lazarillo* has a representative quality, it depicts a general state of affairs. But it would be ridiculous to call *The Unfortunate Traveller* by any such title as *The Englishman's Life*. It has no representative quality at all, and, although the word 'realism' has often been used about it, no pretensions to any such thing. Furthermore, there is nothing in Nashe's work to show that he had even read *Lazarillo*; yet he never hesitated to borrow from such writings as he knew. Nevertheless, the notion that *The Unfortunate Traveller* is in some way or other a novel has persisted, and as recently as 1951 Arnold Kettle still insisted that it is picaresque because, as he sees it, Jack Wilton does not 'belong' to the society in which he finds himself 'or feel himself in any way morally bound to its standards'.[5]

An entirely different view of the work, and one that seems to me to come much nearer to the truth, has been advanced by Miss Agnes C. Latham, who, starting from the verifiable fact that Nashe was deeply interested in literary matters and particularly in problems of style, argues that its main purpose is to parody and burlesque the stock materials and methods of Elizabethan journalism.[6] This conception of it has the great virtue of bringing *The Unfortunate Traveller* much more into line with the rest of its author's

[3] Walter Raleigh, *The English Novel*, London, 1894, pp. 78–9.

[4] V. 23.

[5] Arnold Kettle, *An Introduction to the English Novel*, London, 1951, vol. I. p. 25.

[6] Agnes C. Latham, 'Satire on Literary Themes and Modes in Nashe's "Unfortunate Traveller",' *English Studies 1948*, London, 1948, pp. 85–100.

work, but, like the notion that it is a novel of some kind or other, labours under the handicap of assuming that Nashe was doing one thing and had one main intention in view all through. It also assumes that there was for him a clear-cut line between legitimate over-writing and burlesque; yet we know that the first half of *Christ's Tears* was meant seriously, despite the fact that so much of it reads like a deliberate parody of devotional literature. As I see it, Nashe is essentially an improviser. He works in terms of what may be described as scenes. Interested in the immediate, local effect he can extract from an idea or a situation, he works on it until he has exhausted its possibilities or grown bored with it, and then moves on to something else, unconcerned about its relationship with what has gone before, intent on showing his craftsmanship by treating it in an arresting manner and relying on his virtuosity as a showman to cover up the gaps. Abrupt transitions from the heightened to the burlesque are frequent with him and, on occasions, the one shades into the other. Nor is this feature of his work something peculiar to him. It is also found in much that was being written at the time. The age was, I think, still fascinated by the ease with which ideas and emotions could be conveyed and manipulated within the formal designs and frameworks evolved by the exercise of the arts of rhetoric in the previous decade, 1580–90. Prose was still being influenced by Lyly and blank verse by Kyd. But, in the very process of pushing the rhetorical manner to its limits, writers also became conscious of the limitations of the method. Marlowe's Barabas begins as a kind of Tamburlaine of commerce, but then turns into an Elizabethan Mr. Punch. There are passages in *Romeo and Juliet* that read like a parody of the formal, stylized manner used seriously elsewhere in the same play. *Titus Andronicus* is contemporary with *Love's Labour's Lost* in which Shakespeare bids a lingering farewell to the rhetorical devices he had used so extensively in that play and in *Richard III*. Writers became conscious of the dangers of overwriting in the very process of doing it; excess and the critical exposure of the absurdities it could lead to flourished side by side.

It therefore seems worth while to work patiently through *The Unfortunate Traveller*, in order to see how it is put together, or rather how it grew, and what Nashe is doing in each scene of it, before trying to come to any general conclusions about it. His own remarks about his 'good frends' having encouraged him to try his hand at this kind of writing and about its being in 'a cleane different vaine' from his previous work may be safely ignored. The Dedication from which they come was written after *The Unfortunate Traveller* was finished and when he could see what he had made. They tell us nothing about the intentions with which he began. And the 'good frends' look suspiciously like other 'good friends' who turn up so often as conventional stage properties in Elizabethan dedications and prefaces, invoked to urge or justify publication.

In any case, his friends, whether real or imaginary, can have made no very novel suggestion to Nashe, for the first section of *The Unfortunate Traveller*, which is self-contained and bears no organic relationship to the rest of it when considered in terms of story, belongs to that well established and popular form of writing in the sixteenth century, the jest-book. Nashe had already made use of this kind of material in *Pierce Penilesse*, where he recounts several 'merry tales' and 'rare witty iests', as he calls them; and this fact is a pointer to the intentions with which be began. He was writing a pamphlet, with a difference, and actually says so at the end of the jest-book section, where he writes: 'I must not place a volume in the precints of a pamphlet'.[7] There are other links with the earlier work as well. In it he had drawn on the work of the chroniclers to some extent, though this had not prevented him from criticizing them for their inability to distinguish between the significant and the insignificant and for the flatness of their style. Comparing them with the poets, with whom he identified himself, he had written:

> they want the wings of choise words to fly to heauen, which we haue: they cannot sweeten a discourse, or wrest admiration from men reading, as we can, reporting the meanest accident.[8]

In due course the desire to show the chroniclers how to write, implicit in these words, becomes an important motive in *The Unfortunate Traveller*, but at the beginning the historical account of Henry VIII's siege of Térouanne, or Turwin as Nashe calls it, merely provides a suitable setting for the practical jokes that Jack Wilton plays. Far more important, both for the effect it has on the jest-book matter and ultimately on the work as a whole, is the close resemblance between the idiom that Nashe invents for his

[7] II. 227. [8] I. 194.

page and that which he had given Pierce. Jack speaks directly to his audience in the same intimate, conversational manner, drops in parenthetical asides, quotes Latin tags and makes witty, slangy translations of them, and even invests himself in a livery of mock-titles very like those Pierce had bestowed on the devil, describing himself thus:

> sole king of the cans and blacke iackes, prince of the pigmeis, countie palatine of cleane straw and prouant, and, to conclude, Lord high regent of rashers of the coles and red herring cobs.[9]

To ask where this mere page gets his wit and learning from would be a waste of time. Unlike the novelist—the author of *Lazarillo* for instance—Nashe makes no attempt to provide his hero with anything so mundane, or 'realistic', as parents and education. Jack's only ancestry is literary; his father is Pierce Penilesse.

By endowing Jack with an individual idiom Nashe is able to do new things with the old jest-book matter. A popular collection, such as *A Hundred Merry Tales*, is singularly lacking in any kind of literary artifice. The stories are told baldly and crudely; nothing is done to give them any kind of verisimilitude or dramatic interest; their whole point lies in the practical joke or cunning shift that they relate. The four adventures in which Jack is involved in the first section of *The Unfortunate Traveller* are, in so far as the actual events they deal with are concerned, of exactly this kind. And Nashe makes no secret of it. After the first one, the gulling of a cider-merchant, is over, he has Jack say:

> This was one of my famous atchieuements, insomuch as I neuer light vpon the like famous Foole: but I haue done a thousand better iests, if they had been bookt in order as they were begotten.[10]

But, unlike the authors of the jest-books, Nashe expends art on the telling of his tales. In the first of them, for instance, the story amounts merely to this: that Jack beguiles the cider-merchant into believing that the King regards him as an enemy agent, and leads him to make a free distribution of cider and cheese to the troops in the hope of recovering the King's favour. But in Nashe's hands the beguiling becomes an object lesson in the art of persuasion and the whole situation a little comedy. Jack flatters the merchant with a long complimentary address and then plays on his nerves with

[9] II. 209. [10] II. 217.

rhetorical tricks. With characteristic ingenuity and sophistication Nashe does two things at once: he builds up suspense and parodies the official address to a person of importance. Having described the cider-merchant in burlesque terms as a great Lord, Jack continues thus:

> He and no other was the man I chose out to damne with a lewd monilesse deuice; for comming to him on a day, as he was counting his barels and setting the price in chalke on the head of them, I did my dutie very deuoutly, and tolde his *alie* honor I had matters of some secrecy to impart vnto him, if it pleased him to grant me priuate audience. With me, yong *Wilton*, quoth he, mary, and shalt: bring vs a pint of syder of a fresh tap into the three cups here, wash the pot: so into a backe roome hee lead me, where after he had spitte on his finger, and pickt of two or three moats of his olde moth eaten veluet cap, and spunged and wrong all the rumatike driuell from his ill fauored goats beard, he bad me declare my minde, and thereupon he dranke to mee on the same. I vp with a long circumstaunce, alias, a cunning shift of the seuenteenes, and discourst vnto him what entire affection I had borne him time out of minde, partly for the high descent and linage from whence hee sprong, and partly for the tender care and prouident respect he had of pore souldiers, that, whereas the vastitie of that place (which afforded them no indifferent supply of drink or victuals) might humble them to some extremitie, and so weaken their handes, he vouchsafed in his owne person to be a victualler to the campe (a rare example of magnifisence and honorable curtesy), and diligently prouided that without farre trauell euerie man might for his mony haue syder and cheese his belly full; nor did he sell his cheese by the way onely, or his syder by the great, but abast himself with his owne hands to take a shoomakers knife (a homely instrument for such a high personage to touch) and cut it out equally, lyke a true iusticiarie, in little pennyworths that it would doo a man good for to looke vpon.[11]

The mockery of the formal address is admirably designed to appeal to the cider-merchant's sense of self-importance and to expose him as a fool by its success. The jest-book tale has been transformed into comedy by the infusion into it of drama and literary criticism; a process that Nashe repeats in Jack's second adventure. This time, however, his victim is an 'vgly mechanicall Captain', an indigent individual with pretensions to being

[11] II. 211.

fashionable, and Jack, therefore, suits his gulling speech once more to the characteristic weakness of the man he is practising on, drawing the Captain into the trap he has laid for him by a 'solemne oration' which is a parody of the out-dated Euphuistic style.

In both these stories Nashe puts his gift for imitation and stylistic play to use and makes it serve a fuller purpose than that of mere display. But his success here does not lead him, as it would, I think, have led the born novelist, to do the same kind of thing on a larger scale for the work as a whole by marrying literary artifice to narrative. Instead, he continues with the jest-book matter, though he is now becoming bored with it, relates two more pranks in a rather summary fashion, and then turns to something quite different. The pamphleteer takes over from the story-teller, and the thin thread of narrative is treated in the most arbitrary manner to suit his needs. It becomes no more than a kind of clothes-line on which Nashe hangs a miscellaneous array of satire, moralizing and stylistic *jeux d'esprit*; while Jack is shuttled to and fro between England and the Continent in a way that almost justifies the title of the unfortunate traveller. He is shipped home from the French wars so that he may lord it over the pages at court, and so provide the opportunity for a brilliant little satirical sketch of his own 'Frenchified' dress and behaviour that has a marked similarity to the picture of the upstart, the braggart newly returned from the French wars, in *Pierce Penilesse*.[12] But within a few pages he is overseas again, driven from home by an outbreak of the sweating sickness and by a sudden access of enthusiasm for history on the part of his creator.

Nashe treats the chronicle matter, which he now makes the staple of his work for some time, rather as he had already handled the jest-book stuff at the beginning, mixing literary criticism with humour and showmanship in a series of variations. The main source he drew on, as he says himself,[13] was Lanquet's *Chronicle* but he seems to have made some use of Holinshed and Sleidanus also. To judge from what he does with them, and from his remarks about chroniclers in *Pierce Penilesse*, which I have quoted already, his attitude towards these works was a mixture of interest and contempt: interest in their matter and contempt for their literary shortcomings. His description of the sweating sickness was, I

[12] Cf. II. 227 and I. 168–9. [13] II. 286.

suspect, sparked off by a passage in Holinshed, who writes of the outbreak that occurred in 1517:

> This maladie was so cruell, that it killed some within three houres, some within two houres, some merrie at dinner, and dead at supper.[14]

This rather home-spun attempt to convey the rapidity with which the disease worked apparently aroused Nashe's rather odd sense of humour, for in his account of the epidemic he resorts to wild caricature, mingling the fantastic and the grotesque in his own peculiar fashion and being witty into the bargain. The result is this kind of thing:

> I haue seene an old woman at that season, hauing three chins, wipe them all away one after another, as they melted to water, and left hir selfe nothing of a mouth but an vpper chap. . . .
> It was as much as a mans life was worth, ones to name a freeze ierkin; it was hye treason for a fat grosse man to come within fiue miles of the Court. I heard where they dyde vp all in one Familie, and not a mothers childe escapde, insomuch as they had but an Irish rugge lockt vp in a presse, and not laid vpon anie bed neither.[15]

The extravagant exaggeration is obviously meant to amuse, but it is hard to determine whether Nashe regarded the association of sweating and sudden death as in some way irresistibly comic, or whether he intended the whole thing as a jibe at that taste for wonders and marvels, especially of the more trivial kind, which is so marked in the work of the sixteenth-century chroniclers.

The first alternative seems the more probable in view of what happens next, for, from history as grotesque comedy, he now moves on to history as spectacle, sacrificing chronology to contrast on the way. Fleeing from England to avoid the sweating sickness of 1517, Jack arrives in Italy just in time to witness the battle of Marignano, which took place in 1515, and to give a description of it that is intended, I think, to show the chroniclers what can be made of such matter when a poet takes it in hand. The battlefield is referred to as 'a wonderfull spectacle of blood-shed on both sides', and in the amplification of this statement every detail becomes the subject of a simile:

> here vnweeldie *Switzers* wallowing in their gore, like an Oxe in his dung, there the sprightly *French* sprawling and turning on the

[14] *Holinshed's Chronicles*, London, 1808, vol. 3, p. 626. [15] II. 229

> stained grasse, like a Roach new taken out of the streame: all the ground was strewed as thicke with Battle-axes as the Carpenters yard with chips; the Plaine appeared like a quagmyre, ouerspred as it was with trampled dead bodies.[16]

Nashe could treat his grim subject with this gay élan, because Marignano really meant nothing to him except as a suitable subject for a literary exercise. About the rising of the Anabaptists at Münster, however, and their eventual defeat in 1535, to which Jack 'flies over' immediately after Marignano (happily ignorant that he had twenty years in which to make the journey) he felt very differently. Few events in the sixteenth century made a deeper or more lasting impression on men's minds than this. The communistic state set up by the Anabaptists appeared as a formidable challenge to those deep-rooted ideas about the need for order, subordination and degree which were so widely held at the time, and its eventual overthrow as a vindication of the soundness of those ideas. The conservative-minded Nashe, who was also a Puritan-baiter, had very decided views about it. To him it was a piece of moral history, containing a lesson for his own day which he enforces with vigour.

When he first takes up the subject he does so in a manner that is still in keeping with the comic, burlesque tone that has characterized the work so far. His attitude towards the Anabaptists is one of scorn and contempt, but he expresses it through a rumbustious mock-epic description of their arms and armour, containing such items as these:

> Perchance here and there you might see a felow that had a canker-eaten scull on his head, which serued him and his ancestors for a chamber pot two hundred yeeres, and another that had bent a couple of yron dripping pans armour-wise, to fence his backe and his belly.[17]

Very soon, however, the humorist gives way to the satirist, the Martin-queller and the author of *Christ's Tears*; and all pretensions to fiction go by the board when, treating Jack as though he were a ventriloquist's dummy, Nashe has him say: 'let me dilate a litle more grauely than the nature of this historie requires, or wilbe expected of so yong a practitioner in diuinity.'[18] The last phrase is very similar to that which Nashe uses about himself in the Dedication to *Christ's Tears*, where he tells Lady Carey, 'A young

[16] II. 231. [17] II. 232–3. [18] II. 234.

imperfect practitioner am I in Christs schoole', and it introduces an attack on the Anabaptists and on the Puritans generally, as hypocrites and as the authors of sects and schisms, which is in manner and in matter substantially the same as that which he had already made in *Pierce Penilesse* and was about to repeat in *Christ's Tears*. There are even verbal reminiscences of *Pierce Penilesse*. He had written there:

> 'a number that fetch the Articles of their Beleefe out of *Aristotle*, and thinke of heauen and hell as the Heathen Philosophers, take occasion to deride our Ecclesiasticall State, and all Ceremonies of Deuine worship, as bug-beares and scar-crowes, because (like *Herodes* souldiers) we diuide Christs garment amongst vs in so many peeces, and of the vesture of saluation make some of vs Babies and apes coates, others straight trusses and Diuells breeches: some gally-gascoines or a shipmans hose, like the Anabaptists and adulterous Familists.[19]

In *The Unfortunate Traveller* the same association of ideas recurs when he writes:

> What was the foundation or ground-worke of this dismall declining of Munster, but the banishing of their Bishop, their confiscating and casting lots for Church liuinges, as the souldiers cast lottes for Christes garments, and, in short tearmes, their making the house of God a den of theeues?[20]

There is no trace in this section of the work of burlesque or literary criticism. In the presence of the old enemy, the Puritans, Nashe is deadly serious, and becomes so obsessed with his own satirical sermonizing that when he eventually tries to resume his account of the events at Münster, he drops it after a few lines in order to do some more preaching. And, though even he feels some pity for the merciless way in which the Anabaptists were slaughtered, his final words on the subject are a ferocious warning to the Puritans of his own day:

> Heare what it is to be Anabaptists, to be Puritans, to be villaines; you may bee counted illuminate botchers for a while, but your end will bee, Good people, pray for vs.[21]

This part of *The Unfortunate Traveller* is then undiluted pamphleteering; but even while he was engaged on it Nashe seems to have realized that it was out of keeping with the rest of the work

[19] I. 172. [20] II. 238. [21] II. 241.

and broke the comic tone. Not only does Jack apologize at the beginning for his gravity, in words that equate him with Nashe, but also near the end of it, dropping all pretence that Jack is the narrator, Nashe admits that the style has undergone a radical transformation, and writes:

> This tale must at one time or other giue vp the ghost, and as good now as stay longer; I would gladly rid my handes of it cleanly, if I could tell how, for what with talking of coblers, tinkers, roape-makers, botchers, and durt-daubers, the mark is clean out of my Muses mouth, and I am as it were more than duncified twixt diuinity and poetrie.[22]

It was at this point, I think, that he began to realize that he had already done something new with the pamphlet and that it would be worth while developing the new vein further, instead of re-lapsing into his old manner as he had done with the Anabaptists. At the same time he was obviously very uncertain about how to continue, or, indeed, whether to continue at all. The paragraph with which he rounds off the story of the Anabaptists reads as though it were originally intended to be the final paragraph of the work:

> With the tragicall catastrophe of this Munsterian conflict did I cashier the new vocation of my caualiership. There was no more honorable wars in christendome then towards; wherefore, after I had learned to be halfe an houre in bidding a man *boniure* in Germane sunonimas, I trauelled along the countrie towards England as fast as I could.[23]

At the very least Nashe must have meant to bring his hero back to England, but before he could put his plan into execution he got some new ideas. The first, which would spring naturally from his previous pamphleteering activities, was to find a place in this 'phantasticall Treatise' for an interest which was as strong with him as his hatred of Puritans, namely poetry and poets. The second, which probably developed out of the use he had already made in the work of historical matter, was to involve Jack intimately with a historical figure, instead of using him merely as a spectator of historical events. It also looks as though he may have found a hint for doing this in More's *Utopia*, which he soon introduces into his own work.

As a consequence Jack never reaches England. He gets as far as

[22] II. 241. [23] II. 241.

Middleborough in the Low Countries, but instead of taking ship he falls in with Henry Howard, Earl of Surrey, whom he refers to as 'my late master', though there has been no previous mention of him, and promptly takes service under him. Surrey was chosen by Nashe from among the poets of Henry VIII's reign, because he was for the Elizabethans the most important of them, because he could be seen as a kind of Sir Philip Sidney, and because he had, according to Puttenham, though not in fact, 'trauailed into Italie', which is where he is going when Jack meets him. The association of the high-born poet and the base-born page provides Nashe with a fine opportunity, of which he takes full advantage, for playing off two different attitudes against each other. This was made all the easier and the more interesting by the fact that both attitudes were, to some extent at any rate, his own. He habitually thought of himself as a cut above the average popular entertainer of the time, though this did not prevent him from availing himself of the popular entertainer's devices, and the value he set on poetry and learning was a high one, even an idealizing one, though he was only too well aware of the misery and poverty that the professional writer might endure. This double attitude comes out immediately Jack and Surrey meet. Jack launches into a high-flown eulogy on Surrey and on poets and poetry generally, rather similar to Nashe's praise of them in the *Anatomy of Absurdity* and in *Pierce Penilesse*, but carried that little bit further which makes it extravagant, and then undermines it all by saying: 'Hauing thus met him I so much adored . . . I was not altogether vnwilling to walke along with such a good purse-bearer'.[24]

The same technique is then applied in a more obvious and exuberant fashion to the subject of courtly love, which becomes the central theme of the whole relationship between Jack and the Earl. Nashe takes up Surrey's 'Geraldine' sonnet and expands it into a story of romantic love that provides the motive for Surrey's visit to Italy. But he does it with his tongue in his cheek. Surrey's account of his own feelings is an effective parody of the stock ideas and images, the apostrophes and the adulterated Platonism, that the sonneteers were pouring out at the time that Nashe was writing. Of Geraldine, for instance, Surrey says:

> Her high exalted sunne beames haue set the Phenix neast of my breast on fire, and I my selfe haue brought Arabian spiceries of

[24] II. 243.

sweet passions and praises to furnish out the funerall flame of my follie. Those who were condemned to be smothered to death by sincking downe into the softe bottome of an high built bedde of Roses, neuer dide so sweet a death as I shoulde die, if hir Rose coloured disdaine were my deathes-man.

Oh thrice Emperiall Hampton Court, *Cupids* inchaunted Castle, the place where I first sawe the perfecte omnipotence of the Almightie expressed in mortalitie, tis thou alone that, tithing all other men solace in thy pleasant scituation, affoordest mee nothinge but an excellent begotten sorrow out of the cheefe treasurie of all thy recreations.[25]

The 'love passion', from which this excerpt is taken, comes so close to the thing it parodies that it almost requires Jack's deflating comment, 'fraile earth, fraile flesh, who can keepe you from the worke of your creation?', to make its critical point fully apparent.

The two opposed attitudes to love, incarnate in Surrey and Jack, provide the backbone for the middle section of *The Unfortunate Traveller*, which extends from their meeting in Middleborough to their eventual parting in Florence. But Nashe is still a long way from writing anything like a coherent story. He continues in his usual desultory, random fashion, tacking bits of his reading together, exploiting the stock associations that certain towns had for him and his readers, and ever alert for any opportunity to indulge in satire or burlesque that the journey could be made to provide.

Rotterdam was associated in his mind with the figure of Erasmus. The Earl, therefore, travels by way of that city for no other reason than to give Nashe the chance to mention Erasmus and Sir Thomas More, the one about to write his *Encomium Moriae* (1509) and the other his *Utopia* (1516). It is possible that he also intended to give his tale a touch of verisimilitude by the introduction of these two figures, but, if so, he forgot that Surrey was not born until 1517.

Wittenberg, famous for its university, for its connection with Luther, and with Dr. Faustus and magic offered a much more tempting target. Writing of the Danes in *Pierce Penilesse*, Nashe had described them as 'bursten-bellied sots, that are to bee confuted with nothing but Tankards or quart pots', and had continued: 'God so loue me, as I loue the quicke-witted Italians, and therefore

[25] II. 243.

loue them the more, because they mortally detest this surley swinish Generation.'[26] It would seem that, like many other Elizabethans, he thought much the same of the Germans and regarded them as a drunken, slow-witted and undignified people, much given to disputatiousness and pedantic learning, for he enjoys himself thoroughly at the expense of all these things. Jack and his master reach the town at the moment when the university is giving an official welcome to the Duke of Saxony. Speeches are the order of the day and Nashe provides two of them. The first, which he merely describes, is given by the university orator, who behaves and talks suspiciously like Gabriel Harvey, and is a tilt, by way of burlesque, at Ciceronianism. But the second speech, which is spoken by a representative of the town corporation, is one of Nashe's finest pieces of comic invention. The orator himself is made into an impressive buffoon by the wealth of vivid low similes that is lavished on him; and the 'ridiculous oration' he utters is perfectly in keeping with the figure he cuts; pompous, blundering, undignified and absurd, it consists of trivial matter dressed out in the most superficial commonplaces of rhetoric. Nashe writes:

> A bursten belly inkhorne orator called *Vanderhulke*, they pickt out to present him with an oration, one that had a sulpherous big swolne large face, like a Saracen, eyes lyke two kentish oysters, a mouth that opened as wide euery time he spake, as one of those old knit trap doores, a beard as though it had been made of a birds neast pluckt in peeces, which consisteth of strawe, haire, and durt mixt together. He was apparelled in blacke leather new licourd, and a short gowne without anie gathering in the backe, faced before and behinde with a boistrous beare skin, and a red night-cap on his head. To this purport and effect was this broccing duble beere oration.
>
> Right noble Duke (*ideo nobilis quasi no bilis*, for you haue no bile or colar in you), know that our present incorporation of Wittenberg, by me the tongue man of their thankfulnes, a townesman by birth, a free Germane by nature, an oratour by arte, and a scriuener by education, in all obedience and chastity, most bountifully bid you welcome to Witenberg: welcome, sayd I? O orificiall rethorike, wipe thy euerlasting mouth, and affoord me a more Indian metaphor than that, for the braue princely bloud of a Saxon. Oratorie, vncaske the bard hutch of thy complements, and

[26] I. 180.

> with the triumphantest troupe in thy treasurie doe trewage vnto him. What impotent speech with his eight partes may not specifie, this vnestimable gift, holding his peace, shall as it were (with teares I speak it) do wherby as it may seeme or appeare to manifest or declare, and yet it is, and yet it is not, and yet it may be a diminutiue oblation meritorious to your high pusillanimitie and indignitie. Why should I goe gadding and fisgigging after firking flantado amfibologies? wit is wit, and good will is good will.[27]

Dogberry, nurtured on Cicero, could hardly do better. Parody is hardly the right word to describe this passage, or the oration to which it belongs, since one cannot point to any specific thing that it mocks. What seems to have happened is that the bumbling attempts at eloquence of sixteenth-century officials, the verbal extravagances of the learned and the would-be learned, and Nashe's contempt for the Germans, have all combined to provide him with a jumping-off ground for a flight into sheer nonsense that he takes for the joy of it.

The connection between Wittenberg and magic is skilfully made to contribute to the Geraldine story. Just as Marlowe's Dr. Faustus had summoned up the ghosts of Alexander and his Paramour to entertain the Emperor, so Cornelius Agrippa summons up Cicero to give the inhabitants of Wittenberg a lesson in oratory, and later, while accompanying the travellers to the imperial court, he accedes to their request and shows them Geraldine in a glass. She appears 'sicke weeping on her bed, and resolued all into deuout religion for the absence of her Lord', and the sight leads Surrey to write a love poem that hovers delicately between the conventional and the mocking. So light is Nashe's touch here that only the context makes the element of parody in this poem evident. Detached from the work to which it belongs it could well pass as another Elizabethan lyric.

A spirit of pure fun, the delight that a keen observer takes in the absurdities and the inconsequentiality of human behaviour, animates and irradiates nearly everything that Nashe has to say about Wittenberg. And when he embarks on a topic that is not easily susceptible of comic treatment, which is what happens when he begins to describe the disputation between Luther and Carolostadius, he drops it at once with the significant remark, 'they vttered nothing to make a man laugh, therefore I will leaue

[27] II. 247–8.

them'. Nashe felt, perhaps, that Luther was too big a figure to mock with safety, whereas he could say what he liked about the unconscious mannerisms of the minor participants in the disputation.

The same attitude still remains dominant when the travellers reach Venice, but it is applied to different material. Just as Wittenberg meant Luther and magic to Nashe and his audience, so Venice meant luxury, prostitution and intrigue. Wasting no time on any description of the journey from the Imperial Court to Italy, Nashe goes straight to matter calculated to satisfy his readers' expectations. He writes:

> To cut off blind ambages by the high way side, we made a long stride and got to Venice in short time; where hauing scarce lookt about vs, a precious supernaturall pandor, apparelled in all points like a gentleman and hauing halfe a dosen seueral languages in his purse, entertained vs in our owne tongue very paraphrastically and eloquently, and maugre all other pretended acquaintance, would haue vs in a violent kinde of curtesie to be the guestes of his appointment. His name was *Petro de campo Frego*, a notable practitioner in the pollicie of baudrie. The place whether he brought vs was a pernicious curtizans house named *Tabitha* the Temptresses, a wench that could set as ciuill a face on it as chastities first martyr *Lucrecia*. What will you conceit to be in any saints house that was there to seeke? Bookes, pictures, beades, crucifixes, why, there was a haberdashers shop of them in euerie chamber. I warrant you should not see one set of her neckercher peruerted or turned awrie, not a piece of a haire displast. On her beds there was not a wrinkle of any wallowing to be found, her pillows bare out as smooth as a groning wiues belly, and yet she was a Turke and an infidel, and had more dooings then all her neighbours besides.[28]

The names Nashe gives to the new characters, together with such a tell-tale pointer as the comic simile about the pillows, make the general attitude plain enough, and Miss Latham is surely right when she comments:

> I would . . . suggest that Elizabethan readers, when introduced to a lady called 'Tabitha the Temptress', accepted her in much the same spirit as a modern reader would accept 'Olga Petrovska, the Beautiful Spy', and that her subsequent behaviour is not intended as a realistic comment on the manners of Venice.[29]

[28] II. 255. [29] *Op. cit.*, pp. 94–5.

It does not follow, however, as Miss Latham seems to imply, that because this story of intrigue, plot, counter-plot and counter-counter-plot is treated as a kind of farce, it is a burlesque of stories of Italian villainy. Quite apart from the fact that it is not easy to see just which story Nashe is guying, the whole thing fits in beautifully with that double attitude towards wickedness which was so widespread at the time and which had contributed so much to the success of such figures as Marlowe's Barabas and Shakespeare's Richard III. Wickedness could be fascinating and amusing at the same time that it was shocking, and it is in this spirit that Nashe handles Tabitha the Temptress and Petro de Campo Frego, who is equated with Judas—'he dipt in the same dish with vs euerie daie'—and with the devil—'he was seene in all the seuen liberall deadly sciences, not a sinne but he was as absolute in as sathan himselfe'. Petro, like Richard III, is in a direct line of descent from the Vice and the star characters of the miracle and morality plays, and is meant to produce the same kind of reaction in an audience.

The difference between this kind of writing and burlesque becomes very apparent when, through the 'Italianate wit' of Tabitha and her henchman, Jack and Surrey are cast into prison and there meet Diamante, the wife of a magnifico, who has been incarcerated for 'an vngrounded ielous suspition which her doting husband had conceiued of her chastitie'. Diamante later comes to play a real part in the story, but Nashe seems to have had no thought of using her in this way when he first introduced her. Her purpose is to keep the Geraldine theme alive and, perhaps, to serve for a little skit on Lodge's *Rosalynde* as well, by the contrast she enforces between the courtly and the vulgar attitudes to love and beauty. Jack's description of her is in the same tradition as Chaucer's portrait of Alysoun, the Reeve's wife in the *Miller's Tale*, and embodies the popular idea of female beauty:

> A pretie rounde faced wench was it, with blacke eie browes, a high forehead, a little mouth, and a sharpe nose, as fat and plum euerie part of her as a plouer, a skin as slike and soft as the backe of a swan, it doth me good when I remember her. [A pretty clear indication this, that Nashe had no thought as yet of marrying Jack and Diamante.] Like a bird she tript on the grounde, and bare out her belly as maiesticall as an Estrich. With a licorous rouling eie fixt piercing on the earth, and sometimes scornfully darted on the

> tone side, she figured forth a high discontented disdaine; much like a prince puffing and storming at the treason of some mightie subiect fled lately out of his power.[30]

Surrey, to Jack's great amusement, treats Diamante exactly as Rosader in Lodge's romance treats the disguised Rosalind, deliberately imagining her to be the absent Geraldine, wooing her in the extravagant language of courtly love and writing a sonnet to her in which Nashe makes uproarious mockery of the strained imagery and the language of religious devotion so common in the sonnets of the day. It is an admirable piece of literary criticism and deserves to be given in full:

> If I must die, O, let me choose my death:
> Sucke out my soule with kisses, cruell maide,
> In thy breasts christall bals enbalme my breath,
> Dole it all out in sighs when I am laide.
> Thy lips on mine like cupping glasses claspe,
> Let our tongs meete and striue as they would sting,
> Crush out my winde with one strait girting graspe,
> Stabs on my heart keepe time whilest thou doest sing.
> Thy eyes lyke searing yrons burne out mine,
> In thy faire tresses stifle me outright,
> Like Circes change me to a loathsome swine,
> So I may liue for euer in thy sight.
> Into heauens ioyes none can profoundly see,
> Except that first they meditate on thee.[31]

The final touch to this parody of the Petrarchan manner is supplied by Jack himself, whose comment on it is both ribald and practical:

> Sadly and verily, if my master sayde true, I shoulde if I were a wench make many men quickly immortall. What ist, what ist for a maide fayre and fresh to spend a little lip-salue on a hungry louer? My master beate the bush and kept a coyle and a pratling, but I caught the birde.

It is hard to resist the conclusion that this part of *The Unfortunate Traveller* is an intermediate stage between *Rosalynde* and *As You Like It*, that Shakespeare read it and was influenced by it, and that Rosalind herself owes something to Nashe's witty page.

The way in which Surrey is handled and in which Nashe's attitude towards him changes is clear evidence of the extent to

[30] II. 261. [31] II. 262–3.

which literary interests are uppermost in this part of the work. Introduced into it as the type of the good poet and liberal master, he becomes increasingly the target for satirical criticism, which begins as delicate parody but gradually turns into full-blooded burlesque. A further pointer in the same direction is provided by the casual and unceremonious fashion in which the Tabitha story is packed up and bundled out of the way. Its conclusion is really an excuse for bringing in the figure of Pietro Aretino, who is made mainly responsible for ferreting out the truth and releasing Surrey and Jack from gaol, so that Nashe can write a panegyric on him. Whether Nashe had read much of Aretino's writings is a puzzling question. What matters is that he obviously regarded him as a master-craftsman who could turn his pen to anything, and his description of him is indicative of the ideal that he set himself in much of his own work. He writes:

> Before I goe anie further, let me speake a word or two of this *Aretine*. It was one of the wittiest knaues that euer God made. If out of so base a thing as inke there may bee extracted a spirite, hee writ with nought but the spirite of inke, and his stile was the spiritualitie of artes, and nothing else; whereas all others of his age were but the lay temporaltie of inkehorne tearmes. For indeede they were meere temporizers and no better. His pen was sharp pointed lyke a poinyard; no leafe he wrote on but was lyke a burning glasse to set on fire all his readers. With more than musket shot did he charge his quill, where hee meant to inueigh. No houre but hee sent a whole legion of deuils into some heard of swine or other. If *Martiall* had ten Muses (as he saith of himselfe) when he but tasted a cup of wine, he had ten score when he determined to tyrannize: nere a line of his but was able to make a man dronken with admiration. His sight pearst like lightning into the entrailes of all abuses.[32]

At this point the character of the work begins to change. Having concluded his digression on Aretino, Nashe writes, 'My principall subiect pluckes me by the elbow', and gives the impression that he is about to resume the story. He even does so in an impromptu fashion. Diamante proves to be with child by Jack and her old husband conveniently dies. Her pregnancy, which is promptly forgotten as soon as it has served its purpose, is a reason for leaving Venice, and the money she has inherited by her husband's death

[32] II. 264–5.

furnishes the means. Jack secures her release from prison, and they set off to see Italy together without informing Surrey. The result is a recurrence of the jest-book *motif*. Before arriving in Italy Jack and his master changed places in order to allow Surrey greater freedom of behaviour. Now, even though he has left his master, Jack keeps up the fiction. The confrontation of the false Surrey by the true takes place in Florence and leads to a display of ingenuity on Jack's part in excusing himself that looks forward to Falstaff's performances in the same kind. Before the story can be continued, however, Surrey must be got rid of and the Geraldine theme concluded. It is typical of Nashe's attitude to what he is doing that he should take a lot of trouble over the second task and none at all over the first. The mockery of courtly love here reaches its climax and extends to the chivalric tournament, which still survived in the sixteenth century in a formal and almost theatrical manner. Surrey visits the house in Florence where Geraldine was born and celebrates the occasion with yet another sonnet in which the idea of love as a religion is carried to such a pitch that it becomes ridiculous. Not content with this, he behaves like Lodge's Rosader in Arden and covers the windows with Latin tags expressing his unhappy state. Then, as a grand finale, he issues a challenge to all comers 'in defence of his *Geraldines* beauty'. The tournament that follows is one of Nashe's set pieces. In his description of it he thoroughly and effectively guys that love of significant devices and *imprese* which was so widespread at the English court. Surrey's armour and the trappings of his horse are dealt with in such detail that quotation is impossible, but the likening of his helmet to 'a gardners water-pot' is sufficient indication of Nashe's satiric purpose. His rivals are handled more economically, and the portrait of the second of them will serve to show the opinion Nashe had of the mediaeval revival:

> After him followed the Knight of the Owle, whose armor was a stubd tree ouergrowne with iuie, his helmet fashioned lyke an owle sitting on the top of this iuie; on his bases were wrought all kinde of birdes, as on the grounde, wondering about him; the word, *Ideo mirum quia monstrum*: his horses furniture was framed like a carte, scattering whole sheaues of corne amongst hogs; the word, *Liberalitas liberalitate perit*. On his shield a Bee intangled in sheepes wool; the mot, *Frontis nulla fides*.[33]

[33] II. 273–4.

The attitude is very like that which Nashe had adopted towards courtly love in the *Anatomy of Absurdity*, but the expression of it is entirely different. The general condemnation of the earlier work has given place here to a light raillery that concentrates on the specific and the particular and is far more effective as a result.

Once the tournament is over and there is nothing more to be done with the Geraldine story and the opportunities for literary and social criticism that it offers, Nashe dismisses Surrey without further ado and even speeds him on his way with a jibe:

> post-hast letters came to him from the king his master, to returne as speedily as he could possible into *England*; wherby his fame was quit cut off by the shins, and there was no repriue but *Bazelus manus*, hee must into England; and I with my curtizan trauelled forward in Italy.[34]

Even now, however, with such promising material on his hands as a witty knave and a wanton woman at large in a land that appeared to the Elizabethan imagination as a fascinating compound of heaven and hell, Nashe is in no hurry to work up the story. Jack and Diamante go to Rome, but for some time nothing happens to them there. Jack becomes the sight-seeing English tourist, complete with guide, showing a proper Protestant scepticism for stories about miracles and expressing his militant Christianity by behaviour that is described with a flourish of functional alliteration: 'I was at *Pontius Pilates* house and pist against it'. There is a good deal of matter here which looks as though it is either the fruit of personal experience or has been culled from guide-books, but the conclusion of Mr. E. S. De Beer, who has submitted it all to a careful examination, is that 'there is nothing . . . that could not have been acquired from conversation with travellers or—less likely—from books'.[35] The general impression produced, as Nashe strings together odd scraps of factual information with some satire about the miscellaneous attire of his Englishman, is that he is thumbing over the commonplace book that we know he kept[36] in search of a topic that will give him some scope. He finds it eventually in the elaborate gardens of the wealthy citizens of Rome. Starting with three or four

[34] II. 279.

[35] E. S. De Beer, 'Thomas Nashe: The Notices of Rome in "The Unfortunate Traveller",' *Notes and Queries*, July 1943, pp. 67–70.

[36] See III. 175–6.

separate bits of fact—the great villas around Rome, the Golden House of Nero with a circular revolving roof, and the imitation birds in the garden of the Villa d'Este at Tivoli, which were made to sing by means of a water-organ—[37] Nashe allows his imagination to range freely in the creation of an ideal world, which is utterly unlike the world he portrays elsewhere in *The Unfortunate Traveller* and forms a striking contrast to it. The idea of the golden age is coupled with the Elizabethan conception of the art that outdoes, and is more perfect than, nature itself,[38] to evoke an earthly paradise, 'a miracle of rare device' that has much in common with Spenser's Bower of Bliss. There is no trace of satire or parody here; Nashe delights in the artifice of his 'summer banketting house', surrounded by trees on which 'were pearcht as many sortes of shrill breasted birdes as the Summer hath allowed for singing men in hir siluane chappels', and he concludes his description of it thus:

> No poysonous beast there reposed, (poyson was not before our parent *Adam* transgressed.) There were no sweete-breathing Panthers that would hyde their terrifying heads to betray; no men imitating *Hyaenaes* that chaunged their sexe to seeke after bloud. Wolues as now when they are hungrie eate earth, so then did they feed on earth only, and abstained from innocent flesh. The Vnicorne did not put his horne into the streame to chase awaye venome before hee dronke, for then there was no suche thing extant in the water or on the earth. Serpents were as harmlesse to mankinde as they are still one to another: the rose had no cankers, the leues no cater pillers, the sea no *Syrens*, the earth no vsurers. Goats then bare wooll, as it is recorded in *Sicily* they doo yet. The torride Zone was habitable: only Iayes loued to steale gold and siluer to build their nests withall, and none cared for couetous clientrie, or runing to the Indies. . . . Such a golden age, such a good age, such an honest age was set forth in this banketting house.[39]

The picture drawn here has no pretensions to realism, but, like similar passages in Elizabethan pastoral, it has a function in relation to what follows in that it serves to underline the contrast between what should be and what is, for Nashe now moves on to

[37] De Beer, *op. cit.*, p. 69.
[38] See Madeleine Doran, *Endeavors of Art*, Madison, 1954, pp. 65–70.
[39] II. 284–5.

tell a tale of Italianate villainy and revenge which occupies the rest of the book and is the one piece of coherent story in it. In considering this part of *The Unfortunate Traveller* it is important to notice that the story is really two stories which are involved with one another, but which are treated very differently. The one which concerns Heraclide, Esdras of Granado and Cutwolfe is described by Nashe himself as 'a truculent tragedie', the word *truculent* having here its original Latin meaning of *grim* or *savage*, and seems to me to be meant quite seriously as a moral *exemplum* depicting the inevitable way in which divine justice works to punish human wickedness. The other, dealing with Jack and Diamante and their adventures, which have a fortunate outcome, is a comedy and is handled as such with a thorough exploitation of all the potentialities for parody, burlesque and literary play that it contains.

Nashe makes the transition to these stories by resorting, as he says himself, to Lanquet's *Chronicle* once more. Pitching on the account there of a plague that afflicted Rome in 1522, he jazzes it up in his own grotesque manner and makes it serve as the setting for what seems to be a fiction of his own, the tale of the rape of Heraclide, a virtuous Roman matron in whose house Jack and Diamante are living, by '*Esdras* of *Granado*, a notable Bandetto, authorised by the pope because he had assisted him in some murthers'.[40] Esdras, together with a confederate called Bartol, who is described as 'a desperate Italian', takes advantage of the plague to break into houses that are afflicted with it in order to rob and ravish. Coming to Heraclide's house, where all the family except Heraclide herself and her zany are either dead or sick, Bartol seizes Diamante from Jack, whom he locks up in his room, while Esdras kills the zany and then rapes Heraclide.

The story itself is obviously meant as an example of Italian villainy, but it is not story as such that interests Nashe. Indeed, so careless is he about the mere mechanics of plotting that having locked his narrator in an upper room, he has him recount in detail all that is said and done in a room below, and only after it is all over does he remember to supply Jack with a peep-hole by writing, 'I, thorough a crannie of my vpper chamber vnseeled, had beheld all this sad spectacle'.[41] The actual events are a vehicle for rhetorical display and moralizing. The words with which Nashe takes up the

[40] II. 287. [41] II. 295.

story when the rape is over are a clear indication of his literary purpose. He writes:

> Let not your sorrow die, you that haue read the proeme and narration of this eligiacall historie. Shew you haue quick wits in sharp conceipt of compassion.[42]

In his eyes the story is of the same kind and, therefore, is to be handled in the same manner as the stories used in the poems of complaint so popular at the time, Daniel's *Complaint of Rosamund* for instance, published in 1592, which he had already praised in *Pierce Penilesse*,[43] and Shakespeare's *Rape of Lucrece*, which first appeared in 1594 some eight months after the entry of *The Unfortunate Traveller* in the Stationers' Register. In these poems the narrative is a peg for pathetical description, for still more pathetical declamation and for the moralizing that was expected of a poet. Nashe handles the rape of Heraclide in precisely this manner. The events that precede the moment in which Esdras confronts his victim are despatched quickly in order to leave room for the long speeches on which Nashe lavishes all his art. The transition is made thus:

> First he assayled her with rough meanes, and slue hir *Zanie* at hir foote, that stept before hir in rescue. Then when all armed resist was put to flight, he assaied her with honie speech.[44]

Her reaction, like that of Shakespeare's Lucrece to the arguments of Tarquin, is a long and carefully constructed speech in which she makes an appeal to his conscience, reminds him of the inexorable operation of God's judgment and sets the terrors of damnation before him, as well as trying to arouse his sense of pity. There is much of the Elizabethan theatre about it. It is far closer to the rape of Lavinia in *Titus Andronicus* than to what one expects of narrative. Indeed at one point it looks as though Shakespeare may have borrowed from Nashe, for Chiron's remark at II. iii. 129–30,

> Drag hence her husband to some secret hole,
> And make his dead trunk pillow to our lust,

is very close to Nashe's description of the actual rape: 'Her husbands dead bodie he made a pillow to his abhomination.'[45] Heraclide's words and attitude are throughout those proper to a

[42] II. 292. [43] I. 192. [44] II. 288.
[45] II. 292.

chaste woman and a Christian, while those of Esdras, who is quite ready to justify his actions, are those proper to a villain and an atheist.

The climax to the whole scene comes, of course, as it does in the *Rape of Lucrece*, when the actual rape is over, and Heraclide soliloquizes. Her speech is a 'passion', in which she curses her own beauty, and it concludes with her committing suicide. There are expressions in it, such as her address to the knife, 'Point, pierce, edge, enwiden, I patiently affoorde thee a sheath',[46] which in the light of *A Midsummer Night's Dream* might be taken as parody. Miss Latham lists some others, which seem to her to be too extravagant to be taken *au pied de la lettre*: Esdras's statement, 'My owne mother gaue I a boxe of the eare too, and brake her neck downe a paire of staires, because she would not goe in to a Gentleman when I bad her', and the description of how, as Heraclide swoons under his threats, 'her eies in their closing seemed to spaune forth in their outward sharpe corners new created seed pearle, which the world before neuer set eie on'.[47] On the strength of this evidence she concludes that the whole thing is deliberately overdrawn and is intended as a specimen of the 'twopence coloured' style. The foundation seems to me to be altogether too weak to support the conclusion that is built on it. The author of *Christ's Tears* was capable of any degree of excess in lachrymose matters; Christ says of himself there, 'I . . . haue wasted myne eye-bals well-neere to pinnes-heads with weeping (as a Barber wasteth his Ball in the water)'.[48] A much better guide to Nashe's general intention is provided by the affinities between this tale and the *Rape of Lucrece*, by his description of it as 'an eligiacall historie' and, above all, by the terms in which Heraclide pleads. Damnation and impiety were no topics for jesting with Nashe or his audience. When they heard Heraclide speak as follows to Esdras, they knew what to expect:

> How thinkest thou, is there a power aboue thy power? if there be, he is here present in punishment, and on thee will take present punishment if thou persistest in thy enterprise. . . . Gods hand like a huge stone hangs ineuitably ouer thy head.[49]

The story evolves in due course along exactly the lines Heraclide lays down here. It is meant as a frightful warning and the

[46] II. 295. [47] *Op. cit.*, p. 94. [48] II. 36.
[49] II. 289.

sensational element in its telling, like that in Tourneur's *The Atheist's Tragedy*, which has the same end in view, is to enforce that warning and make it more effective.

The 'tragic' quality that Nashe seeks to underline in his account of the rape is endorsed by the abrupt change in the style that comes when he turns from this subject to the story of Jack, which is 'comic'. No sooner has Heraclide stabbed herself than this follows:

> So (throughlie stabd) fell she downe, and knockt her head against her husbands bodie: wherwith he, not hauing been aired his ful foure and twentie howres, start as out of a dreame: whiles I, thorough a crannie of my vpper chamber vnseeled, had beheld all this sad spectacle. Awaking, he rubbed his head too and fro, and wyping his eyes with his hand, began to looke about him.[50]

The revived husband discovers Jack locked up and accuses him of the murder, but the tone in which this is related leaves one in no doubt about the outcome of this adventure, or, for that matter, of Jack's other adventures in Italy. Nashe writes:

> Vppon this was I laide in prison, should haue been hanged, was brought to the ladder, had made a Ballad for my Farewell in a readines, called *Wiltons wantonnes*, and yet for all that scapde dauncing in a hempen circle. He that hath gone through many perils and returned safe from them, makes but a merriment to dilate them.[51]

The rest of Jack's story is handled in the spirit of this passage. Merriment is mixed with melodrama, moralizing with mockery. A tale of terror and warning becomes a fertile source of laughter and amusement, without losing its more elementary qualities of excitement and suspense. In the manner proper to an Elizabethan 'thriller', Jack is saved from the gallows at the last moment by the intervention of 'a banisht English Earle', who confirms the truth of Jack's tale—and, incidentally, carries the Esdras story a stage further—by relating how he heard the dying confession of Bartoll, killed by Esdras in order to gain possession of Diamante. The Earl then proceeds to give Jack a long lecture on the dangers of foreign travel, on national characteristics and on the advantages of remaining in one's own country, which can have cost Nashe very little effort to write, since it is substantially a repetition of

[50] II. 295. [51] II. 295.

what he had said on this subject in *Pierce Penilesse*. There he had described Italy as 'the Academie of man-slaughter, the sporting place of murther, the Apothecary-shop of poyson for all Nations'.[52] The Earl's remarks are in the same Aschamite tradition. He tells Jack:

> *Italy*, the Paradice of the earth and the Epicures heauen, how doth it forme our yong master? It makes him to kis his hand like an ape, cringe his necke like a starueling, and play at hey passe repasse come aloft, when he salutes a man. From thence he brings the art of atheisme, the art of epicurising, the art of whoring, the art of poysoning, the art of Sodomitrie. The onely probable good thing they haue to keepe vs from vtterly condemning it is that it maketh a man an excellent Courtier, a curious carpet knight: which is, by interpretation, a fine close leacher, a glorious hipocrite. It is nowe a priuie note amongst the better sort of men, when they would set a singular marke or brand on a notorious villaine, to say, he hath beene in *Italy*.[53]

The Earl concludes his grave, fatherly advice with the words: 'Get thee home, my yong lad, laye thy bones peaceably in the sepulcher of thy fathers, waxe olde in ouerlooking thy grounds, be at hand to close the eyes of thy kindred.' But, just as it is in keeping with the rules of decorum that he, an old, grave man, should speak in this fashion, so it is equally in keeping with those rules that Jack should dismiss his advice as a bore, and should pay for his disregard of it by promptly falling into a cellar and so into the clutches of Zadoch the Jew. Nashe is having it both ways here. Jack's misadventures are a dramatic exposition of the dangers the traveller in Italy runs and, at the same time, a brilliant mockery of the whole admonitory tradition, for, as we shall see, the true moral to be drawn from them is the exact reverse of the overt one.

Zadoch promptly sells Jack to a fellow countryman of his 'one Doctor *Zacharie*, the Pope's Phisition', who is a recreation of the figure of Greedinesse in *Pierce Penilesse*, as Nashe carefully indicates when, having described his house and his cheeseparing habits, he says of him 'He was dame Niggardize sole heire and executor.' The words are a plain indication that we are now in the world of melodramatic fantasy seen from the comic point of view. Zacharie has bought Jack in order to use him for vivisection in an

[52] I. 186. [53] II. 301.

anatomy lecture, and Nashe enjoys himself hugely, as he describes his hero's feelings at this cheerful prospect, in a passage where humour and sensationalism mingle with one another:

> O, the colde sweating cares which I conceiued after I knewe I should be cut like a French summer dublet. Me thought already the blood began to gush out at my nose: if a flea on the arme had but bit me, I deemed the instrument had prickt me. Wel, well, I may scoffe at a shrowd turne, but theres no such readie way to make a man a true Christian, as to perswade himselfe he is taken vp for an anatomie. Ile depose I praid then more than I did in seuen yeare before. Not a drop of sweate trickled downe my breast and my sides, but I dreamt it was a smooth edgd razer tenderly slicing downe my breasts and sides. If anie knockt at doore, I supposd it was the Bedle of surgeons hal come for me.[54]

This description sets the tone for the treatment of the rest of Jack's adventures, which, from the point of view of plot, are much the most carefully articulated part of the whole work. When Jack falls into Zadoch's cellar, he finds Diamante there. They are separated almost at once, but Nashe follows the fortunes of both until they eventually meet again at the house of Juliana, the pope's mistress, and make their escape from it together. Moreover, he accounts for the other main figures involved, Juliana, Zadoch and Zacharie and he also rounds off the tale of Esdras of Granado. It would, however, be wrong to assume that even in this section of the work story-telling is his chief concern. He certainly seems to have intended a contrast between the two tales, that of Jack and that of Esdras, for, while both are horrific accounts of intrigue and villainy, the one is handled 'comically' and the other 'tragically'. But both are made vehicles for literary display. Nowhere else in the book is there so much ostentatious sign-posting as here, where Nashe, the showman, runs the humorous, the savage, the gruesome and the sadistic together in a manner that is at once dazzling and disturbing.

The comic intention is at its most evident in the way Juliana is handled. The trouble she goes to in order not to allow her relations with Jack to become too public draws the comment from him: 'Heere was a wily wench had her liripoop without book, she was not to seeke in her knackes and shifts', and her death, caused by the accidental administration of poison to revive her from a swoon, is

[54] II. 305.

dismissed in a carefree sentence: 'It reuived her with a verie vengeaunce, for it kild her outright; onely she awakened and lift vp her hands, but spake nere a worde.' But Juliana is a subsidiary figure. Zadoch interests Nashe far more, because he can be used as a means of outdoing Marlowe. The situation that arises when Juliana, having failed to get Jack from Zacharie by fair means, resorts to intrigue, convinces the Pope that Zacharie has sought to poison him, and thus secures the banishment of the Jews from Rome and the confiscated goods of Zacharie for herself, is very similar to that which exists in *The Jew of Malta* after the governor of the island has mulcted the Jewish community of half their possessions and confiscated the entire wealth of Barabas. The reactions of Zadoch, when Zacharie tells him of what has happened, are like those of Barabas; he breaks into curses and vows every kind of vengeance. But Nashe first indicates the spirit in which it is all to be read by a mocking preliminary sentence in which he writes: 'Descriptions, stand by, here is to bee expressed the furie of Lucifer when he was turnde ouer heauen barre for a wrangler.' Zadoch's performance is meant to have the same effect as that of Herod in the miracle plays, to excite fear and derision at the same time. It does so, until he is caught, before he can put his plans into effect, and condemned to be executed. But at this point the comic tone is broken. Nashe becomes absorbed in the spectacle of the execution and its attendant tortures and describes them with a ferocious glee, exulting in every ghastly detail. It is hard to escape the conclusion that there is sadism here as well as savage anti-Semitism.

The same quality also makes itself felt in the other execution that is wedged into these last pages, that of Cutwolfe of Verona, the brother of Bartoll, who makes public confession immediately before his death of the means he used to ensure that his revenge on Esdras for his brother's murder should be complete and result in Esdras's soul going to hell. Cutwolfe glories in his achievement, and his impiety infuriates the crowd to such an extent that they urge the executioner to get on with his task. Nashe really conveys the fury of the mob in his prose and then this follows:

> The executioner needed no exhortation herevnto, for of his owne nature was he hackster good inough: olde excellent he was at a bone-ach. At the first chop with his wood-knife would he fish for a mans heart, and fetch it out as easily as a plum from the

bottome of a porredge pot. He woulde cracke neckes as fast as a cooke cracks egges: a fidler cannot turne his pin so soone as he would turne a man of the ladder. Brauely did he drum on this *Cutwolfes* bones, not breaking them outright, but, like a sadler knocking in of tackes, iarring on them quaueringly with his hammer a great while together. No ioint about him but with a hatchet he had for the nones he disioynted halfe, and then with boyling lead souldered vp the wounds from bleeding: his tongue he puld out, least he should blaspheme in his torment: venimous stinging wormes hee thrust into his eares, to keep his head rauingly occupied: with cankers scruzed to peeces he rubd his mouth and his gums: no lim of his but was lingeringly splinterd in shiuers. In this horror left they him on the wheele as in hell; where, yet liuing, he might beholde his flesh legacied amongst the foules of the aire.[55]

The whole passage surely transmits the kind of feelings that the London mob must have experienced at the public executions that they flocked to see. Nashe's participation in the executioner's task is, like his remarks about Bull in the *Almond*,[56] the admiration of one artist for another. He belongs to a world in which executions were just as much a spectacle and an entertainment as the theatre itself, and the similes with which he garnishes his account express his virtuoso appreciation of the performance. A hundred years later John Dryden in his *Discourse concerning the Original and Progress of Satire* also sees a parallel between the satirist and the hangman when he writes:

there is still a vast difference betwixt the slovenly butchering of a man, and the fineness of a stroke that separates the head from the body, and leaves it standing in its place. A man may be capable, as Jack Ketch's wife said of his servant, of a plain piece of work, a bare hanging; but to make a malefactor die sweetly was only belonging to her husband.[57]

The pleasure in a job well done palliates some of the unpleasantness of the description and makes it less nasty than the account of the execution of Zadoch, where the emphasis is on physical horror throughout. It is also in keeping with the manner in which Nashe manages the Cutwolfe story as a whole, which he clearly looked on as a great *tour de force* and a proper climax to the work. It is intro-

[55] II. 327. [56] III. 348.
[57] *Critical Essays of Dryden*, ed. W. P. Ker, Oxford, 1900, II. 93.

duced with a sweeping showman's gesture. Nashe addresses the reader direct and begins as follows:

> Prepare your eares and your teares, for neuer tyll this thrust I anie tragecall matter vpon you. Strange and wonderfull are Gods iudgements, here shine they in their glory. Chast *Heraclide*, thy bloud is laid vp in heauens treasury, not one drop of it was lost, but lent out to vsurie: water powred forth sinkes downe quietly into the earth, but bloud spilt on the ground sprinkles vp to the firmament. Murder is wide-mouthd and will not let God rest till he grant reuenge. Not onely the bloud of the slaughtred innocent, but the soul, ascendeth to his throne, and there cries out and exclaimes for iustice and recompence. Guiltlesse soules that liue euery houre subiect to violence, and with your dispairing feares doe much empaire Gods prouidence, fasten your eies on this spectacle that will adde to your faith. Referre all your oppressions, afflictions, and iniuries to the euen ballanced eie of the Almightie; he it is, that when your patience sleepeth, will be most exceeding mindfull of you.[58]

Miss Latham quotes the first sentence of this paragraph and then continues thus:

> Is this sign-posting a little suspicious? Is it how a serious writer prepares for a climax, or is it that irreverent creature, Tom Nashe, announcing that he is about to tear a cat? The very jingle of *eares* and *teares* is comical, and 'thrust I vpon you' destroys the dignity of the 'tragecall matter'.

She concludes by saying: 'This is a revenge story to end all revenge stories, a *reductio ad absurdum* of revenge. It is not realism, it is criticism, and the form it takes is literary satire.'[59] On this issue it seems to me that she is wrong and credits Nashe with a sophistication beyond his reach. Sign-posting is common enough in his serious writing; *Christs Tears* is full of it, and it is not all dignified. The way he introduces the Miriam story is a case in point:

> Mothers of LONDON, (each one of you to your selues) doe but imagine that you were *Miriam*, wyth what hart (suppose you) could ye go about the cooquerie of your own chyldren?[60]

Moreover, the sentence quoted as evidence of a comic intention is only the beginning of a paragraph, which, viewed as a whole could well come from a sermon or a homiletic work. The idea that 'blood

[58] II. 320.
[59] *Op cit.*, pp. 89–90.
[60] II. 71.

will have blood' was deeply rooted and widely held. I find it inconceivable that any Elizabethan, and least of all that conventionally minded defender of the Anglican Church, Thomas Nashe, should write of God's justice and its inexorable working in a manner that has anything whatever to do with burlesque. A phrase such as 'fasten your eies on this spectacle that will adde to your faith' puts the matter beyond all doubt. It comes incongruously from the lips of Jack Wilton, but Nashe has forgotten all about Jack, he is speaking *in propria persona*. The story of Cutwolfe's revenge, like the rape of Heraclide to which it is a sequel, is meant quite seriously, and the horrific quality in it, which leads Miss Latham to say that it is a *reductio ad absurdum* of revenge, is merely the result of Nashe's desire to do the job better than any of his predecessors and teach a more forceful lesson. The whole of 'this truculent tragedie', as he calls it, is in perfect keeping with his account of the Anabaptists, whose fate he describes as 'the tragicall catastrophe of this Munsterian conflict'. Nashe's conception of tragedy was simple and crude, to him it meant bloody and violent action from which a moral could be drawn.

Jack draws the appropriate moral. His account of the execution of Cutwolfe ends with these words:

> Vnsearchable is the booke of our destinies. One murder begetteth another: was neuer yet bloud-shed barren from the beginning of the world to this daie. Mortifiedly abiected and danted was I with this truculent tragedie of *Cutwolfe* and *Esdras*. To such straight life did it thence forward incite me that ere I went out of *Bolognia* I married my curtizan, performed many almes deedes; and hasted so fast out of the *Sodom* of *Italy*, that within fortie daies I arriued at the king of *Englands* campe twixt *Ardes* and *Guines* in *France*.[61]

But, like much else in 'this phantasticall treatise', the moral ending has, of course, its ambiguous side, for the most obvious conclusion to be drawn from Jack's adventures, as distinct from the story of Esdras, is that crime pays, provided the criminal is lucky and skilful enough. Before Jack and Diamante escape from Juliana's house they steal all they can lay their hands on:

> Against our countesse we conspire, packe vp all her iewels, plate, mony that was extant, and to the water side send them: to conclude, couragiously rob her, and run away.[62]

[61] II. 327. [62] II. 318.

And prior to this Jack has been living on the money Diamante inherited from her husband. In what sense he is the unfortunate traveller it is hard to see. He is singularly lucky not only in the number of hair-breadth escapes from disaster that he has, but also in the way he is immune from the workings of the divine justice that pursues the other rogues in the story so relentlessly.

Is Nashe, then, really making fun of the whole moral tradition? I do not think so. The cause of the discrepancies between the overt morality of the tale and its true significance is quite simply his incompetence as a story-teller. He is incapable of keeping Jack, the actor and narrator, distinct from himself, the moralist and the literary critic. A failure to see this elementary fact has led to a good deal of nonsense being written about the book. Brett-Smith credits Jack with a conscience,[63] and R. G. Howarth writes as follows:

> There is no doubt that Jack is a masterly piece of character-creation. He is as alive as Nashe himself: indeed it is almost as though Nashe had undergone these adventures, so vivid is his imagination. Throughout Jack remains in intimate contact with his hearers, who scarcely feel themselves to be readers. Nashe had here discovered and skilfully used the best method of narration yet known.[64]

In fact Jack has neither conscience nor character. As a realized human being he does not exist at all. The mischievous page of the beginning and the courageous robber of the end belong together, but they are wholly irreconcilable with the ferocious preacher who lambasts the Anabaptists and the stern moralist who tells the tale of Heraclide and of how her rape was avenged. Dr. Kettle's picture of Jack as the outcast rogue, who has a certain place in society but does not ' "belong" to that society or feel himself in any way morally bound to its standards', is a happy fiction, concocted to serve a general theory of the picaresque. There is no Jack in the proper sense of the word, and, so far as I can see, there is no society either. Where in the story does Dr. Kettle find anything that has any pretensions whatever to being a realistic picture of England, of Italy, or of Europe generally?

At the back of all this theorizing lies the tacit assumption that in some way or other *The Unfortunate Traveller* is a novel, but, since Nashe shows no interest either in the telling of a coherent

[63] *The Unfortunate Traveller*, ed. H. Brett-Smith, Oxford, 1920, p. ix.

[64] R. G. Howarth, *Two Elizabethan Writers of Fiction*, Cape Town, 1956, p. 29.

tale, or in the depiction of a consistent character, still less in the development of that character in response to events within a society that has some relation to actuality, it is hard to see how the assumption can be justified. As I see it the evolution of the book was determined by two factors which apply to most of Nashe's other writings and which have no necessary connection with the novel at all: first, the need of the pamphleteer-journalist to get something down on paper, and secondly, the overpowering urge that this particular pamphleteer-journalist had to show his paces in as many kinds of writing as possible. The 'story' is sheer improvisation; its course and Jack's movements are dictated not by the economic and social pressures that govern the life of a *picaro*, but by the materials Nashe had at hand, his own earlier writings, the chronicles, his commonplace book, the associations in his mind between places and people and, above all, the expectations that particular places and scenes could be relied on to raise in the minds of his readers. Equally important was the contemporary literary scene with its jest-books, its chronicles, its anti-Puritan pamphlets, its Petrarchan love poetry, its pastorals depicting an ideal world, its attacks on Italian luxury and loose-living, its elegiacal histories and, above all, its revenge plays, of which *The Jew of Malta* seems to have been most in Nashe's mind. The hero is and does whatever Nashe's strictly literary purpose at any particular moment demands that he should be and do. When his creator seeks to outdo the writers of jest-books, Jack is the accomplished practical joker; when he seeks to outdo the chroniclers, Jack is the most vivid of chroniclers; when Petrarchism is under fire, he becomes a gifted literary critic and a clever parodist; when the golden age is to be depicted, he turns into a pastoral poet. And so one could go on. *The Unfortunate Traveller* is held together, as *Pierce Penilesse* and *The Terrors of the Night* are held together, by one thing only, the personality of the author. Like the chameleon, Nashe changes his colour in a flash, slipping from one way of writing to another in a dazzling display of sheer virtuosity, carried through with such rapid changes of direction and intention that the reader has difficulty in keeping up with them.

It may well be that most of Nashe's contemporaries were bewildered by his quick transitions and lightning switches from one subject and attitude to another. At any rate *The Unfortunate Traveller* went through only two editions and did not have the success that Nashe seems to have hoped for it when he concluded it with the following half promise:

> All the conclusiue epilogue I wil make is this; that if herein I haue pleased anie, it shall animat mee to more paines in this kind. Otherwise I will sweare vpon an English Chronicle neuer to bee out-landish Chronicler more while I liue.[65]

It remains as his only essay in this kind and, indeed, a thing *sui generis*, which is a pity, for, while it embodies nothing that can be called a view of life, it does succeed in conveying a number of discrepant attitudes to morals and to literature with peculiar force and vitality, giving them the quality of immediate sensations.

[65] II. 328.

# VII

# THE GREAT FLYTING—NASHE AND GABRIEL HARVEY

## I

NASHE found himself as a writer when he became involved in the Martin Marprelate controversy. The reason is not far to seek. His great deficiency as a creative artist lay in the fact that he had comparatively little to say, no passionately held or original view of life to offer, no cause, except that of poetry, to which he was devoted. What he had instead were strong prejudices, a good deal of second-hand information, much of it of an odd and out of the way kind, which he could use as capital and dress out in a startling and bizarre fashion by his mastery of language, a love of battle and contention, and the compulsion to appear in print and to keep himself in the public eye provided by sheer necessity. His strength lay in his gift for improvisation, in his flair for the topical, in his unfailing interest in novelties and ingenuities of style, and in his facility for satire, parody, caricature and abuse. Controversy, therefore, was his natural element, since he could then rely on his opponent to produce material for him to play with, refute, burlesque and hold up to scorn. Better still, this opponent might himself be made into a fertile theme for the exercise of wit. Already in the *Almond* Nashe had discovered in his handling of Penry how much could be accomplished by an adroit mixture of scandal, invective and gross caricature. But the Marprelate controversy came to an end before he could develop the possibilities latent in it for the old mediaeval literary game of flyting beyond the scope of a single pamphlet. At its conclusion one can imagine him looking eagerly round for a fresh victim and butt to take the place of Penry and his associates. He did not look for long; first Richard Harvey, and then his elder brother, Gabriel, supplied him with exactly the occasion and the material that he needed. And, having found the perfect target and foil in Gabriel, Nashe made such use of him that ultimately their quarrel came to account for more of his writings than any other topic.

The dispute was for much of its course largely a matter of personalities; only now and then did it broaden out into wider problems of a more general and permanent interest. Its course was, moreover, intricate, perplexed, and at times obscure. Nevertheless, a survey of it is justified, I feel, on several grounds. First, because it is the biggest thing of its kind in our literature; secondly, because behind the personalities, and emerging from time to time from them, there was a genuine clash of ideas and attitudes concerning society, education and literature; and thirdly, because it was conducted, at least on Nashe's part, with great gusto and skill. So successful was his onslaught that Harvey's reputation has never recovered from it. The true Harvey lies buried under the figure of fun created by Nashe much as the true Shadwell is lost in MacFlecknoe.

The origins of the quarrel and its subsequent course have been carefully established and charted by McKerrow.[1] My account of them is based substantially on his. The contention arose out of the Marprelate controversy and began with the publication, probably in 1590, of Richard Harvey's pamphlet, *Plain Perceval the Peace Maker of England*. The avowed intention of this work was, according to the title-page, 'to botch vp a Reconciliation between Mar-ton and Mar-tother', but its tone is far from pacific and it amounts to no more than an extended version of Mercutio's cry, 'A plague on both your houses'. Richard Harvey, however, does not show Mercutio's impartiality; he is more bitter about the anti-Martinists than about Martin himself. Offended, shocked and alarmed by their scurrility and violence, he describes them as, 'Whip Iohns, and Whip Iackes: not forgetting the Caualiero Pasquill, or the Cooke Ruffian, that drest a dish for Martins diet, Marforius and all Cutting Hufsnufs, Roisters, and the residew of light fingred younkers, which made euery word a blow, and euery

[1] V. 65–110.

booke a bobbe'.[2] Whether Nashe had yet published the *Almond* is not certain, but as one engaged in writing against Martin he must have felt himself under attack whether his pamphlet had actually appeared in print or not, and he may well have concluded that he was one of those referred to as 'light fingred younkers'.

In the same year, 1590, Richard Harvey published a further treatise, entitled *The Lamb of God*. To it, after its original publication, he added an Epistle, addressed 'To the fauorable or indifferent *Reader*', which Nashe was to describe as 'arrogantly censoriall'.[3] The greater part of it is devoted to an attack on Martin, who is taken to task for his lack of learning, of charity and of manners. The attack concludes with some words that Nashe was to remember and to apply to Richard Harvey himself:

> The Lamb of God make him a better Lamb heereafter then he hath beene heeretofore, and teach him now to dispute rather *ad rem*, then *ad personam*, especially till he hath reformed his owne person, as corruptible, on my word and his owne proofe, as the person of any of his mard Prelates.[4]

At this point Harvey transfers his attention to

> one *Thomas Nash* . . . who taketh vppon him in ciuill learning, as *Martin* doth in religion, peremptorily censuring his betters at pleasure, Poets, Orators, Polihistors, Lawyers, and whome not? and making as much and as little of euery man as himselfe listeth. . . . Iwis this *Thomas Nash*, one whome I neuer heard of before (for I cannot imagin him to be *Thomas Nash* our Butler of *Pembrooke Hall*, albeit peraduenture not much better learned) sheweth himselfe none of the meetest men, to censure Sir *Thomas Moore*, Sir *Iohn Cheeke*, Doctor *Watson*, Doctor *Haddon*, Maister *Ascham*, Doctor *Car*, my brother Doctor *Haruey*, and such like. . . . let not *Martin*, or *Nash*, or any such famous obscure man, or any other piperly makeplay or makebate, presume ouermuch of my patience as of simplicitie, but of choice.[5]

The ground of Nashe's offence in Richard Harvey's eyes, which led to this onslaught on him, was, of course, the readiness with which the young writer, fresh from Cambridge, had expressed his opinion of contemporary learning and letters in his Preface to Greene's *Menaphon*, which had appeared in the previous year. The resentment the older man felt at this procedure is understandable, though he might have been less censorious and super-

[2] V. 75. [3] I. 271. [4] V. 179. [5] V. 179–80.

cilious in his expression of it. So is the resentment of the younger at being reproved in this fashion and, above all, I suspect, at being classed with Martin, to whom his antagonism was genuine enough.

The odd thing about it all is that neither Nashe, the only anti-Martinist actually named by Richard Harvey, nor any of the other writers attacked by him, saw fit to reply for some two years. The first to do so was Robert Greene who found a place for some biting personal abuse not only of Richard Harvey, but also of his two brothers, Gabriel and John, in his pamphlet *A Quip for an Upstart Courtier*, published in 1592. The passage concerning the three brothers was cancelled, and at the time when McKerrow published his great edition of Nashe no copy of *A Quip* containing it was known to be extant. Subsequently, however, in 1919, a copy in which the all important passage had not been cancelled turned up. In it Greene meets in the dream, which is the subject of *A Quip*, John Harvey, a rope-maker and one of the leading citizens of Saffron Walden, the father of the three brothers. The following dialogue then takes place.

> And whether are you a going quoth I? Marry sir quoth he, first to absolue your question, I dwel in Saffron Waldon, and am going to Cambridge to three sons that I keep there at schoole, such apt children sir as few women haue groned for, and yet they haue ill lucke. The one sir [Richard Harvey] is a Deuine to comfort my soule, and he indeed though he be a vaine glorious asse, as diuers youths of his age bee, is well giuen to the shew of the world, and writte a late the lambe of God, and yet his parishioners say he is a limb of the deuill, and kisseth their wiues with holy kisses, but they had rather he should keep his lips for madge his mare. The second sir [John], is a Physitian or a foole, but indeed a physitian, and had proued a proper man if he had not spoiled himselfe with his Astrological discourse of the terrible coniunction of Saturne and Iupiter. For the eldest [Gabriel], he is a Ciuilian, a wondrous witted fellow, sir reuerence sir, he is a Doctor, and as Tubalcain was the first inuenter of Musick, so he Gods benison light vpon him, was the first that inuented Englishe Hexamiter: but see how in these daies learning is little esteemed, for that and other familiar letters and proper treatises he was orderly clapt in the Fleet, but sir a Hawk and a Kite may bring forth a coystrell, and honest parents may haue bad children.[6]

[6] *A Supplement*, pp. 75–6. On the authorship of this passage see my Appendix, pp. 254–5.

It is characteristic of Greene, a prodigal in everything, but especially so in the giving of gratuitous moral advice and the making of enemies, that he should have included the whole family of the Harveys in his rejoinder to one of them. It is also characteristic of him that he knew exactly how best to hurt them. Nashe was only too happy to follow his lead, and much that he was to say springs from this short passage. Green's assertion that Richard Harvey, the vicar of Chislehurst, was guilty of loose living was repeated more than once by him, but the jeers that really caught his fancy were those levelled at the Harveys' failure as astrologers and at Gabriel's part in the attempt to naturalize the hexameter in English poetry. The astrologers in the family were Richard and John. In 1583 Richard had issued

> An Astrological Discourse vpon the great and notable Coniunction of the two superiour Planets, SATURNE AND IUPITER, which shall happen the 28. day of April, 1583.

The prediction was a serious and scholarly work, but its prophecies of disaster, which seem to have caused widespread alarm, were not fulfilled and their author became the object of much ridicule. John shared in it, for he put out *An Astrologicall Addition* to his brother's *Discourse* and, unperturbed by the failure of its forecasts, went on publishing astrological treatises until three years before his death. This took place in July 1592, and had an important bearing on the quarrel, for it was in this month that Greene's *Quip* was entered in the Stationers' Register. It was, I think, Greene's attack on the dead John Harvey—though Greene did not know of John Harvey's death when he wrote it—that brought Gabriel into the fray, and that goes a long way towards explaining and even mitigating the savagery of his attack on the dead Greene. Furthermore, if we assume that Greene did not hear of John Harvey's death until after the publication of *A Quip*, we have a sound explanation of why the offending passage was cancelled. Greene was hot-tempered, but not vindictive, and would not be the man to make war on the dead, or the mourners. Such an explanation makes far better sense than those offered by Gabriel Harvey and by Nashe. Gabriel says that Greene offered ten or twenty shillings to the printer to suppress the passage 'with confession of his great feare to be called *Coram* for those forged imputations';[7] but this statement is nonsense, since there is nothing in Greene's attack that would provide grounds for legal proceedings. Nashe's version is that Greene cancelled the passage at the request of a physician who attended him in his last illness and who did not like to see a member of his own profession treated in the way Greene had treated John Harvey.[8] This explanation is improbable and, even if true, could account only for the omission of the remarks on John Harvey, not of the whole passage.

Nashe seems to have regarded Greene's attack as a step in the right direction, but an inadequate one. He took up the quarrel on his own account in *Pierce Penilesse*, where, in the section of the Supplication dealing with the Sin of Wrath, he says that if he is well treated by a patron he will delight in honouring him, but,

> if I bee euill intreated, or sent away with a Flea in mine eare, let him looke that I will raile on him soundly: not for an houre or a day, whiles the iniury is fresh in my memory, but in some elaborate, pollished Poem, which I will leaue to the world when I am dead, to be a liuing Image to all ages, of his beggerly parsimony and ignoble illiberaltie: and let him not (whatsoeuer he be) measure the weight of my words by this booke, where I write *Quicquid in buccam venerit*, as fast as my hand can trot; but I haue tearmes (if I be vext) laid in steepe in *Aquafortis*, and Gunpowder, that shall rattle through the Skyes, and make an Earthquake in a Pesants eares.[9]

The reference to patrons is misleading. Before *Pierce Penilesse* went to press Nashe, emboldened no doubt by Greene's attack on the Harveys, had seen his quarry in the shape of Richard Harvey, and after this threatening and swashbuckling prelude he proceeds to give a demonstration of his own qualities as a railer by launching into a torrent of picturesque abuse of him. The old taunt about the failure of the *Astrological Discourse* is expanded and filled out with an account of the ridicule it exposed Richard Harvey to; in keeping with Nashe's general attitude towards the new dialectic, scorn is poured on him for his support of Ramus while he was a student at Cambridge; Nashe makes far more than Greene had done of the fact that John Harvey, the father, was a rope-maker; makes uproarious fun of *The Lamb of God*, which he describes as a 'Sheepish discourse'; and finally rounds off his performance with

[7] Gabriel Harvey, *Foure Letters*, ed. G. B. Harrison, London, 1922, p. 13.
[8] I. 279–80. [9] I. 195.

these words, which are clearly intended to goad his enemy into print by their incisive parody of Harvey's admonition to Martin:

> The Lambe of God make thee a wiser Bell-weather then thou art, for else I doubt thou wilt be driuen to leaue all, and fall to thy fathers occupation, which is, to goe and make a rope to hang thy selfe.[10]

Richard Harvey made no reply to Nashe's taunts, but Gabriel did. Coming to London at the end of August 1592, about some legal business arising out of the death of his brother John, he lodged at the house of the printer John Wolfe. Smarting under the insults that Greene had heaped on him and his family, Gabriel made it his business 'to enquire after the famous Author: who was reported to lye dangerously sick in a shoemakers house near Dow-gate: not of the plague, or the pockes, as a Gentleman saide, but of a surfett of pickle herringe and rennish wine'.[11] His intention had been, according to what he says, to take legal action against Greene,[12] though so far as I can see he had no case, but within a few days he learned that Greene had died on 3 September 1592. The sequence of events that followed has been unravelled by McKerrow[13] and by Francis R. Johnson.[14] Greene's death had denied Gabriel the opportunity of legal redress. Moreover, at the beginning of the year his fellowship at Trinity Hall had expired[15] and it may be presumed he was short of money. Greene's death in misery and squalor was a sensational event of high news value. Harvey and Wolfe took immediate advantage of it. Within a few days, probably, Johnson thinks, by 7 or 8 September, Harvey wrote and Wolfe published an account of Greene's end, that took the form of what Nashe describes as a 'butter-fly Pamphlet against *Greene*',[16] and as 'a short Pamphlet of six leaues, like a paire of summer pumps'.[17] No copy of this work has come to light, but McKerrow and Johnson agree in identifying it as the second of the *Four Letters*, the one in which Harvey describes Greene's death. Harvey then went on to write the third and the fourth letters—the first, which is a letter of introduction, he presumably brought to

[10] I. 198. [11] *Foure Letters*, p. 13.
[12] *Op. cit.*, p. 18. [13] IV. 152–3.
[14] *The Library*, vol. XV, 1935, pp. 212–23.
[15] See Gabriel Harvey's *Marginalia*, ed. G. C. Moore Smith, Stratford-upon-Avon, 1913, p. 61, note 2.
[16] III. 130. [17] I. 263.

London with him—and the first edition of the whole work was probably on sale by the end of September. It would seem to have sold well, for Wolfe embarked on a second edition at once, and Johnson takes the view that this had been 'completed and issued before the book was entered to John Wolfe in the Stationers' Register on 4 December, 1592'.[18]

Since it was the publication of the *Four Letters* that brought Harvey into the controversy with Nashe, since the readiness of a man of his standing to enter into a slanging match with a dissolute and unscrupulous journalist needs some explanation, and since much of the controversy was to be concerned with events in his earlier career, it seems appropriate at this point to give a brief account of Harvey's life.

Born in 1550 or 1551, he came of a middle-class family which, to judge from the mantel-piece in his father's house,[19] had a considerable feeling for beauty, and which also set a high value on education. Gabriel, the eldest son, went to Christ's College, Cambridge. He was a brilliant student and after taking his B.A. in 1569–70 he was elected to a fellowship at Pembroke Hall. It should have been the beginning of a successful academic career, but his personality prevented him from gaining the advancement that his intelligence deserved. He was unpopular, partly because he seems to have had a sense of social inferiority which led him to take offence readily, and partly because he was keenly interested in new ideas and did not hesitate to show his contempt for those who were content to stick in the mud. In 1573 he applied for the degree of Master, but was opposed in it by two fellows of his own college, not on academic but on personal grounds. He was accused of being unsociable, of being arrogant, of not valuing his fellowship highly enough and of supporting anti-Aristotelian ideas, i.e. of being a Ramist. The impression created by these charges and by Harvey's defence of himself against them is of a man of ability, conscious of his own worth, disliked by his fellows because of his ability, and driven in consequence to take up an intransigent position that aggravated the whole situation.

Eventually, however, Harvey won the support of Dr. Young, the Master of the College, and received his master's degree. In October 1573 he became college lecturer in Greek and in April

[18] *Op cit.*., p. 219.

[19] See picture facing p. 7 in *Gabriel Harvey's Marginalia*.

1574 he was made University Praelector or Professor in Rhetoric. It was at this time that he became friendly with Edmund Spenser, and their friendship continued after Spenser left the university in 1576. This successful and happy period reached its culmination in July 1578, when Queen Elizabeth visited the great house of Audley End not far from Saffron Walden. Harvey was one of the scholars from Cambridge (which had to all intents and purposes moved to Audley End for the occasion) chosen to dispute before the Court. He made the most of this opportunity to attract attention and the patronage which might follow it, for at this stage in his career he had no intention of staying in Cambridge, but hoped for some kind of public employment. The Queen noticed him, told Leicester that he had the look of an Italian and allowed him to kiss her hand. This apparent success seems to have gone to Harvey's head. He celebrated the whole proceedings in a book of Latin verse, the *Gratulationes Valdinenses*, in which he devotes a poem to the Queen's remark about his Italian appearance and another to his kissing her hand. The whole thing is a rather naïve and blatant bid for favour and patronage, though it must be remembered that at the time there was no other way of advancement.

Ultimately the poem recoiled on Harvey's head, since it provided material for Nashe, but at first it looked as though something might come of the efforts he had made at Audley End. Leicester was seriously considering taking him into his service and sending him abroad, but the plan fell through. At much the same time his fellowship at Pembroke expired, but he was elected to a new fellowship at Trinity Hall shortly afterwards. At this stage in his career his friendship with Spenser led to his appearing in *The Shepheardes Calender*, under the name of Hobbinol, and to the publication in 1580 of five letters which had passed between them —two from Spenser to Harvey and three from Harvey to Spenser —under the titles of *Three Proper and Wittie, familiar Letters* and *Two Other very commendable Letters*. It was presumptuous and rather ridiculous of the two young men, who both took themselves too seriously, to imagine that their private correspondence would be of general interest, even though it was concerned with a subject of some literary importance, the attempt to introduce classical metres into English poetry. The situation in brief was that Harvey was an exponent of the case for classical metres, but a moderate and sensible advocate of them, who was well aware that the experiment could only succeed if it took account of the natural rhythms and accentuation of English speech. Spenser, on the other hand, after being opposed to the whole idea at first, had become a convert to the extreme and purely mechanical rules for determining length propounded by Archdeacon Drant and practised by Sir Philip Sidney and Sir Edward Dyer. To Harvey's credit it deserves to be remembered that he warned Spenser against these rules and showed far more sense about the whole business of the English hexameter than the unscrupulous Nashe was later to credit him with. Nothing could be less pedantic or more to the point than Harvey's comment:

> In good sooth, and by the faith I beare to the Muses, you shal neuer haue my subscription or consent (though you should charge me wyth the authoritie of fiue hundreth Maister *Drants*,) to make your *Carpēnter* our *Carpĕnter*, an inche longer, or bigger, than God and his Englishe people haue made him.[20]

While he was sensible enough about the hexameter, Harvey made two mistakes of another kind in publishing these letters which were to cause him trouble.[20a] In the third of them he printed some English verses of his own, including a poem entitled *Speculum Tuscanismi*. This is a piece of satire on the Englishman Italianate, but John Lyly seems to have done his best to convince the Earl of Oxford that it was intended as a satire on him and, though there is no evidence that Oxford took any action in the matter, Nashe was to make good use of the story. More serious in its effect on Harvey was a reference in the second letter, during the course of a derogatory sketch of Cambridge, to a person whom he describes to Spenser as 'youre olde Controller', and of whom he writes:

> A busy and dizy heade, a brazen forehead: a ledden braine: a wodden wit: a copper face: a stony breast: a factious and eluish hearte: a founder of nouelties: a confounder of his owne, and his friends good gifts: a morning bookeworm, an afternoone maltworm: a right Iuggler, as ful of his sleights, wyles, fetches, casts of Legerdemaine, toyes to mock Apes withal, odde shiftes, and knauish practizes, as his skin can holde. He often telleth me, he loooueth me

[20] *The Poetical Works of Edmund Spenser*, ed. J. C. Smith and E. de Selincourt, Oxford, 1912, p. 630.

[20a] For the view that Harvey did publish them see A. C. Judson, *The Life of Edmund Spenser*, Baltimore, 1945, p. 60.

> as himselfe, but out lyar out, thou lyest abhominably in thy throate.[21]

Writing like this in 1580, Harvey was clearly no novice in the art of railing; but, unfortunately for him, despite the fact that the 'old Controller' was plainly a Cambridge man, Sir James Croft, the Controller of the Queen's Household, took it as an attack on himself and, according to Nashe, had Harvey clapped in the Fleet. Harvey, of course, denied that he underwent this indignity. He certainly did not deserve it, for the 'old Controller' he had in mind when he wrote the passage was Dr. Perne, the Master of Peterhouse, a most wily politician, whom he had every reason to dislike. In 1579 the Public Orator, Dr. Bridgewater, had resigned, but the resignation did not become generally known in the university until April 1580. By the time Harvey came to hear of it, two other candidates for the vacant post, both of them junior to him, were already in the field. Realizing that there would be a struggle and that there was strong opposition to his own candidature, despite the fact that he had the best academic qualifications for the post, Harvey took the step of writing to the Chancellor of Cambridge, Lord Burleigh, to solicit his support. But, even though Burleigh replied with a favourable letter, it was not sufficient to overcome the local opposition, and when a new orator was finally elected in March 1581 it was not Harvey. By the summer of 1580 Harvey knew that his own candidature had failed, and he was almost certainly right in seeing Perne as the organizer of the opposition.

The loss of the Public Oratorship, which was regarded as the stepping-stone to a distinguished career in the public service, was a severe blow to Harvey's ambitions and aspirations. Five years later came another. In 1585 the Master of Trinity Hall died. Harvey confidently expected to succeed him, but once again, as a result of intrigues in which Perne seems to have played a leading part, his hopes were thwarted. By January 1592, when another man was admitted to the fellowship at Trinity Hall that he had held for twelve or thirteen years, Harvey was not only a disappointed man, bitterly aware of great abilities that had come to nothing and of hopes frustrated by university politicians, but also a poor man with nothing to fall back on except his pen and his qualifications as a lawyer—he was made a Doctor of Civil Laws at Oxford in 1585 in rather curious circumstances[22]—which, accord-

[21] *Op. cit.*, p. 622. [22] See *Gabriel Harvey's Marginalia*, pp. 49–50.

ing to Nashe,[23] never brought him a case. To a man with this history and in this situation Greene's attack in *A Quip* on his family and on himself must have appeared as a kick in the teeth, a public manifestation of the same kind of snobbery, backbiting and contempt which had thwarted his ambitions and ruined his career at Cambridge.

It is hardly surprising, therefore, that Harvey should have seen in Greene's death a heaven-sent opportunity to level old scores and to justify his own behaviour in the past. But, while these were almost certainly the basic motives that led to the publication first of the 'butter-fly Pamphlet' and then of the *Four Letters*, Harvey must have been delighted also to have a chance to use his pen on some saleable news.

## 2

Harvey begins the first of the *Four Letters* by reproducing a letter, dated 29 August 1592, from one Christopher Bird, a citizen of Saffron Walden, to a certain Emanuell Demetrius of Lime Street in London, recommending Harvey to him as a scholar interested in history and in foreign affairs. Bird then adds a postscript in which he refers to Greene's *Quip*, calling it 'as fantasticall and fond a Dialogue, as I haue seene',[24] and then takes Greene to task for libelling John Harvey, the father, 'a right honest man of good reckoninge'. He also mentions that John Harvey, the son, 'returning sicke from *Norwich* to *Linne*, in Iuly last, was past sence of any such malicious iniury, before the publication of that vile Pamphlet', and ends up with a sonnet abusing Greene in a crude and violent manner as

> A rakehell: A makeshift: A scribling foole.

Bird's letter is clearly intended by Harvey to serve as a piece of independent witness, but its value in this respect is somewhat undermined by the sonnet, which, as Nashe spotted, reads suspiciously like the work of Harvey himself, and which contains the line

> Now sicke, as a Dog: and euer brainesick,

a reference to Greene's illness that one would hardly expect from a worthy citizen of Saffron Walden.

[23] III. 73, and 85–6.
[24] *Foure Letters*, ed. Harrison, p. 11.

The second letter, dated 5 September, from Harvey to Bird, deals with Greene's death in a manner calculated to make the work sell and to invite answers. After describing how he learned on arriving in London that Greene was ill, Harvey attacks him as a railer and loose liver and then says, 'here is matter inough for a new ciuill war, or shall I say for a new Troyan siedge, if this poore Letter should fortune to come in print'.[25] Since Harvey was living in Wolfe's house at the time and knew perfectly well that the letter would be in print in a day or two, it looks very much as though he was spoiling for a fight and hoped to stir up his adversaries. He then goes on to write about satire in general which, he says, may have its uses, but draws the line at libellous attacks on his family, and relates that he was considering exactly what steps he ought to take against Greene, when,

> I was suddainely certified, that the king of the paper stage (so the Gentleman tearmed *Greene*) had played his last part, and was gone to *Tarleton*: whereof I protest, I was nothing glad, as was expected, but vnfainedly sory; aswell because I could haue wished, he had taken his leaue with a more charitable farewell: as also because I was depriued of that remedy in Law, that I entended against him in the behalfe of my Father, whose honest reputation I was in many dueties to tender. Yet to some conceited witt, that could take delight to discouer knaueries, or were a fitte person to augment the history of Conny-catchers: O Lord, what a pregnant occasion were here presented, to display leaud vanity in his liuely coullours, and to decipher the very misteries of that base Arte?[26]

There is more than a touch of Pecksniff about this passage; Harvey's sorrow proves to be canting hypocrisy, for he now proceeds to do exactly what he says 'some conceited witt' would do in these circumstances; he relates with great relish what everyone in London, according to him, knew and thought of Greene. This piece of sustained abuse must be quoted, not only because it explains why Nashe took up Greene's defence, but also because it shows that Harvey could, when he wished, write a very forceful colloquial prose and was no mean opponent in a flyting. He writes:

> who in London hath not heard of his dissolute, and licentious liuing; his fonde disguisinge of a Master of Arte with ruffianly haire, vnseemely apparell, and more vnseemelye Company: his

[25] *Ibid.*, p. 14.

[26] *Ibid.*, pp. 18–19.

vaine-glorious and Thrasonicall brauinge: his piperly Extemporizing and Tarletonizing: his apishe counterfeiting of euery ridiculous, and absurd toy: his fine coosening of Iuglers, and finer iugling with cooseners: hys villainous cogging, and foisting; his monstrous swearinge, and horrible forswearing; his impious profaning of sacred Textes: his other scandalous, and blasphemous rauinge; his riotous and outragious surfeitinge; his continuall shifting of lodginges: his plausible musteringe, and banquetinge of roysterly acquaintaunce at his first comminge; his beggarly departing in euery hostisses debt; his infamous resorting to the Banckeside, Shorditch, Southwarke, and other filthy hauntes: his obscure lurkinge in basest corners: his pawning of his sword, cloake, and what not, when money came short; his impudent pamphletting, phantasticall interluding, and desperate libelling, when other coosening shifts failed: his imployinge of Ball (surnamed, cuttinge Ball) till he was intercepted at Tiborne, to leauy a crew of his trustiest companions, to guarde him in daunger of Arrestes: his keeping of the foresaid Balls sister, a sorry ragged queane, of whome hee had his base sonne, *Infortunatus Greene*: his forsaking of his owne wife, too honest for such a husband: particulars are infinite: his contemning of Superiours, deriding of other, and defying of all good order?[27]

Once launched, Harvey cannot stop, the hoarded up bitterness of years comes pouring out as he goes on to gloat over Greene's penury, to relate that 'he was attended by lice' and to suggest in a covert sneer that his mistress suffered from the pox, interspersing his evident delight in it all with such smug comments as, 'I pittied him from my hart', and, 'I am none of those, that bite the dead'. He even goes so far as to say that he hopes God will forgive Greene, while at the same time carefully indicating that he thinks it highly improbable.

The only mention of Nashe in this letter is an innocuous one. Harvey says that Greene in his extremity could get no help from his friends and adds:

Alas, euen his fellow-writer, a proper yong man, if aduised in time, that was a principall guest at that fatall banquet of pickle herring, (I spare his name, and in some respectes wish him well) came neuer more at him: but either would not, or happily could not performe the duty of an affectionate, and faithfull frend.[28]

To this Nashe could hardly take exception; it is obviously conciliatory; but there was plenty of matter in the rest of the letter

[27] *Ibid.*, pp. 19–20. [28] *Ibid.*, p. 21.

to arouse his resentment. He was friendly with Greene and must have found Harvey's mingling of gloating regret and downright abuse singularly distasteful and nauseating. It was altogether too like the canting attitude, for which he had so frequently attacked the Puritans, to be ignored.

Harvey's mild tone about Nashe in this letter is to be explained by the fact that he had not yet seen *Pierce Penilesse* when he finished writing it (5 September). He had read it, however, when he wrote his third letter, which is dated 8 and 9 September, and it looks rather as though it came to his notice while he was actually engaged in the writing. Addressed 'to euery Reader, fauourablie, or indifferently affected', this opens in a very different manner from the second letter. Harvey here appears at his best. With moderation, restraint and dignity, he defends himself against the charges Greene had made against him in *A Quip*. Beginning with his correspondence with Spenser and the consequences that followed on its publication, he admits that he was rather rash and naïve at the time, that he was deeply annoyed at being passed over for the office of Public Orator and that his chagrin led him into attacking Dr. Perne. He then goes on to say, however, that he showed what he had written to some of his friends who, either out of malice or indiscretion, 'aduentured to imprint in earnest, that was scribled in iest'.[29] The excuse savours of special pleading. Harvey had, so far as we know, made no protest when the letters were published, or in the twelve years that had elapsed since. About his share in the invention of the English hexameter he is rightly unrepentant. He writes:

> If I neuer deserue anye better remembraunce, let mee rather be Epitaphed, The Inuentour of the English Hexameter: whom learned Master Stanihurst imitated in his Virgill; and excellent Sir Philip Sidney disdained not to follow in his *Arcadia*, and elsewhere: then be chronicled, The greene maister of the Black Arte.[30]

But when he turns to Greene's remarks about his family, which were clearly the thing that really rankled with him, the level tone disappears. He slips into abuse once more, accuses his enemy of every crime under the sun and rides rough-shod over Greene's readers as well as his writings. On several occasions he tries to stop, but is unable to do so until eventually he is diverted by a new

[29] *Ibid.*, p. 31.

[30] *Ibid.*, pp. 32–3.

target, which has suddenly presented itself and which he introduces thus:

> Flourishing Master Greene is most-wofully faded, and whilest I am bemoaning his ouer-pittious decay; and discoursing the vsuall successe of such ranke wittes, Loe all on the suddaine, his sworne brother, Master *Pierce Pennilesse*, (still more paltery but what remedy? we are already ouer shoes, and must now go through) Loe his inwardest companion, that tasted of the fatall herringe, cruelly pinched with want, vexed with discredite, tormented with other mens felicitie, and ouerwhelmed with his own misery; in a rauing, and franticke moode, most desperately exhibiteth his supplication to the Diuell.[31]

The note of light raillery so evident here is sustained all through Harvey's answer to Nashe which is, in its own kind, a most accomplished piece of writing. There is none of the rancour about it that marks his attack on Greene. It is carried out in a spirit of good humour and with genuine literary sense. Harvey picks up Nashe's own terms and plays with them, turning them inside out and creating the impression that their author is a silly young man, 'an od wit, and a mad hooreson',[32] as he puts it. He makes fun of Nashe's pretentious display of learning and thoroughly enjoys himself at the expense of the poem at the beginning of *Pierce Penilesse*, of which he writes:

> Now, good sweete Muse, I beseech thee by thy delicate witte, and by all the queintest Inuentions of thy deuiseful braine, cast not thy drearie selfe headlong into the horrible Gulf of Desperation: but being a Creature of so singular, and wonderfull hope, as thy inspired courage diuinelie suggesteth, and still reare-vp mountaines of highest Hope; and either gallantlie aduance thy vertuous self, maugre Fortune: (what impossible to aspiring industry?) or mightilie enchant some magnificent Mecænas, (for thou canst doe it) to honour himselfe in honouring thee: and to blisse the eies of the gazing worlde, with beholding those Miracles, which some round liberality, and thy super-thankfull minde, would hugelie enable thee to work.[33]

Irony was exactly the right weapon to use against Nashe, and Harvey handles it lightly yet effectively. Moreover, even when he becomes more serious, as he does when he takes up Nashe's aspersions on his father and his brother, he still retains control

[31] *Ibid.*, p. 44. [32] *Ibid.*, p. 45. [33] *Ibid.*, pp. 46–7.

over what he is saying and does not lapse into bitterness. On the contrary there is real dignity and courage in his assertion that 'fewe Sonnes have felinger cause to loue, or reuerence, or defend their Fathers, then my selfe'. By and large, however, Harvey treats the whole altercation as a game, entering freely into the spirit of the flyting, ready on the one hand to call a halt and to 'bee made friendes with a cup of white wine, and some little familiar conference, in calme and ciuile termes', or on the other to carry on the battle if composition is refused, since there are 'a number of greedy Eares, that egerly longe, and as it were daunce attendaunce, to heare those dreadfull inuincible termes, steeped in *Aquafortis*, and Gunpowder'.[34]

There can be no doubt, I think, that at this early stage in the quarrel Harvey was in two minds about it. On the one side he wished it to go no farther and was prepared to treat Nashe generously and forbearingly, regarding him as a young man of parts, who had been led astray by others. Indeed he even goes so far as to couple him with such poets as Spenser and Daniel and to thank him, along with them, for 'their studious endeuours, commendably employed in enriching, and polishing their natiue Tongue, neuer so furnished, or embellished as of-late',[35] a very handsome compliment indeed from a scholar of his eminence. But, on the other side, it is also plain that he rather enjoyed the opportunity Nashe had given him for displaying his own wit and learning, and that he was not averse, in his need, from taking a further part in a paper battle that was arousing such interest among the reading public of the day.

The final letter, dated 11 and 12 September, endorses this conclusion. It is mainly the work of Harvey, the scholar and man of letters, rather than of Harvey, the hack-writer. It is a justification of his own action in bothering to answer his enemies, and is given up to an exposition of his general attitude to life and his preference for action as opposed to theory. It also expresses his fear that the growth of a sensational and irresponsible journalism might do real damage to the cause of letters and learning. Harvey seems to be genuinely weary of the whole dispute now and once again gives Nashe a chance to end it all. He writes:

> Might *Pierce* be entreated, to quallifye his distempered veine; and to relcaime his unbrideled selfe . . . I assuredly would be

[34] *Ibid.*, pp. 65–6. [35] *Ibid.*, p. 68.

> the first, that should wrapp-vp such memorials, not in a sheete of wast-paper, but in the winding-sheete of Obliuion.[36]

But there is another thread running through this elevated discourse. In spite of his professions of magnanimity, Harvey cannot refrain from gibes at Greene and Nashe, whom he refers to as 'woeful *Greene*, and beggarly *Pierce Pennylesse*', as 'Asses in print' and as 'The vayne Peacocke, with his gay coullours, and the pratling Parrat with his ignorant discourses',[37] a plain indication that he regarded Nashe as the author of the *Almond for a Parrot.*

The work is rounded off with some twenty-two sonnets in which Harvey substantially repeats the matter of the letters, praising his father and his brothers, abusing Greene and proclaiming his belief in the value of learning and letters in undistinguished verse that makes a lame conclusion, except for the fact that he has the sense to print Spenser's sonnet in his praise right at the very end.

Taken all in all the *Four Letters* are a very curious and in some ways puzzling piece of work. Harvey's careful presentation of his credentials, in the shape of the letter from Christopher Bird with which he opens and the sonnet by Spenser with which he ends, contrasts oddly with the general consciousness of his own worth and importance found elsewhere in the work. His violent abuse of Greene and his evident satisfaction in that writer's miserable end sort ill with his professions of magnanimity and high-mindedness. His statements that he is sick of the whole quarrel and wishes for a reconciliation with Nashe do not tally with the obvious pleasure he takes in repaying Nashe's raillery in kind. The *Four Letters* are the expression of a divided mind, and not least so in their style, which varies from the skilful and easy use of an allusive irony against Nashe to the clumsy, clotted verbiage of many of the sonnets. As a target they are everything that an opponent could wish for, inconsistent both in style and in attitude, the work of one who, for all his insistence on the importance of marrying practice to theory, never came within sight of doing it himself.

At the time when the *Four Letters* were first published, probably, as Mr. Johnson has shown, at the end of September, Nashe was absent from London. Either some time elapsed before he saw a copy of them, or else he took longer to reply than his friends

[36] *Ibid.*, p. 73. [37] *Ibid.*, p. 77.

expected, for Henry Chettle's pamphlet *Kind Heart's Dream*, which was registered on 8 December 1592, contains a letter from the ghost of Greene to Pierce Penilesse, upbraiding him for his delay and ending with the following call to action:

> Awake (secure boy) reuenge thy wrongs, remember mine: thy aduersaries began the abuse, they continue it: if thou suffer it, let thy life be short in silence and obscuritie, and thy death hastie, hated, and miserable.[38]

It is unlikely that Nashe needed any such spur, but Chettle's remarks may well have caused him to realize that there was a public keenly interested in the whole debate and impatiently expecting the next round. They did not have to wait for long after the publication of *Kind Heart's Dream*. On 12 January 1593, Nashe's answer to Harvey was entered in the Stationers' Register by John Danter under the title *The Apologie of Pierce Pennylesse or strange newes of the intercepting certen letters, and a convoy of verses as they were goinge to victuall the Lowe Cuntries*. This title is most ingenious. It burlesques the topical news-sheets of the day, it has a martial air and it implies that the *Four Letters* are already so much waste paper and, as such, destined for the basest of uses. It also expresses the confidence with which Nashe goes to work. He was now on familiar ground. The situation was in some ways similar to that which had existed a few years earlier between Martin Marprelate on the one side and Dr. Bridges and Bishop Cooper on the other, though the issues were, of course, different. Like the two Anglican apologists, Harvey was a man of great learning, but not one who was at home in the market-place and had an instinctive sense of how to win the interest and the sympathies of the general public. Waspish though he could be and touchy as he was, he was no brawler. Nashe, like Martin, was; and *Strange News* owes something to *Oh read over Dr. Bridges* and to *Hay Any Work for Cooper*.

That Nashe intended *Strange News* to have a popular appeal is evident from the Dedicatory Epistle. It is not addressed to an aristocratic patron for the obvious reason that the work it prefaces was hardly one that he could expect any person of rank to countenance or approve of. Instead it is a mock dedication addressed to one *Maister Apis lapis*, a name which McKerrow plausibly con-

[38] V. 146.

jectures refers to someone named Beeston. Nothing is known of Beeston, apart from this mention, but from what Nashe says about him it would seem that he was something of a ballad-maker, that he frequented taverns and that he enjoyed a certain notoriety as a drinker and a wencher. This choice of dedicatee—the antithesis of Harvey's honest father and worthy friends—and the indecorous, hearty, swashbuckling tone of the whole epistle are good index of what is to follow. Nashe here adopts the *rôle* of plain man and jester, not to mention boon companion, who will make short work of vanity and pretentiousness and show no respect whatever for pedantry. This impression is reinforced by an epistle addressed 'to the Gentlemen Readers' in which Nashe first enters a protest against those who had sought to find personal satire in *Pierce Penilesse*, and then goes on to hold Harvey up to ridicule as one 'that bepist his credite, about twelue yeeres ago, with *Three proper and wittie familiar letters*', and who, not content with this, 'must be running on the *letter*, and abusing the Queenes English without pittie or mercie'.[39] In the accent of a town crier he places his enemy in the stocks and reels off an indictment of him as a praiser of himself and a coiner of ink-horn terms, ending up with a swaggering challenge:

> Heere lies my hatte, and there my cloake, to which I resemble my two Epistles, being the vpper garments of my booke, as the other of my body: Saint Fame for mee, and thus I runne vpon him.

The brawling metaphor is appropriate to Nashe's conduct of his own case. His method of answering Harvey's attack is very like that adopted by Martin when answering Bishop Cooper. He works his way through the *Four Letters*, quoting passages from them which he either rebuts, or comments on in a humorous fashion. Nor is he above misquoting or misrepresenting the sense of a passage when it is to his advantage to do so. For instance, Harvey had excused his own entry into the conflict as follows:

> I was first exceeding loath to penne, that is written: albeit in mine owne enforced defence, (for I make no difference betweene my deerest frendes, and my selfe): and am now much loather to diuulge, that is imprinted: albeit against those, whose owne Pamflets are readier to condemne them, then my Letters forwarde to accuse them.[40]

[39] I. 261. [40] *Foure Letters*, p. 7.

Nashe quite unscrupulously turns the last part of this statement upside down, yet represents his version of it as direct quotation. He writes of how Greene and he had opposed the Harveys, and then continues:

> Hee forbeares to speake much in this place of the one or the other, *because his letters are more forward to accuse them than their owne books to condemne them.*[41]

It is not easy to say whether Nashe here intended to deceive the public or not, but the misrepresentation is so blatant that it seems likely that he expected them to notice it and to treat it as an amusing but outrageous joke. Indeed he almost says so himself when, after accusing Harvey of lying repeatedly in the *Four Letters*, he continues thus in a passage that Shakespeare seems to have remembered when he makes the Prince tell Falstaff in *1 Henry IV*, IV. iv.: 'These lies are like their father that begets them, gross as a mountain, open, palpable':

> Had they been wittie lies, or merry lies, they would neuer haue greeu'd mee: but palpable lies, damned lies, lies as big as one of the Guardes chynes of beefe, who can abide?[42]

Certainly the tone of *Strange News* as a whole is that of a popular entertainment; it is very much a piece of knock-about farce. Nashe's characteristic love of self-display is here flamboyant in the extreme. He accuses Harvey of being ashamed of his father's occupation and then states how he would have reacted had his own father been a ropemaker:

> Thou dost liue by the gallows, and wouldst not haue a shooe to put on thy foot, if thy father had no traffike with the hangman. Had I a Ropemaker to my father, and somebody had cast it in my teeth, I would foorthwith haue writ in praise of Ropemakers, and prou'd it by sound sillogistry to be one of the seuen liberal sciences.[43]

And he leaves one in no doubt that this is no mere empty boast. Much of his strength lies in the fact that he brings scholarly techniques of argument to bear on trivial matters purely for the fun that they give rise to. It is no accident that Shakespeare remembered *Strange News* when he was writing *Henry IV*. In some measure at least the disputations and slanging matches that the Prince and Falstaff engage in derive from the way Nashe goes to work here. Words such as *therefore* and *ergo*, the small change of

[41] I. 267. [42] I. 269. [43] I. 270.

the logic schools, abound. The whole thing is conceived of in terms that recall either those used in a learned disputation, or those used in a court of law. Nashe heads his attack on the Third Letter, the one in which Harvey had had most to say about him, 'The Arrainment and Execution of the third Letter', and then prefaces a quotation from it with the words: 'Text, stand to the Barre. Peace there below'. And on the same page a further quotation is introduced by a neat combination of logical terminology and comic simile: 'Heere enters Argumentum a *testimonio humano*, like *Tamberlaine* drawne in a Chariot by foure Kings'.[44]

To make his opponent look ridiculous, one of the arts of rhetoric that Nashe was most skilled in, he invents burlesque names for him, much as he had done for the devil in *Pierce Penilesse*. Harvey appears under such absurd misnomers as Gabriell Howliglasse, Gilgilis Hobberdehoy, Gregory Haberdine, Gabriel Hangtelow, Timothy Tiptoes, Gibraltar and Galpogas. He is exposed to volleys of riotous and exuberant abuse in which, for the modern reader at any rate, any offensive quality disappears in the admiration excited by the inventive faculty that could produce such a wealth and variety of picturesque and scurrilous phrases. Harvey had shown some talent in this kind in the names he had heaped on Dr. Perne and on Greene. Nashe took them as a challenge. He quotes some of them and then turns on their author:

> Why, thou arrant butter whore, thou cotqueane and scrattop of scoldes, wilt thou neuer leaue afflicting a dead Carcasse, continually read the rethorick lecture of Ramme-Allie? a wispe, a wispe, a wispe, rippe, rippe, you kitchinstuffe wrangler.[45]

One does not need to know the exact meaning of every word there in order to feel something of the gusto with which Nashe draws this comparison between Harvey, abusing Greene, and a foul-mouthed slattern, 'letting rip' as she gossips at a kitchen door.

To stress that the general character of *Strange News* is humorous, that it is essentially comic in an irreverent, irrepressible cockney fashion, is not, of course, to deny that it has any serious purpose at all. It is clear, I think, that Nashe had been stung by Harvey's reflections on his insignificance and on his lack of learning, and that there is a generous impulse behind his defence of Greene. He felt that the abuse of the dead man was unpardonable and that the

[44] I. 293.  [45] I. 299.

contrast between Harvey's professions of charity and the savage delight with which he had pictured the misery of Greene's end could only be explained as sheer hypocrisy. He accuses him of playing the Pharisee[46] and, in order to clear Greene's name from the worst of his charges, he writes a character sketch of his old friend, which is for brilliance of observation and liveliness of expression the most striking picture we have of any Elizabethan writer and, as such, deserves to be given in full:

> In short tearmes, thus I demur vpon thy long Kentish-tayld declaration against *Greene*.
>
> Hee inherited more vertues than vices: a iolly long red peake, like the spire of a steeple, hee cherisht continually without cutting, whereat a man might hang a Iewell, it was so sharpe and pendant.
>
> Why should art answer for the infirmities of maners? Hee had his faultes, and thou thy follyes.
>
> Debt and deadly sinne, who is not subiect to? with any notorious crime I neuer knew him tainted; (and yet tainting is no infamous surgerie for him that hath beene in so many hote skirmishes).
>
> A good fellow hee was, and would haue drunke with thee for more *angels* then the Lord thou libeldst on *gaue thee in Christs Colledge*; and in one yeare hee pist as much against the walls, as thou and thy two brothers spent in three.
>
> In a night and a day would he haue yarkt vp a Pamphlet as well as in seauen yeare, and glad was that Printer that might bee so blest to pay him deare for the very dregs of his wit.
>
> Hee made no account of winning credite by his workes, as thou dost, that dost no good workes, but thinkes to bee famosed by a strong faith of thy owne worthines: his only care was to haue a spel in his purse to coniure vp a good cuppe of wine with at all times.
>
> For the lowsie circumstance of his pouerty before his death, and sending that miserable writte to his wife, it cannot be but thou lyest, learned *Gabriell*.
>
> I and one of my fellowes, *Will. Monox* (Hast thou neuer heard of him and his great dagger?) were in company with him a month before he died, at that fatall banquet of Rhenish wine and pickled hearing (if thou wilt needs haue it so), and then the inuentorie of his apparrel came to more than three shillings (though thou saist the contrarie). I know a Broker in a spruce leather ierkin with a great number of golde Rings on his fingers, and a bunch of keies at his girdle, shall giue you thirty shillings for the doublet alone, if you can helpe him to it. Harke in your eare, hee had a very faire Cloake

[46] I. 268.

with sleeues, of a graue goose turd greene; it would serue you as fine as may bee: No more words, if you bee wise, play the good husband and listen after it, you may buy it ten shillings better cheape than it cost him. By St. Siluer, it is good to bee circumspect in casting for the worlde, theres a great many ropes go to ten shillings. If you want a greasy paire of silk stockings also, to shew your selfe in at the Court, they are there to be had too amongst his moueables. *Frustra fit per plura quod fieri potest per pauciora*: It is policie to take a rich peniworth whiles it is offred.[47]

Not only has Greene been set before us in his habit as he lived, but a most telling contrast has been drawn between his essential generosity and Harvey's meanness of spirit. Moreover, the attitude Nashe adopts here is a good pointer to the fundamental opposition between Harvey and himself. Both of them members of the same middle class, both products of Cambridge, both literary men genuinely concerned about the state of letters in their time, they looked at life from two diametrically opposed points of view, which were not theirs alone, but those of the age they were living in. Harvey had a true passion for learning, but even that passion was not a pure one. At the back of it lay the desire to get on, to achieve position and power. Conscious of his own ability, he had no hesitation in asserting the importance of intelligence as opposed to any accident of birth, he was at one with Machiavelli, whom he admired, in the value he set on *virtù*. Yet his apparent boldness in this matter is evidence of a deeper uncertainty, insecurity and self-distrust. He could not escape from or disregard the social temper of the age he was living in. At Cambridge, as we have seen, he was difficult to get on with, because he was constantly on the look-out for the slights and the contempt he expected and resented. Extremely conscious of his own humble origins, he was pathetically eager for any recognition of his qualities by the great and, when he received it, could not help making a parade of it. There was much in him that was admirable. He had a good mind, he was not afraid of new ideas, he was attached to his family; but he was all too ready at all times to fawn on his social superiors, to regard his equals as involved in a conspiracy against him and to take an arrogant, hectoring tone with those whom he looked on as his inferiors. He was a misfit with a remarkable capacity for irritating others.

[47] I. 287–8.

In almost every respect Nashe was Harvey's antithesis. There was nothing deep or exact about his learning; he was not interested in new ideas and disapproved of them; socially he was a conformist. But he was free from self-regarding suspicion. His relations with people of all classes seem to have been easy; he can pay a compliment, or express thanks for a benefit, without fawning and take a rebuff without resentment. Aware of his own limitations, as Harvey was not, he seems never to have expected too much of life. Even his complaints about the neglect of scholars are saved from nagging peevishness by the grace of humour, a quality entirely missing from Harvey's writings. He lived by his pen, but with all his professionalism there is throughout his work a devotion to the cause of poetry that never falters; for him literature is not a means to an end, as it was for Harvey, but an end in itself. And what he looks for in good writing is wit, inventive fertility and imaginative vitality. Therefore, when Harvey attacks Greene's way of life, Nashe retorts by pointing to Greene's qualities as a writer, and by adopting other standards than those of Harvey to assess Greene's life by. For him the capacity to enjoy and the readiness to be generous count for more than strict morality. The opposition between them was the old one between virtue and cakes and ale. Harvey was no Puritan in the religious sense of the word, but, in so far as his own experience had made him sour, grudging and envious, he did share some of the less admirable traits of Nashe's old enemies. Moreover, Nashe's experience of the world, that practical knowledge of men and manners that he had actually acquired while Harvey had been busy writing about it, enabled him to see with devastating clarity just what Harvey's state of mind was. He describes it with great force in a summing up which, despite its exaggerations—a part of the game—is essentially convincing and true:

> Gentlemen, by that which hath been already laid open, I doe not doubt but you are vnwaueringly resolued, this indigested Chaos of Doctourship, and greedy pothunter after applause, is an apparant Publican and sinner, a selfe-loue surfetted sot, a broken-winded galdbacke Iade, that hath borne vp his head in his time, but now is quite foundred and tired, a scholer in nothing but the scum of schollership, a stale soker at *Tullies Offices*, the droanc of droanes, and maister drumble-bee of non proficients. What hath he wrote but hath had a wofull end? When did he dispute but hee duld all

his auditorie? his Poetry more spiritlesse than smal beere, his Oratory Arts bastard, not able to make a man rauishingly weepe, that hath an Onion at his eye. In Latin, like a louse, he hath manie legges, many lockes fleec'd from *Tullie*, to carry away and cloath a little body of matter, but yet hee moues but slowly, is apparaild verie poorely.[48]

Nashe saw that in Harvey he had an opponent whose best days were over, a man already defeated by life. It is little wonder that he sailed into battle with a fine confidence that his rival could not hope to emulate. But in addition to this kind of knowledge he had also the advantage of a finer literary sense. He does not hesitate to take Harvey up on matters of fact, and will even admit to the truth of accusations against himself that are not really damaging when by so doing he can make a telling rejoinder. For instance he acknowledges that he had been imprisoned in the Counter for debt, but instead of being ashamed of the fact he glories in it and says, 'there is no place of the earth like it, to make a man wise'.[49] In this way he builds up his own veracity and, at the same time, makes Harvey look a fool as well as a liar for denying that he had been imprisoned in the Fleet. But he reserves his sharpest and most damaging attacks for an assault on his opponent's style. He accuses him of writing 'reasty Rhetoricke' and 'pan-pudding prose', phrases in which the kitchen references bring out beautifully the painful absence of flavour and lightness from some of the prose of the *Four Letters*. He quotes the opening of the *Third Letter* and then adds the deadly comment: 'The body of mee, hee begins like a proclamation'.[50] Of Christopher Bird's letter he writes:

it is no letter, but a certificate (such as Rogues haue) from the headman of the Parish where hee was borne, *that* Gabriel *is an excellent generall Scholler, and his Father of good behauiour.*[51]

Again and again he makes use of his lively interest in all sorts of writing to draw odious comparisons. And, like Martin attacking Dr. Bridges, he jumps on the unwieldy length of Harvey's sentences:

I talke of a great matter when I tell thee of a period, for I know two seuerall periods or full pointes, in this last epistle, at least fortie lines long a piece.[52]

[48] I. 301–2. [49] I. 310. [50] I. 293.
[51] I. 273. [52] I. 329.

It is, however, in his vividly accurate diagnosis of Harvey's most fatal shortcoming as a satirist, his inability to be witty, that Nashe is most effective and most memorable. He sums up Gabriel's unavailing efforts at wit thus:

> High grasse that florisheth for a season on the house toppe, fadeth before the haruest cals for it, and maye well make a fayre shewe, but hath no sweetnesse in it. Such is this Asse *in presenti*, this grosse painted image of pride, who would faine counterfeite a good witte, but scornfull pittie, his best patron, knows it becomes him as ill, as an vnweldy Elephant to imitate a whelpe in his wantonnes.
>
> I wote not how it fals out, but his inuention is ouer-weapond; he hath some good words, but he cannot writhe them and tosse them to and fro nimbly, or so bring them about, that hee maye make one streight thrust at his enemies face.
>
> Coldly and dully *idem per idem*, who cannot indite? but with life and spirit to limne deadness it selfe, *Hoc est Oratoris proprium.*[53]

It is precisely the witty invention so evident here, the easy way in which the allusion to fencing is sustained so that the whole picture leaps to life, that Harvey cannot manage. The image of the 'vnweldy Elephant' is exactly right for him and to call him 'this Asse *in presenti*' is brilliantly clever. It is a punning allusion to Lily's Latin Grammar, in which the mnemonic for verbs of the first conjugation runs 'As in presenti, perfectum format in aui. Vt no nas naui: vocito vocitas vocitaui'. Nashe implies, of course, that Harvey (aui) is the perfect form of Ass (as).

It is not only the prose of the *Four Letters* that is pilloried in *Strange News*. The sonnets Harvey chose to include in it and his earlier experiments with the English hexameter receive even harder usage. It is possible to put up some kind of apology for his prose, but his poetry is quite indefensible. Cragged in diction, clumsy in metre and utterly shapeless, it should never have been published at all. It cries out to be burlesqued, and Nashe was not the man to let it cry in vain. At the beginning of his confutation of the *Four Letters* he makes for the poems at once, and says, 'there are a great many barefoote rimes in it, that goe as iumpe as a Fiddle with euery ballet-makers note'.[54] Later he amplifies this criticism. At the end of the First Letter Harvey had reproduced a sonnet on Greene, which, according to him, was the work of

[53] I. 282. [54] I. I. 265.

Christopher Bird. Nashe, however, chose to regard it—and he was probably right to do so—as the work of Harvey himself. It opens with these lines:

> *Greene*, the Connycatcher, of this Dreame the Autor,
> For his dainty deuise, deserueth the hauter.
> A rakehell: A makeshift: A scribling foole:
> A famous bayard in Citty, and Schoole.[55]

Nashe burlesques them thus:

> *Put vp thy smiter, O gentle Peter,*
> *Author and halter make but ill meeter.*
> I scorne to answer thy mishapen rime,
> Blocks haue cald schollers bayards ere this time.
>
> I would trot a false gallop through the rest of his ragged Verses, but that if I should retort his rime dogrell aright, I must make my verses (as he doth his) run hobling like a Brewers Cart vpon the stones, and obserue no length in their feete; which were *absurdum per absurdius*, to infect my vaine with his imitation.[56]

There is really no more to be said about the sonnet, though Nashe torments it further; the parody and the comment, with its expressive simile, place it very fairly in the ranks of doggerel where it belongs.

Nashe's superiority over Harvey, both in literary sense and in literary ability, makes itself felt again in his treatment of his opponent's experiments with the English hexameter. Unlike G. M. Young, who credits Harvey with a sense of humour for which his prose provides little evidence, and who suggests that he saw that the English hexameter lent itself to comic uses and exploited it for this purpose,[57] Nashe chose to regard the experiments as seriously meant. To him they appeared as ill-timed, unnatural and, above all, as something that was contrary to the natural genius of the English language. This conviction he expressed as follows:

> The Hexamiter verse I graunt to be a Gentleman of an auncient house (so is many an english begger), yet this Clyme of ours hee cannot thriue in; our speech is too craggy for him to set his plough in: hee goes twitching and hopping in our language like a man

[55] *Foure Letters*, pp. 11–12. [56] I. 275.

[57] G. M. Young, 'A Word for Gabriel Harvey' in *English Critical Essays: Twentieth Century*, ed. Phyllis M. Jones, London, 1933.

running vpon quagmiers, vp the hill in one Syllable, and down the dale in another, retaining no part of that stately smooth gate, which he vaunts himselfe with amongst the Greeks and Latins.[58]

There is no other piece of Elizabethan criticism more pointed and muscular than this. The uncertain movement of the English hexameters of the day, in all their clumsiness and ineptitude, has been caught and rendered in a series of arresting and accurate images, drawn from daily life. With these words the whole experiment has been placed, judged and found wanting. There are occasions in Nashe's writings when he shows some of the more tiresome traits of the humanists, but this is not one of them. His feeling for the native thew and sinew of English speech enables him to resist the claims of authority.

When he attacks Richard Harvey and then Gabriel on the grounds that they are excessively addicted to the employment of 'inkhorn terms', however, his criticism is far from ingenuous; he wields a stick that seemed convenient for beating his opponents with, without considering whether it fitted his hand or not. In fact it did not. He had never hesitated to coin new words himself whenever he felt the need for them, and, as we have seen already, when he came to write *Christ's Tears* he not merely invented neologisms on a large scale, but also in the new Address to the Reader, which he wrote for the issue of 1594, he defended his activities in so doing with considerable spirit, arguing that any man who sought to write moving prose had of necessity to borrow words from other tongues in order to counteract the excessively monosyllabic character of English. Nevertheless, he was not prepared to extend to Harvey the liberty that he claimed for himself. Accusing him of writing 'ouer-rackt absonisme', he culled from the *Four Letters* a collection of words and phrases that seemed to him to be examples of 'inkehornisme'. The result is the following list:

*Conscious mind*: *canicular tales*: *egregious an argument*; when as *egregious* is never vsed in *english but in the extreame ill part. Ingenuitie*: *Iouiall mind*: *valarous Authors*: *inckehorne aduentures*: *inckehorne pads*: *putatiue opinions*: *putatiue artists*: *energeticall persuasions*: *Rascallitie*: *materiallitie*: *artificiallitie*: *Fantasticallitie*: *diuine Entelechy*: *loud Mentery*: *deceitfull perfidy*: *addicted to Theory*: *the worlds great Incendiarie*: *sirenized furies*: *soueraigntie*

[58] I. 298–9.

> *immense*: *abundant Cauteles*: *cautelous and aduentrous*: *cordiall liquor*: *Catilinaries and Phillipicks*: *perfunctorie discourses*: *Dauids sweetnes olimpique*: *the Idee high and deepe Abisse of excellence*: *The only Vnicorne of the Muses*: *the Aretinish mountaine of huge exaggerations*: *The gratious law of Amnesty*: *amicable termes*: *amicable end*: *Effectuate*: *addoulce his melodie*: *Magy*: *polimechany*: *extensiuely emploid*: *precious Traynment*: *Nouellets*: *Notorietie*: *negotiation*: *mechanician.*[59]

It is a fascinating list, because it shows not, as Nashe intended it to do, the absurdities into which Harvey's fondness for new words led him, but the extent to which modern English is indebted to Harvey, and to scholars like him, for the wealth of its vocabulary. And there is no denying that in this part of the controversy Harvey showed himself more sensible and less shortsighted than his adversary, for in *Pierce's Supererogation* he retorted to this passage with a list of curious words and phrases, drawn from *Strange News*, that most modern readers will find far more outlandish than that brought together by Nashe out of the *Four Letters*. What he writes is of such general interest that it deserves to be quoted in full:

> He is of no reading in comparison that doth not acknowledge euery terme in those Letters [*Four Letters*] to be autenticall English; and allow a thousand other ordinary Pragmaticall termes, more straunge then the straungest in those Letters, yet current at occasion. The ignorant Idiot (for so I will prooue him in very truth) confuteth the artificiall wordes, which he neuer read: but the vayne fellow (for so he proooueth himselfe in word, and deede) in a phantasticall emulation presumeth to forge a mishapen rablement of absurde, and ridiculous wordes, the proper badges of his newfangled figure, called Foolerisme: such as *Inkhornisme*, *Absonisme*, *the most copious Carminist*, *thy Carminicall art*, *a Prouiditore of young Schollars*, *a Corrigidore of incongruitie*, *a quest of Caualieros*, *Inamoratos on their workes*, *a Theologicall Gimpanado*, *a Dromidote Ergonist*, *sacrilegiously contaminated*, *decrepite capacitie*, *fictionate person*, *humour unconversable*, *merriments vnexilable*, *the horrisonant pipe of inueterate antiquitie*; and a number of such Inkhornish phrases, as it were a pan of outlandish collops, the very bowels of his profoundest Schollerisme. For his eloquence poseth my intelligence, that cleapeth himselfe a *Callimunco* for pleading his Companions cause in his owne Apology, and me a *Pistlepragmos*, for defending

[59] I. 316.

my frendes in my Letters: and very artificially *interfuseth Finicallitie, sillogistrie, disputatiue right, hermaphrodite phrases, declamatorie stiles, censoriall moralizers, vnlineall vsurpers of iudgement, infamizers of vice, new infringement to destitute the inditement, deriding dunstically, banging abominationly, vnhandsoming of diuinityship, absurdifying of phrases, ratifying of truthable and Eligible English, a calme dilatement of forward harmfulnesse, and backward irefulnesse,* and how many sundry dishes of such dainty fritters? rare iunkets, and a delicate seruice for him, that compiled the most delitious Commentaries, *De optimate triparum.* And what say you Boyes, the flatteringest hope of your moothers, to a *Porch of Panim Pilfryes, Pestred with Prayses.* Dare the pertest, or deftest of you, hunt the letter, or hauke a metaphor, with such a Tite, tute, tate?[60]

This answer seems to me to gain in cogency from Harvey's readiness to admit that some of Nashe's odd phrases are the result of an attempt to burlesque the style of the *Four Letters,* and to be as complete a refutation of Nashe's charges as anyone could wish for. Nashe, however, obviously did not think so. Having cast his opponent for the *rôle* of the pedant, he stuck to this identification and renewed the onslaught on his vocabulary in *Have With You to Saffron-Walden,* a work already promised in *Strange News* which ends with a comic sonnet breathing defiance and including the lines:

> Ile heare no truce, wrong gets no graue in mee,
> Abuse pell mell encounter with abuse:
> Write hee againe, Ile write eternally.
> Who feedes reuenge hath found an endlesse Muse.
>
> . . . . . .
>
> Awaite the world the Tragedy of wrath;
> What next I paint shall tread no common path.[61]

The mockery here of the conventions of revenge tragedy is a plain enough indication that the threat is not meant over seriously, but the gusto with which the attitude is struck shows equally clearly that Nashe had thoroughly enjoyed writing *Strange News* and was ready to continue the war of words, should Harvey take up his bragging challenge. Furthermore, the manner in which *Strange News* is written emphasizes the essential difference between that

[60] *The Works of Gabriel Harvey,* ed. A. B. Grosart, The Huth Library, 1884, II. 275–6.

[61] I. 333–4.

work and the *Four Letters*. Varied though the materials of which it is composed are, Nashe's pamphlet, because it has a unity of tone deriving from the personality of its author, has some claim to be regarded as a work of art. From beginning to end it has one aim in view: to show Harvey as a vainglorious braggart, a hunter after applause, a man ashamed of his own humble origins and an incompetent writer in verse and prose, and, by so doing, to make him look ridiculous. Pursuing this one end, it achieves it. Any personal animus Nashe may have felt is subdued to a point where it does not conflict with the jeering, mocking technique he perfected to carry his purpose out. By comparison the *Four Letters*, with its multitude of targets and its inability to control and discipline the bitter resentments which gave rise to it, is not a work of art at all. Harvey does not dramatize his personality, as Nashe does, extending his humour even to himself; instead, he pours out his feelings in the manner of one obsessed by them. He is all too like the bear at the stake, deprived of freedom of movement by his emotional involvement in the things he writes about and, therefore, all the more vulnerable to the taunts of the skilful baiter.

## 3

Harvey's reaction to *Strange News* was immediate. That work was entered in the Stationers' Register on 12 January 1593, and probably published then or very soon afterwards. By 27 April he had finished a lengthy reply to it, entitled *Pierces Supererogation or a New Prayse of the Old Asse*, but at this point the story becomes extremely complicated. Publication did not follow for some time and Harvey went on adding bits to the pamphlet. There is a prefatory letter, dated 16 July 1593, 'at London', and there is a kind of appendix, made up of letters and sonnets from friends of Harvey, as well as some of his own sonnets. Included among these is a letter from John Thorius, an Oxford scholar, which is dated 3 August 1593. But still the work did not come out. There seem to be two reasons for the delay, which may well have worked together. First, if Nashe is to be believed, Harvey lodged with Wolfe, the printer, for 'three quarters of a yere',[62] i.e. from September 1592 to mid-July 1593, and he agreed to defray the charges of printing *Pierce's Supererogation*. His board and the cost of the

[62] III. 87.

printing together put him in Wolfe's debt to the tune of thirty-six pounds, a sum he was unable to pay.[63] Wolfe, therefore, had good cause to delay publication so long as he had any hope of recovering the money from Harvey. Secondly, there can be no doubt that friends of Nashe and Harvey were doing their best during the summer of 1593 to patch up a reconciliation between them. Both writers refer to these negotiations. According to Harvey, he tried to see Nashe personally but was unsuccessful. In his *New Letter*, which carries at the end the date 16 September 1593, he writes:

> I haue earnestly, and instantly craued personall conference: but that should seeme to make little for his purpose, or might haue bene graunted with less suite. All must be done by mediation of a third, and a fourth; and such an intercourse, as I may probably haue in some ielousie, though I conceiue well of the interposed persons.[64]

Nashe says much the same thing and insists that the first overtures for peace came from Harvey. In the new Epistle to the Reader, which he wrote for the second issue of *Christ's Tears* in 1594, he writes:

> Impious *Gabriell Haruey*, the vowed enemie to all vowes and protestations, plucking on with a slauish priuat submission a generall publike reconciliation, hath with a cunning ambuscado of confiscated idle othes, welneare betrayed me to infamie eternall, (his owne proper chaire of torment in hell.) I can say no more but the deuil and he be no men of their words.[65]

He repeats the same charge in *Have With You to Saffron-Walden*, where he says that Harvey published *Pierce's Supererogation* 'after (through your Frends intreatie) wee were reconcilde'.[66]

It is clear then that there were negotiations. It is also clear that by the beginning of September 1593, Nashe had been convinced that Harvey desired peace, for in the Epistle to the Reader, prefixed to *Christ's Tears* which was entered in the Stationers' Register on 8 September, he makes a very thorough and handsome apology for his earlier attacks. In the mood of repentance and con-

[63] III. 71 and 96.
[64] *The Works of Gabriel Harvey*, I. 286–7.
[65] II. 179–80. [66] III. 118.

trition out of which *Christ's Tears* came he bids farewell to 'fantasticall Satirisme' and then continues thus:

> Nothing is ther nowe so much in my vowes, as to be at peace with all men, and make submissiue amends where I haue most displeased. Not basely feare-blasted or constraintiuely ouer-ruled, but purely pacifycatorie suppliant, for reconciliation and pardon doe I sue to the principallest of them, gainst whom I profest vtter enmity. Euen of Maister Doctor *Haruey*, I hartily desire the like, whose fame and reputation (though through some precedent iniurious prouocations, and feruent incitements of young heads) I rashly assailed: yet now better aduised, and of his perfections more confirmedly perswaded, vnfainedly I entreate of the whole worlde, from my penne his worths may receiue no impeachment. All acknowledgements of aboundant Schollership, courteous well gouerned behauiour, and ripe experienst iudgement, doe I attribute vnto him. Onely with his milde gentle moderation, heervnto hath he wonne me.
>
> Take my inuectiue against him in that abiect nature that you would doe the rayling of a Sophister in the schooles, or a scolding Lawyer at the barre, which none but fooles wil wrest to defame.[67]

This is indeed an *amende honorable* which, one is safe in assuming, even the religious impulse that led to the writing of *Christ's Tears* would not have been sufficient in itself to prompt, had not Nashe had every reason to believe that Harvey really wished for peace and was ready to accept his apology in the spirit in which it was made. He had, therefore, good cause to feel annoyed and cheated when Harvey's only response to his offer was the publication of a further attack on him in the shape of *Pierce's Supererogation.* That this appeared after the publication of *Christ's Tears* is placed beyond all doubt by an explicit reference to it in the second Epistle to the Reader, where Nashe writes:

> vpon his [Harvey's] prostrate intreatie I was content to giue him a short Psalme of mercie: nowe, for repriuing him when he was ripe for execution, thus he requites me. Sixe and thirtie sheets of mustard-pot paper since that hath he published against me, wherein like a drunken begger he hath rayled most grossely, and imitated the rascally phrase of sunne-burnt rogues in the field.[68]

Six and thirty sheets is exactly the length of *Pierce's Supererogation* and the *New Letter* together, and this fact, coupled with Nashe's

[67] II. 12. [68] II. 180.

treatment of them as though they were one work, not two, leads McKerrow to conclude that they were issued together.[69]

Why did Harvey not accept Nashe's apology, and why was *Pierce's Supererogation* published after the apology had been made? These two problems admit of no easy answer; all one can do is to suggest possible motives and courses of events. As we have seen, Harvey was still in London on 16 July 1593, when he wrote the prefatory matter to *Pierce's Supererogation*, which, he tells his friends, 'was long sithence finished in writing, and is now almost dispatched in Print'.[70] Soon after this date, however, he must have returned to Saffron Walden, because it was from there that he wrote a long rambling letter to Wolfe, which was later published as *A New Letter of Notable Contents*. It is dated at the end 16 September 1593, and must have taken days to write. In it he thanks Wolfe for sending him a parcel of books and pamphlets and then, after some general remarks about books and contemporary writers, he passes on to the subject of his quarrel with Nashe, the projected reconciliation and *Christ's Tears*. His allusions to these matters are, however, so vague and obscure that it is impossible to say whether he had actually seen a copy of *Christ's Tears*, or whether he had merely heard about it from Wolfe or someone else. McKerrow, who tends to fall over backwards in his anxiety to be fair to Harvey, thinks that he had not seen Nashe's pamphlet when he wrote this letter and quotes the following passage from it as conclusive evidence on the matter:

> Till a *publique iniurie* be publiquely confessed, and *Print* confuted in Print, I am one of St. Thomas disciples: not ouer-prest to beleeue, but as cause causeth: and very ready to forgiue, as effect effecteth. They that know the daunger of *Truces*, and the couen of *Treatyes*, vt supra, must begge leaue to ground their repose vpon more *cautels* then one; and to proceede in terms of *suspence*, or *Pause*, till they may be resolued with infallible *assurance*. For mine owne determination, I see no credible hope of *Peace*, but in *Warre*: and could I not commaunde, that I desire, I am persuaded, I should hardly obteine, that I wish. I loue *Osculum Pacis*; but hate *Osculum Iudae*: and reuerence the *Teares of Christ*; but feare the *Teares of the Crocodile*.[71]

McKerrow says that it would have been absurd for Harvey 'to clamour for a "public injury to be publicly confessed" when he

[69] V. 102. [70] *Works of Gabriel Harvey*, II. 10. [71] *Ibid.*, I. 287.

had Nashe's confession and apology in print before him',[72] but he does not consider the possibility that Harvey may have been quite capable of behaving absurdly. Instead, he assumes that Harvey would have wished to suppress *Pierce's Supererogation* and, to account for its appearance, puts forward the hypothesis that it was published by Wolfe, without its author's consent, in order to recoup some of the money he had laid out in printing it before he discovered that he was not to be paid for his labour.[73] Even if it is sound, however, this hypothesis does nothing to exonerate Harvey from the responsibility for continuing the dispute, because, if publication took place against his wish, he could easily have made the fact public and still accepted Nashe's apology. He never did so, and his silence argues tacit compliance at the least, if not active participation.

I read the *New Letter* rather differently from McKerrow. He sees it as the work of a man 'who regrets the waste of time and would be glad to come to terms with his adversary, provided that he could with honour do so'.[74] But, in fact, I can see no difference between the assumption of superiority and moral magnanimity in this work and similar assumptions in the *Four Letters*. In both Harvey wishes to have it both ways: to create the impression that he is above such peccadilloes and to trounce his opponent. Moreover, the *New Letter* also makes it plain that he regarded *Pierce's Supererogation* as a knock-down blow and that he would have found it a very painful matter to suppress it. Nothing is more typical of the man than the high value he set on his own writings and the strong desire he felt to see himself in print. Nor am I as sure as McKerrow is that Harvey had not read *Christ's Tears* when he wrote the *New Letter*. For one who had never seen it he certainly knows a great deal about it. He is aware, for instance, that it is written in a different style from Nashe's other writings and says of it:

> I would be loth to aggrauate the least, or greatest particular against a Penitentiall soule: but still to haunt infamous, or suspected houses, tauernes, lewd company, and riotous fashions, as before, (for to this day his behauiour is no turnecoate, though his stile be a changeling) is a greater liberty in my small diuinity, then accordeth with that deuoute and most holy-holy profession.[75]

[72] V. 102. [73] V. 104. [74] V. 104.
[75] *Works of Gabriel Harvey*, II. 288.

He knows too that it contains some kind of recantation by Nashe. He writes:

> Did I not intend to deale a bountiful almes of Curtesie, who in my case would giue eare to the law of *Obliuion*, that hath the Law of *Talion* in his handes; or accept of a silly recantation, as it were a sory plaister to a broken shinne, that could knocke Malice on the head, and cut the windpipe of the railing throate?[76]

The physical violence of the last two images in this passage is indicative of the strength of Harvey's feelings on the matter, and in the end, I think, these feelings got the better of his more rational intention to behave generously. Nashe's apology could be interpreted as an abject submission and Harvey found the temptation to take it this way and to triumph over his enemy too much for him. In short, I think *Pierce's Supererogation* was published because its author was proud of it, because he thought it would put the seal on his victory over Nashe and because he wished it to be published. The statement about print 'being confuted in print' could easily be got round. Nashe's apology, though generous, is also vague. It refers only to Gabriel Harvey, not to his father or his brothers, and could, therefore, be stigmatized as inadequate in scope.

*Pierce's Supererogation* falls far short of Harvey's own opinion of it. It bears all the marks of hurried composition and does not lend itself easily to analysis. There is first an elaborate mass of prefatory matter, made up of an address 'To my very gentle and liberall frendes, Master Barnabe Barnes, Master Iohn Thorius. Master Antony Chewt', thanking them for their letters supporting him and condemning Nashe; of three sonnets, couched in a fantastic style, which purport to come from an 'excellent Gentlewoman', who proclaims her eagerness to take on Nashe with his own weapons; of a letter from Barnabe Barnes, requesting Harvey to publish *Pierce's Supererogation* forthwith, and of two sonnets from the same pen, one holding Nashe up to scorn as lewd of life and an enemy to learning, the other in praise of Harvey. And even then there is still 'The Printers Aduertisement to the Gentleman Reader' as a final obstacle between the audience and the text. The preliminaries over, Harvey begins by expressing his regret that he should be forced into wasting his precious time in writing

[76] *Ibid.*, I. 276.

pamphlets against 'the two impudentest mates [Greene and Nashe] that euer haunted the presse',[77] and promptly contradicts this avowal by launching into page after page of heavy-handed irony, designed to show that, for all his bragging, Nashe is a poor hand at raillery and abuse when compared with the old masters in these arts. Eventually he refers explicitly to *Strange News*, stating that his opponent has no proper sense of the value of letters, or of the achievements and importance of his contemporaries (a subject, incidentally, on which Harvey is both well informed and perceptive) and then goes on to protest against Nashe's cavalier handling of the *Four Letters*. He writes:

> He can raile: (what mad Bedlam cannot raile?) but the fauour of his railing, is grosely fell, and smelleth noysomly of the pumpe, or a nastier thing. His gayest floorishes, are but Gascoignes weedes, or Tarletons trickes, or Greenes crankes, or Marlowes brauados: his iestes, but the dregges of common scurrilitie, the shreds of the theater, or the of-scouring of new Pamflets: his freshest nippitatie, but the froth of stale inuentions, long since lothsome to quick tastes: his shrouing ware, but lenten stuffe, like the old pickle herring: his lustiest verdure, but rank ordure, not to be named in Ciuilitie, or Rhetorique: his only Art, and the vengeable drift of his whole cunning, to mangle my sentences, hack my arguments, chopp and change my phrases wrinch my wordes, and hale euery sillable most extremely; euen to the disioynting, and maiming of my whole meaning.[78]

There are some shrewd knocks here at Nashe's pride in his own originality, but in accusing him—quite rightly—of treating the *Four Letters* unfairly Harvey was playing into the hands of the humorist.

At this point Harvey drops the subject of Nashe entirely for the time being and turns his attention to another enemy in the person of John Lyly, using for the purpose a piece of invective which he had had lying by him for the last four years, since it is dated 5 November 1589. It is a reply to Lyly's attack on him in *Pap with a Hatchet* and is a contribution to the Marprelate controversy. Its resurrection after such a long interval is clear evidence of Harvey's readiness to bear a grudge and of his unwillingness to allow anything he had written to go unprinted, but it has no place whatever in *Pierce's Supererogation* and merely makes the work even more chaotic than it would otherwise have been.

[77] *Ibid.*, II. 34.    [78] *Ibid.*, II. 115.

Eventually he returns to Nashe once more, beginning more or less where he left off by attacking him for his railing and then, with complete illogicality, competing with him in the art of abuse. In the process he comes close to writing sheer nonsense, as when he describes the extraordinary terms that the mysterious gentlewoman, his ally, had used of Nashe:

> She doth him no wrong, that doth him right, like Astræa, and hath stiled him with an immortal penne; the *Bawewawe* of Schollars, the *Tutt* of Gentlemen, the *Tee-heegh* of Gentlewomen, the *Phy* of Citizens, the *Blurt* of Courtiers, the *Poogh* of good Letters, the *Faph* of good manners, and the *whoop-hoe* of good boyes in London streetes. Nash, Nash, Nash, (quoth a louer of truth, and honesty) vaine Nash, railing Nash, craking Nash, bibbing Nash, baggage Nash, swaddish Nash, rogish Nash, Nash the bell-weather of the scribling flocke, the swish-swash of the presse, the bumm of Impudency, the shambles of beastlines, the poulkat of Pouls-churchyard, the schrichowle of London, the toade-stoole of the Realme, the scorning-stocke of the world, and the horrible Confuter of foure Letters.[79]

He does much better when he resumes his jesting at the expense of Nashe's affectation of relying on mother-wit for his inventiveness and places him in the same category as, 'Thomas Delone, Philip Stubs, Robert Armin, and the common Pamfletters of London',[80] the popular writers whom Nashe despised. But even now he cannot keep to his main theme. He inserts a bitter attack on his old enemy, Dr. Perne, before he finally returns to Nashe and threatens him with more productions from the pen of the prolific and abusive gentlewoman already referred to. Eventually a conclusion is reached, but there still remains an appendix of letters and sonnets and, as though all this were not sufficient, 'The Printers Post-script', stating that he still has more matter by him from the pen of Thorius.

Interesting for what it tells us of Harvey's general attitude to life and of his awareness of much that was happening at the time, *Pierce's Supererogation* does not even begin as a literary composition, still less as an answer to Nashe. There are some sharp thrusts in it; Harvey enjoys tracking his opponent to his commonplaces and pouring scorn on his pretensions to originality; but the effect of his blows is largely lost in the irrelevances, reiterations and

[79] *Ibid.*, II. 272–3.   [80] *Ibid.*, II. 280–1.

general obscurity that surrounds them. The final impression one is left with is one of incoherence, disorder and, above all, of a complete inability on Harvey's part to know when he has said enough. Middleton in his *Father Hubburd's Tales* (1604) dismisses the whole flyting as 'but the running a Tilt of wits in Bookesellers shops, on both sides of *Iohn* of *Paules Churchyard*',[81] implying that the disputants engaged in it as a public entertainment to make money and, perhaps, that they were egged on by their respective publishers, but the evidence of the *Four Letters* and of *Pierce's Supererogation* points the other way. Both are the work of an angry man with whom the abuse and the impudence of Greene and Nashe really rankled, and became involved with other long-cherished resentments such as those he felt towards Dr. Perne and John Lyly.

About Nashe, on the other hand, Middleton is probably right. For him the quarrel was primarily the occasion for a literary exercise. It is true that he was obviously annoyed, as we have seen, by the publication of *Pierce's Supererogation* and took the first occasion that came his way to say to by producing a new Address to the Reader for the second issue of *Christ's Tears*, but even there he keeps his sense of humour, picking out the central weakness of *Pierce's Supererogation* and promising to return a fitting answer to it in due course:

> Maister *Lillie*, poore deceassed *Kit Marlowe*, reuerent Doctor *Perne*, with a hundred other quiet senslesse carkasses before the conquest departed, in the same worke he hath most notoriously and vilely dealt with; and to conclude, he hath proued him selfe to be the only *Gabriel* Graue-digger vnder heauen. Thrice more conuenient time I wil picke out to stretch him forth limbe by limbe on the racke, and a field as large as *Achilles* race to baite him to death with darts according to the custome of bayting buls in Spaine.[82]

The threat in the last sentence was duly carried out, and in 1596 John Danter published

> Haue with you to Saffron Walden. Or, Gabriell Harueys Hunt is vp. *Containing a full Answere to the eldest sonne of the Halter-maker*. Or, Nashe his Confutation of the sinfull *Doctor*. The Mott, or Posie, in stead of *Omne tulit punctum*: *Pacis fiducia nunquam. As much to say, as* I sayd I would speake with him.

[81] Quoted at V. 151. [82] II. 180–1.

The title conveys beautifully Nashe's sense that he had started the perfect quarry and that all that remained to be done was to set off in full cry after it, but, nevertheless, he took his time over the writing and exactly three years had elapsed since the appearance of the *New Letter* and *Pierce's Supererogation* when *Have With You to Saffron-Walden* was published. Aware of the discrepancy between the impression of spontaneity he sought to give and the actual facts of the case, Nashe begins his Address to the Reader by admitting that he has spent two or three years on and off working on it, but, he continues, he has had to do other things as well in order to live, for flyting pamphlets are not at all profitable. At the same time he also makes plain his own cool, detached attitude towards the whole business and his ability to see it all from the outside as a spectator might have done. To the imaginary critic, who accuses him of unnecessary delay, he answers:

> *Patientia vestra*, there is not one pint of wine more than the iust Bill of costs and charges in setting forth, to be got by anie of these bitter-sauced Inuectiues. Some foolish praise perhaps we may meete with, such as is affoorded to ordinarie Iesters that make sport: but otherwise we are like those fugitiue Priests in *Spaine* and *Portugall*, whom the Pope (verie liberally) prefers to Irish Bishoprickes, but allowes them not a pennie of any liuing to maintaine them with, saue onely certaine Friers to beg for them.
>
> High titles (as they of Bishops and Prelates), so of Poets and Writers, we haue in the world, when, in stead of their begging Friers, the fire of our wit is left, as our onely last refuge to warme vs.
>
> *Haruey* and I (a couple of beggars) take vpon vs to bandie factions, and contend like the *Vrsini* and *Coloni* in *Roome*; or as the *Turkes* and *Persians* about *Mahomet* and *Mortus Alli*, which should bee the greatest: and (with the *Indians*) head our inuentions arrowes with Vipers teeth, and steep them in the bloud of Adders and Serpents, and spend as much time in arguing *pro et contra*, as a man might haue found out the quadrature of the Circle in: when all the controuersie is no more but this, he began with mee, and cannot tell how to make an end; and I would faine end or rid my hands of him, if he had not first begun.
>
> I protest I doo not write against him because I hate him, but that I would confirme and plainly shew, to a number of weake beleeuers in my sufficiencie, that I am able to answere him: and his frends, and not his enemies, let him thanke for this heauie load of disgrace

> I lay vpon him, since theyr extreame disabling of mee in this kinde, and vrging what a triumph he had ouer me, hath made me to ransacke my standish more than I would.[83]

I have quoted this passage in full, first, because it shows that interest in the quarrel was confined largely to a restricted circle, that of poets and writers, which explains why *Have With You* went through only one edition, and secondly, because it is precisely the attitude expressed here which makes the pamphlet such a devastating reply. Nashe adds other reasons to account for his delay. One of them, that he had found it necessary to prostitute his pen in writing amorous poems for new-fangled gentlemen, I have discussed already in another connection;[84] the other is that he expected some of the other writers whom Harvey had attacked, and especially John Lyly, to assist him by defending themselves in print. The main reason, however, is surely that, unlike Harvey who dashed off *Pierce's Supererogation* in a hurry and a heat, Nashe took his time in order to make something really worth while of his answer, for in its own curious way *Have With You* is a most accomplished piece of writing, a rich mixture of parody, literary criticism, comic biography and outrageous abuse that nevertheless hangs together by virtue of the art that is lavished on it and of the sheer joy in caricature and in linguistic extravagance and inventiveness that informs it from beginning to end. All traces of malice disappear in the free play of a humour that transforms the frustrated, disappointed and in many ways depressing figure of Gabriel Harvey into a great comic character, a kind of Don Quixote for whom pedantry takes the place of chivalry. Nashe himself refers to *Have With You* at one point in it as a 'Comedie'.[85] To me the title seems to be fully justified.

The quickest and most obvious way of establishing that Harvey is indeed metamorphosed into a comic creation is to point to the picture drawn of his physical appearance. It occurs during the course of an account Nashe gives of how he and Harvey accidentally found themselves in the same inn at Cambridge some six months or so before *Have With You* was published. Harvey apparently desired to have some kind of meeting or conference when he discovered that his enemy was under the same roof with

[83] III. 18–19. [84] See pp. 52–9 above. [85] III. 69.

him, but Nashe refused for several reasons, not all of them serious and the last one far from it. He writes:

> If I had (I say) rusht in [to Trinity Hall] my selfe, and two or three hungrie Fellowes more, and cryde, Doo you want anie guestes? what, nothing but bare Commons? it had beene a question (considering the good-will that is betwixt vs) whether he wold haue lent me a precious dram more than ordinarie, to helpe disgestion: he may be such another craftie mortring Druggeir, or Italian porredge seasoner, for anie thing I euer saw in his complexion. That word complexion is dropt foorth in good time, for to describe to you his complexion and composition, entred I into this tale by the way, or tale I found in my way riding vp to *London.* It is of an adust swarth chollericke dye, like restie bacon, or a dride scate-fish; so leane and so meagre, that you wold thinke (like the Turks) he obseru'd four Lents in a yere, or take him for the Gentlemans man in the *Courtier*, who was so thin cheekd and gaunt and staru'd, that, as he was blowing the fire with his mouth, the smoke tooke him vp, like a light strawe, and carried him to the top or funnell of the chimney, wher he had flowne out God knowes whether, if there had not bin crosse barres ouerwhart that stayde him; his skin riddled and crumpled like a peice of burnt parchment; and more channels and creases he hath in his face than there be Fairie circles on *Salsburie Plaine*, and wrinckles and frets of old age than characters on Christs Sepulcher in *Mount Caluarie*, on which euerie one that comes scrapes his name and sets his marke to shewe that hee hath been there: so that whosoeuer shall behold him,
>
> *Esse putet Boreae triste furentis opus*,
>
> will sweare on a booke I haue brought him lowe, and shrowdly broken him: which more to confirme, look on his head, and you shall finde a gray haire for euerie line I haue writ against him; and you shall haue all his beard white too, by that time hee hath read ouer this booke. For his stature, he is such another pretie *Iacke a Lent* as boyes throw at in the streete, and lookes, in his blacke sute of veluet, like one of these ieat droppes which diuers weare at their eares in stead of a iewell.[86]

The whole technique of exaggeration by way of fantastic similes with which this figure is set before us has obvious affinities with that Shakespeare was soon to endow Falstaff with, and the portrait of Harvey here seems to me to anticipate the description given of Mr. Justice Shallow in *2 Henry IV*, III. 2, where he is said to be 'like a man made after supper of a cheeseparing'. By the

[86] III. 93–4.

time Nashe has finished his picture, Harvey has ceased to be a historical figure, bounded by place and time, and has become a timeless artefact. I would also like to stress the relative unimportance that Nashe attaches to the actual meeting, as compared with the portrait that it provided him with an excuse for writing. In this respect the passage quoted is a faithful reflection of the whole work. *Have With You*, once the lengthy, but effective, preliminaries are over, falls into three clearly defined sections: an oration by Harvey, made by stringing together passages and phrases culled from his works; a 'biography' of him, which forms the central part of the pamphlet; and, finally, a reply to *Pierce's Supererogation*. Of these three sections the last is far and away the scrappiest and least interesting. Nashe clearly put off writing it, because rebutting Harvey's charges mattered little or nothing to him in comparison with the creative impulse towards comedy that finds expression in the other two sections.

The 'Life', which is practically self-contained, is a clever compound of two different things. On the one hand, it is a genuine biography—in my view the liveliest life written in England in the sixteenth century, though historians of the biographical art all ignore it—in the sense that Nashe has taken the trouble to set out the main facts of his 'hero's' career in chronological order, and even to provide rough indications of when some, at least, of the events in it took place. It is distinctly possible that he did a certain amount of research for this purpose, for at the opening of *Have With You*, when meeting the allegation that he has taken far too long in composing it, he writes:

> nothing else in my defence I will alledge but *Veritas Temporis filia*, it is onely time that reuealeth all things: wherefore, though, in as short time as a man may learne to run at Tilt, I could haue gone thorough with inuention inough to haue run him thorough and confounded him, yet I must haue some further time to get perfect intelligence of his life and conuersation, one true point whereof, well set downe, wil more excruciate and commacerate him, than knocking him about the eares with his owne stile in a hundred sheetes of paper.[87]

But, while it is based on fact, the 'Life', as well as being the antithesis to the hagiographical biography, common at the time, in its exclusive concentration on all that is absurd, discreditable or

[87] III. 29.

unfortunate in its subject's history, is also a mock life, a piece of parody, as Nashe informs us immediately before he begins it when he remarks by way of introduction:

> here haue I set downe his whole life from his infancie to this present 96, euen as they vse in the beginning of a Book to set down the life of anie memorable ancient Author.[88]

The aptness of this particular model in the case of Harvey, the scholar and humanist, needs no underlining, and the choice of it leads to some excellent fooling. With the classical myths, the writings of the ancient biographers and, above all, the work of Livy, whom he explicitly mentions, in mind, Nashe invents a whole series of ominous dreams for Gabriel's mother which she dreams while she is pregnant with him, and then interprets them in terms of Harvey's later activities as omens of his contentiousness and addiction to scribbling. The last of them shows his witty fantasy in its liveliest and most mordant vein.

> At the same time (ouer and aboue) shee thought that, in stead of a boye (which she desired), she was deliuerd and brought to bed of one of these kistrell birds, called a wind-fucker [a kestrel]. Whether it be verifiable, or onely probably surmised, I am vncertaine, but constantly vp and downe it is bruted, how he pist incke as soon as euer hee was borne, and that the first cloute he fowld was a sheete of paper; whence some mad wits giu'n to descant, euen as *Herodotus* held that the *Aethiopians* seed of generation was as blacke as inke, so haply they vnhappely wold conclude, an *Incubus*, in the likenes of an inke-bottle, had carnall copulation with his mother when hee was begotten.[89]

In the same manner Nashe has his hero's birth accompanied by ridiculous prodigies and adds to them an appropriate conjunction of the planets. Moreover, there is a burlesque letter, purporting to come from his tutor at Cambridge to his father, predicting a great future for the hopeful lad, praising him for the wrong things in a whole series of neat, ironical thrusts at his ambitions and his pedantry, and, to keep the balance even, ending with some warnings about certain weaknesses in his character, including his tendencies towards vanity and contention.

The effect of this kind of thing is to turn Harvey into something not far removed from a mock-epic hero, and the actual incidents from his life that are selected for detailed treatment and

[88] III. 55. [89] III. 62.

elaboration endorse this impression. His whole career becomes a chronicle of blunders. When he attempts to become a courtier, as he did when the Queen visited Audley End, he makes himself a laughing-stock. When he attacks his old enemy, Dr. Perne, in print, Sir James Croft misinterprets it as an attack on himself and sends him to the Fleet. Where other men write pamphlets and sell them to a printer, Harvey has to pay the printer in order to get his published at all, and, consequently, runs into debt. In his poverty he is reduced to all kinds of shifts in order to maintain his dignity, yet they ultimately have the opposite effect and make him more absurd than ever in the eyes of the world. From all these experiences he learns nothing. No rebuff, however harsh, pierces the armour of his self-conceit. His last adventure, which is probably an invention of Nashe's, clinches the point in a truly dramatic fashion. In debt to his printer, Wolfe, to the tune of some thirty-six pounds—fact this—he is arrested by a couple of bailiffs and carried to Newgate gaol. Thereupon the following dialogue takes place between him and his captors:

> whither, quoth he, you villaines, haue you brought mee? To Newgate, good Master Doctour, with a lowe legge they made answer. I knowe not where I am. In Newgate, agayne replyed they, good Master Doctour: Into some blinde corner you haue drawne me to be murdred: to no place (replyed they the third time) but to Newgate, good Master Doctour. Murder, murder, (he cryed out): some body breake in, or they will murder mee. No murder but an action of debt, sayd they, good Master Doctour. O you prophane *Plebeyans*, exclaymed hee, I will massacre, I will crucifie you for presuming to lay hands thus on my reuerent person.[90]

Factually dubious, to say the least of it, these exchanges are artistically right in the way they sustain to the very end the character that Nashe has built up for his hero-victim of a man rendered impervious to fact by his own arrogance and lack of self-knowledge. There is more than a touch of Malvolio about it all, and Nashe's Harvey in Newgate is as much, or as little, deserving of pity, as Olivia's steward in the dark room. They belong to the same order of created being.

The presentation of Harvey in the 'Life' has already been prepared for and foreshadowed in *Have With You* by the Oration which Nashe puts into his mouth and which forms the first part

[90] III. 99.

of the work proper. It consists of 'miscreant words and sentences in the Doctours Booke' (i.e. *Pierce's Supererogation* and *A New Letter*), as Nashe describes them, words, phrases, and on occasions, passages of some length, culled from all over the place and then strung together to form a continuous whole. The prime function of the oration is, as McKerrow says, 'to exemplify and ridicule his style'.[91] Rare words and inkhorn terms, therefore, abound in it, but more than Harvey's vocabulary is involved in Nashe's criticism. Harvey deliberately cultivated what George Williamson has described as 'the Lipsian, hopping manner' of prose writing,[92] that is to say the use of terse, jerky phrases in opposition to the melodious copiousness, characteristic of so much Elizabethan prose. In his quest for pregnancy of utterance coupled with force, Harvey frequently becomes extremely obscure, and Nashe was able to lift two passages from one page of *Pierce's Supererogation* and run them together with the following result:

> Tell mee (I pray you), was euer *Pegasus* a cow in a cage, *Mercury* a mouse in cheese, Dexteritie a dog in a dublet, Legerdemaine a slow-worme, Viuacitie a lazy bones, Entelechie a slug-plum, Humanitie a spittle-man, Rhetorique a dummerell, Poetrie a tumbler, Historie a banqrout, Philosophie a broker?[93]

The passage condemns itself, and the same thing may be said of the rest of the 'Oration'; it is an admirable piece of literary criticism as well as an instrument for destroying Harvey. Faults of style, in the narrower sense of the word, are only part of what Nashe condemns and holds up to scorn in this section of *Have With You*. In *Pierce's Supererogation*, and still more in the *New Letter*, terseness of phrase is combined with an intolerable prolixity of statement. One enigmatic utterance is piled on another to form an untidy and often impenetrable heap of verbiage. In his crabbed eloquence Harvey loses all touch with reality. His periods have no relation to any clear or definite idea. This feature of his writing Nashe also seizes on in the 'Oration', and the mode of utterance he endows him with in it is exactly in keeping with the character he gives him in the 'Life'. Moreover, if one reads the 'Oration' through as a continuous whole, ignoring the interruptions from the audience that break it into fragments, it links up with

[91] IV. 302.

[92] George Williamson, *The Senecan Amble*, London, 1951.

[93] III. 43.

the 'Life' in another way. Purporting to be a self-defence, it proves to be a piece of self-applause. Harvey reckons up his various writings with the utmost complacency, places himself with Sir Philip Sidney as a poet and a humanist, dismisses Nashe and Greene as 'Impudencie and Slaunder' and, while protesting that he is above such petty squabbles, ends by virtually challenging Nashe to battle. The whole bent of the mind that produces the 'Oration' is the same as that which leads to the blunders and the disasters depicted in the 'Life'.

In these two sections of *Have With You* then, Nashe does something much more original and effective than what he had done in *Strange News*. The nearest that he comes to the method of the earlier work is in the final section, where he takes up and refutes some of the charges Harvey had brought against him. But even this part of the pamphlet is drawn into the comic mode of the whole, because he still retains in it the same dramatic form of presentation that he employs for the first two sections and which is a logical development from his earlier writings. In his prose generally he is always conscious of his audience, addressing them directly, inviting them to participate in what he is doing and even engaging in snatches of dialogue with them. In *Pierce Penilesse* he takes a further step in the direction of a more dramatic manner by introducing a second person in the shape of the Knight of the Post. In *Have With You* he goes further still; five characters are involved and the whole thing is cast in dialogue form, complete with speech headings. He says himself that he took his cue for doing so from William Bullein's popular *Dialogue against the Fever Pestilence* (1564),[94] but Bullein's example can have done no more than confirm a tendency already implicit in his earlier work. The four other characters who take part in *Have With You* are apparently based on historical figures with whom Nashe was friendly at the time.[95] Unfortunately it is impossible to establish their identity, though I would like to think that Domino Bentivole, who, 'beside true resolution and valure (wherewith he hath ennobled his name extraordinarie) and a ripe pleasant wit in conuersing, hath in him a perfect vnchangeable true habit of honestie',[96] is really Ben Jonson. In an appropriate setting, provided by 'some nooke or blind angle of the *Black-Friers*', the five friends meet and 'clap vp a *Colloquium* amongst them'. It takes the form

[94] III. 20. [95] III. 21. [96] III. 22.

of a judicial enquiry, shot through with hints of a doctoral disputation as well: a most ingenious mixture when one recalls that Harvey was a Doctor of Civil Law and that he apparently broke down in performing his Acts for that degree at Oxford in 1585.[97] Nashe himself plays the part of the Respondent, facing the charge that he has failed to answer Harvey and making good his defence by means of the 'Oration', the 'Life' and his 'Analysis' of *Pierce's Supererogation.* It is, of course, Harvey who is really on trial. The parts of the other four are best described in Nashe's own words:

> *Imprimis, Senior Importuno*, the Opponent.
>
> The second, *Grand Consiliadore*, chiefe Censor or Moderator.
>
> The third, *Domino Bentiuole*, one that stands, as it were, at the line in a Tennis-court, and takes euerie ball at the volly.
>
> The fourth, *Don Carneades de boone Compagniola*, who, like a busie Countrey Iustice . . . sets downe what proportion of iustice is to be executed vpon him [Harvey], and, when his backe hath bled sufficient, giues a signall of retrayt.[98]

The chief performer throughout is naturally Nashe himself, but the presence of the other four adds liveliness and variety and gives the whole thing the qualities of a debate. Of them, only Importuno sticks by and large to the task assigned him of stating the view, prevalent in literary circles at the time, that Nashe is unable to answer Harvey. The *rôle* of the others is substantially summed up in the analogy, drawn from tennis, that is used to describe Bentivole's part. They participate in a game of verbal tennis, or what Shakespeare calls 'a set of wit'. Nashe, the respondent, tosses the ball to them in the shape of some 'inkhornism', or absurdity of phrasing, taken from *Pierce's Supererogation*, and they then bat it gaily to and fro. If only these other performers had some distinguishing marks of character, or even of attitude, *Have With You* would be well on the way to something like a Peacock novel. But they have not. All Nashe can endow them with is his own verbal dexterity and an aptitude for indulging in elaborate logic-chopping, which results in some good learned fooling, as in the discussion about the relationship between a halter and despair,[99] which recalls similar things in *Summer's Last Will and Testament*, a work written with something like the same audience in view.

[97] See Gabriel Harvey's *Marginalia*, p. 50.

[98] III. 21. [99] III. 59–60.

The presence of these other figures, shadowy though they are in themselves, and the comments that they make, serve to underline Nashe's stylistic virtuosity. And this is as it should be, for *Have With You* is, after all, Nashe against Harvey, and the final impressions one is left with after reading it are, first, of the truly comic figure that Harvey cuts in it, and, secondly, of the sheer skill of his opponent as a conjurer with words. Never before had Nashe handled the English language with quite the same audacity and ease, or put it to such a variety of uses, as he does here. To find a parallel to it, apart from Urquhart's translation of Rabelais, one has to look ahead for more than three hundred years to the work of James Joyce. At one end of the scale he can, when he wishes, produce a simple, direct, conversational prose that sounds completely natural and authentic. The words with which Importuno greets Nashe at the opening of the work are of this kind. He says:

> What, *Tom*, thou art very welcome. Where hast thou bin this long time; walking in Saint *Faiths* Church vnder ground, that wee neuer could see thee? Or hast thou tooke thee a Chamber in *Cole-harbour*, where they liue in a continuall myst, betwixt two Brew-houses?[100]

At the other end of the scale, there is the elaborate, punning, allusive manner of the opening words of the Dedicatory Epistle, which begins with mock formality and then suddenly explodes like a fire-cracker, into a dazzling display of inventiveness that comes close to pure nonsense. The dedicatee in this case was not a great man, but Richard Lichfield, the barber of Trinity College, and the dedication itself is a burlesque. Lichfield was chosen for a number of reasons—all of them literary. In the first place, being a barber he was by definition an enemy to barbarism; and barbarism, in the sense of violence to, and misusage of, the English language, was one of the main things Harvey was to be convicted of. Secondly, his two main activities, the letting of blood and the trade of shaving and trimming, of lopping off superfluities, were both relevant to Nashe's purpose. Thirdly, Lichfield, whether 'a respectable man' or not, bore the name Richard, which was also the name of Harvey's astrological brother, and Nashe had already had rare fun in the main body of the work

[100] III. 25.

out of tossing the name 'Dick' about. All these fertile possibilities are exploited to the full in the Dedication, which begins thus:

> To the most Orthodoxall and reuerent Corrector of staring haires, the sincere and *finigraphical rarifier of prolixious rough barbarisme, the thrice egregious and censoriall animaduertiser of vagrant moustachios, chiefe scauinger of chins, and principall Head-man of the parish wherein he dwells, speciall superuisor of all excrementall superfluities for Trinitie Colledge in* Cambridge, *and (to conclude) a not able and singular benefactor to all beards in generall,* Don Richardo Barbarossa de Caesario, Thomas Nashe *wisheth the highest* Toppe *of his contentment and felicitie, and the* Shortning *of all his enemies.* Acute and amiable Dick, not *Dic mihi, Musa, virum,* Musing Dick, that studied a whole yeare to know which was the male and female of red herrings: nor *Dic obsecro,* Dick of all Dickes, that, in a Church where the Organs were defac'd, came and offred himselfe with his pipe and taber: nor old Dick of the Castle, that, vpon the newes of the losse of *Calis,* went and put a whole bird-spit in the pike of his buckler: nor Dick Swash, or Desperate Dick, that's such a terrible Cutter at a chyne of beefe, and deuoures more meate at Ordinaries in discoursing of his fraies and deep acting of his slashing and hewing, than would serue halfe a dozen Brewers Dray-men: nor *Dick of the Cow,* that mad Demilance Northren Borderer, who plaid his prizes with the Lord *Iockey* so brauely: but paraphrasticall gallant Patron Dick, as good a fellow as euer was Heigh, fill the pot, hostesse: curteous Dicke, comicall Dicke, lively Dicke, louely Dicke, learned Dicke, olde *Dicke of Lichfield, Iubeo te plurimum saluere,* which is by interpretation, I ioy to heare thou hast so profited in gibridge.[101]

The learned and the popular, Horace's *Ars Poetica* and the border ballad, have been laid under contribution by an imagination that works in terms of puns, verbal association and parody to create an impression of ebullient high spiritedness. Nashe slaps the barber on the back with words.

Between the two extremes represented by these two passages Nashe ranges freely, and his stylistic technique is adequate to every demand he makes on it, whether it be for wild exaggeration, as when he describes the arrival of Harvey's book at his door, for comic threats, for a mock grace, for picturesque abuse, or for the vigorous literary criticism that, after stating that *Pierce's Super-*

[101] III. 5–6.

*erogation* is divided into four parts, dismisses the whole thing with the deadly accurate remark:

> Neither are these parts seuerally distinguished in his order of handling, but, like a Dutch stewd-pot, iumbled altogether, and linsey-wolsey wouen one within another.[102]

Whether Harvey recognized just how devastating *Have With You* is and how unanswerable, it is impossible to say. The fact remains that he did not answer it. In 1597 one further contribution to the controversy, in the shape of a pamphlet called *The Trimming of Tom Nashe* from the pen of one Don Richardo de Medico Campo, was published by Philip Scarlet, after being entered in the Stationers' Register to Cuthbert Burby on 11 October. This has been attributed to Harvey, but to me the attribution seems wrong. In the first place the style, which is direct and pedestrian, apart from a few Euphuistic touches, is quite unlike Harvey's characteristic mixture of the terse and the elaborate. Secondly, there is no sign whatever in *The Trimming* of the erudition so evident in all his authentic writings. Finally, and I think quite conclusive in its implications, there is the fact that not one of Nashe's gibes at Harvey and his brothers, or of his stories against him in *Have With You*, is so much as touched on. It is inconceivable that Harvey could have written any kind of answer without giving his own version of why he did not accept Nashe's apology, or of what happened in London while he was writing *Pierce's Supererogation*, without refuting the charge that Wolfe had him clapped into Newgate for debt, and without so much as mentioning the occasion when he and Nashe stayed at the same inn in Cambridge. If one thing is certain about Gabriel Harvey, it is his extreme touchiness in all matters affecting his dignity. *Have With You* must have hurt him badly by its presentation of him as a blundering, grotesque clown. But the author of *The Trimming* has not been hurt at all and, as McKerrow points out,[103] he does not concern himself at all with *Have With You* proper, he deals simply and solely with the Dedicatory Epistle to it. In fact there are no grounds for attributing the authorship to anyone other than Richard Lichfield himself, 'Barber Chirurgion to Trinitie Colledge in Cambridge', as he is described on the title-page.

According to what the author of it says, *The Trimming* was

[102] III. 117. [103] V. 107.

composed in some three weeks or so during the spring of 1597, but this statement cannot be true of all of it, since about two-thirds of the way through it refers to the trouble Nashe got into with the Privy Council on account of his share in *The Isle of Dogs*, the playing of which was restrained on 28 July 1597. Nashe almost certainly meditated an answer to *The Trimming*, for at the opening of *Lenten Stuff* he remarks:

> in my exile and irkesome discontented abandonment, the silliest millers thombe or contemptible sticklebanck of my enemies is as busie nibbling about my fame as if I were a deade man throwne amongest them to feede vpon . . . But let that passe, though they shal find I wil not let it passe when time serues, I hauing a pamphlet hot a brooding that shall be called the *Barbers warming panne*.[104]

From this it looks as though he did not think *The Trimming* was the work of Harvey, whom he could hardly have regarded as small fry. But in any case any further development of the controversy was checked abruptly on 1 June, when Whitgift and Bancroft issued an order prohibiting the further printing of satires and ended their list of banned works with the following injunction:

> That all NASSHES bookes and Doctor HARVYES bookes be taken wheresoeuer they may be found and that none of theire bookes be euer printed hereafter.[105]

The order seems to have been aimed primarily at works which were regarded as pornographic, or as dangerously critical of existing institutions and attitudes, but it is not easy to see how the writings that came out of the Harvey-Nashe controversy could fall into either of these categories. Perhaps the chief offence of the disputants in the eyes of the bishops lay in the fact that they raked up the embers of the old Marprelate troubles in which their quarrel had had its beginnings.

[104] III. 153.
[105] *Transcript of the Stationers' Registers*, ed. Arber, iii. 677.

# VIII

## 'NASHE'S LENTEN STUFF'

WE know that in 1595 Nashe, when he was in London, lived at the house of the printer and book-seller John Danter,[1] much as Harvey lived with his printer Wolfe, and it is quite likely that he had been doing so since 1593. In these circumstances he may well have found himself engaged in dull and boring hack-work, including, perhaps, the correction of proofs. Something of the kind certainly seems to be implied, as E. H. Miller points out,[2] by two passages in the *Parnassus Plays* where Ingenioso admits 'I remaine thrise humblie and most affectionatly bounde to the right honorable printing house for my poore shiftes of apparell', and also states 'if pouerty presse not too much; Ile correct no presse but the presse of the people'.[3] But, whatever it was that he did, it hardly sufficed to keep his head above water, as we discover from the private letter which he wrote to William Cotton some time between 10 August and 9 October 1596.[4] Bawdy and scatological, the letter nevertheless paints a most interesting picture of his difficulties and of his reactions to them. He relates how he has stayed on in London during the summer vacation, even though he has been 'earnestly inuited elsewhere', waiting 'vpon had I wist hopes, and an after haruest I expected by writing for the stage and for the presse'. Neither patrons, the stage, nor the press, however, have brought him any gain. The players in question, the Lord Chamberlain's Men, were involved in a dispute with the Lord Mayor and

[1] III. 115.

[2] E. H. Miller, *The Professional Writer in Elizabethan England*, Harvard University Press, 1959, p. 168.

[3] *Op. cit.*, pp. 143 and 228.

[4] V. 192–6.

Corporation of London, who had finally succeeded in expelling them 'from the City inns which had long been their head-quarters', and had gone to Faversham,[5] while the book-sellers were interested only in topical ballads dealing with Essex's recent voyage. He also has a good deal to say about the stir caused by Harington's pamphlet the *Metamorphosis of Ajax*. He is in fact still reiterating the old complaint he had voiced at the beginning of his career in the *Anatomy of Absurdity* that work of merit stands little chance in competition with trash and with the topical and the sensational. Nevertheless, he is in good spirits and he concludes as follows:

> well some men for sorrow singe as it is in the ballet of Iohn Carelesse in the booke of martirs, and I am merry whe[n] I haue nere a penny in my purse. God may moue you though I say nothing, in which hope that that which wilbee shalbe I take my leaue.

Impecunious and reduced to begging, Nashe is not importunate and still keeps up the gay, carefree attitude to poverty that he had adopted as his own in *Pierce Penilesse* and made an essential part of his literary personality, which is exactly the same in this private letter, that has survived by chance, as it is in his public writings. It is little wonder that those who knew him wrote of him with affection. His spirit in the face of adversity compels admiration.

It may be presumed that the publication of *Have With You* at about the time that the letter to Cotton was written brought him in something, but he soon had to turn to his pen once more. He began a comedy called the *Isle of Dogs* which he describes in *Lenten Stuff* as 'that infortunate imperfit Embrion of my idle houres', carefully adding the following side-note by way of explanation:

> An imperfit Embrion I may well call it, for I hauing begun but the induction and first act of it, the other foure acts without my consent, or the least guesse of my drift or scope, by the players were supplied, which bred both their trouble and mine to.[6]

These words need to be interpreted with some caution. We can be sure that Nashe would not have handed over the imperfect work to the players—in this case probably Pembroke's Men[7]—without being paid for it. The sale of an incomplete work was not uncommon and, once it had been handed over and paid for, the author

[5] E. K. Chambers, *The Elizabethan Stage*, II. 195.
[6] III. 153–4.
[7] E. K. Chambers, *The Elizabethan Stage*, III. 454.

had no further rights in it. Nashe, therefore, had no legitimate grounds for complaining, as he does, about what the players did with it and, in all probability, would never have thought of complaining but for the trouble that followed. The play was then completed by the young Ben Jonson and put on some time in the summer of 1597 before 28 July, when the theatres were closed. Its performance led an informer to state to the Privy Council that it was 'a lewd plaie . . . contanynge very seditious and sclanderous matter',[8] and on the strength of this intelligence orders were given for a restraint to be put on all the theatres. On top of this, Ben Jonson and two of the players concerned were committed to prison, and Richard Topcliffe, the well-known intelligencer, was given the task of searching Nashe's lodgings and perusing his papers. Nashe, however, appears to have got wind of what was happening, which rather argues that he may have been expecting trouble and, to use his own words, 'was glad to run from' the storm, a description of his behaviour which he later expands thus:

> Auoide or giue grounde I did; *scriptum est*, I will not goe from it: and *post varios casus*, variable Knight arrant aduentures and outroades and inroades, at greate Yarmouth in Norfolke I arived in the latter ende of Autumne.[9]

From this account it would appear that his journey to Yarmouth had been by roundabout ways, in order to avoid apprehension, and by no means free from incident. But on his arrival there his troubles seem to have ended, for he goes on to relate that he was treated with great kindness and hospitality and that he stayed for some six weeks. The idea of writing a pamphlet in praise of Yarmouth, as a mark of appreciation for the refuge it gave him, appears to have come to him during the course of his stay, but the actual writing was done in the Lent of 1598[10] 'in the countrey'.[11] Exactly what this last phrase means it is hard to say, beyond the fact that it clearly implies he was not in London, which was still, presumably, too hot for him to venture there. This conclusion is endorsed by the fact that he also mentions 'my learned counsell' at this point, from which it would appear that he was taking legal advice. But by the

[8] V. 31, note 2.

[9] III. 154.

[10] III. 151 and 160.

[11] III. 176.

time the work was in the press he must either have made his peace with the authorities, or the storm raised by the *Isle of Dogs* had blown itself out, for he tells us at the end of his Epistle to the Reader, 'I am cald away to correct the faults of the presse, that escaped in my absence from the Printing house.'[12] He must, therefore, have been back in London round about 11 January 1599, when the work was entered in the Stationers' Register. Publication must have followed soon afterwards, for on 1 June, as we have seen, came the order prohibiting the printing of any further work by Nashe or Harvey.

*Lenten Stuff* is very much a product of the circumstances in which it was written. It is quite the most idiosyncratic and, in some ways, also the most brilliant and witty of all Nashe's writings. It is peculiarly fitting that it should be the last of his works, for in it he carries his manner and method to their logical conclusion. It is difficult to see how he could possibly have developed them further. Some indication of the pamphlet's character is given by its title:

> Nashes Lenten Stuffe, Containing, The Description and first Procreation and Increase of the towne of Great Yarmouth in Norffolke: With a new Play neuer played before, of the praise of the RED HERRING. Fitte of all Clearkes of Noblemens Kitchins to be read: and not vnnecessary by all Seruing men that haue short boord-wages, to be remembred. *Famam peto per vndas.*

It is a catchpenny title. In using his own name in this way, as well as in his reference to 'a new Play', Nashe was almost certainly cashing in on the general interest aroused by the whole business of the *Isle of Dogs*. There is also, however, the implication that Nashe's Lenten Stuff will have a distinct flavour from anyone else's. It looks as though he now felt that he had finally achieved the objective he had set himself of creating a recognizable literary personality. Moreover, Lenten Stuff, the food proper to Lent, also has several significances. Referring primarily, of course, to the red herring, his ostensible theme, it also indicates the time when the pamphlet was composed, the penurious and trying state he was in and, perhaps, his readiness to do penance for his misdemeanours and regain the favour of the Privy Council. It could even be a pointer to the exiguous materials out of which the whole

[12] III. 152.

thing was spun, for there are no personalities and very little social satire in *Lenten Stuff*, apart from the girding at the activities of intelligencers as a class, of which there is a good deal. Indeed, the whole work could well be regarded as a challenge to these men to exercise their talents for misinterpretation on the heterogeneous materials of which it is composed. But for the fact that the Oxford English Dictionary can produce no example of the metaphorical use of the term 'red herring', in the sense of a false scent, before 1892, I would think that it was this meaning of the word that Nashe had uppermost in his mind when writing *Lenten Stuff*, for it consists of one red herring after another. And, in spite of the evidence produced by the Dictionary, I am loath to abandon the idea, since Nashe himself knew and mentions the use of the red herring by hunters. In the last part of his pamphlet, where he is reckoning up the virtues of the fish and the wide variety of uses it can be put to, he writes: 'Next, to draw on hounds to a sent, to a redde herring skinne there is nothing comparable.'[13]

What is clear in any case is that after the trouble over the *Isle of Dogs* Nashe had to step warily. He could be certain that anything from his pen would be submitted to close scrutiny and he therefore had to mute any impulse towards social satire that he may have felt. To allow his talents for observation and caricature full play would have been dangerous. Consequently he was thrown back on books and learning as a source of material. But here also there were obstacles. The circumstances of his flight from London had prevented him from taking his note-books with him. He laments their absence when, after describing how the idea of writing something in praise of Yarmouth came to him, he continues thus:

> But this I must giue you to wit, how euer I haue tooke it vpon me, that neuer since I spouted incke was I of woorse aptitude to goe thorow with such a mighty March brewage as you expect, or temper you one right cup of that ancient wine of *Falernum*, which would last fourty yeere, or consecrate to your fame a perpetuall temple of the Pine-trees of *Ida*, which neuer rot. For besides the loud bellowing prodigious flaw of indignation stird vp against me in my absence and extermination from the vpper region of our celestiall regiment, which hath dung mee in a maner downe to the infernall bottome of desolation, and so troubledly bemudded with

[13] III. 221.

> griefe and care euery cell or organ-pipe of my purer intellectuall faculties, that no more they consort with any ingenuous playful merriments, of my note-books and all books else here in the countrey I am bereaued, whereby I might enamell and hatch ouer this deuice more artificially and masterly, and attire it in his true orient varnish and tincture; wherefore heart and good wil, a workman is nothing without his tooles; had I my topickes by me in stead of my learned counsell to assist me, I might haps marshall my termes in better aray, and bestow such costly coquery on this *Marine magnifico* as you would preferre him before tart and galingale, which *Chaucer* preheminentest encomionizeth aboue all iunquetries or confectionaries whatsoeuer.[14]

The effect of this deprivation was to stimulate Nashe's inventiveness and to make him rely on materials accessible in Yarmouth itself. The main sources of *Lenten Stuff* are two: first, works that he knew well and had used often, such as Cornelius Agrippa and Hakluyt; secondly, Camden's *Britannia* and 'a Chronographycal Latine table'[15] which hung in the Guildhall at Yarmouth and of which there seems to have been an English translation. McKerrow deduces the existence of the translation from the large number of close parallels between Nashe's account of the history of Yarmouth and that contained in the so-called Manship Manuscript. Supposed to have been written by one Henry Manship the elder round about 1562, this manuscript, at the time when Nashe was at Yarmouth, was probably in the possession of Manship's son, also called Henry, who later compiled a history of the town.[16] The exact relationship between the manuscript and the relevant passages of *Lenten Stuff* is obscure, but there can be no doubt that they go back to a common original. The matter is of some importance, because a comparison between the passages in the manuscript and Nashe's handling of the same material provides some useful insights into his manner of working.

The difficulties forced on him by his fear of informers on the one hand, and the inaccessibility of his note-books on the other, Nashe took as a challenge to his virtuosity. In the prefatory epistle addressed 'To his Readers, hee cares not what they be', he makes a full and valuable statement about his intentions and the means he has used to carry them out. After answering an imaginary inter-

[14] III. 175–6. [15] III. 161. [16] IV. 372–3.

locutor, who wants to know the significance of the title, he continues:

> This is a light friskin of my witte, like the prayse of iniustice, the feuer quartaine, *Busiris*, or *Phalaris*, wherein I follow the trace of the famousest schollers of all ages, whom a wantonizing humour once in their life time hath possest to play with strawes, and turne molehils into mountaines.
>
> Euery man can say Bee to a Battledore, and write in prayse of Vertue and the seuen Liberall Sciences, thresh corne out of the full sheaues and fetch water out of the Thames; but out of drie stubble to make an after haruest, and a plentifull croppe without sowing, and wring iuice out of a flint, thats *Pierce a Gods name*, and the right tricke of a workman. Let me speake to you about my huge woords which I vse in this booke, and then you are your own men to do what you list. Know it is my true vaine to be *tragicus Orator*, and of all stiles I most affect and striue to imitate *Aretines*, not caring for this demure soft *mediocre genus*, that is like wine and water mixt togither; but giue me pure wine of it self, and that begets good bloud, and heates the brain thorowly: I had as lieue haue no sunne, as haue it shine faintly, no fire, as a smothering fire of small coales, no cloathes, rather then weare linsey wolsey. Apply it for me, for I am cald away to correct the faults of the presse, that escaped in my absence from the Printing-house.[17]

*Lenten Stuff*, then, belongs to a definite literary tradition, that of learned trifling, the mock encomium, of which the most important and distinguished example in the sixteenth century was Erasmus's *Encomium Moriae*. As such it is to be burlesque in character and to rely for its effect on a comic contrast between low matter and a high-faluting style. Mockery is to be of its essence. Nevertheless, there seems to be serious intent in Nashe's refusal to have anything to do with 'this demure soft *mediocre genus*' of prose. This description must be derived from Vives's *De Ratione Dicendi*, where, in distinguishing the middle style of writing from the lofty on the one side and the low on the other, the great humanist writes: *Est alia mediocris, et ut Seneca dicit, plana et placida*.[18] Nashe's scornful version of Vives's words contrasts vividly with Ben Jonson's approving appropriation of them in the *Discoveries*.[19] Much as he and Jonson had in common in some

[17] III. 151–2.
[18] Quoted from *Ben Jonson*, ed. Herford and Simpson, XI. 271.
[19] *Ibid.*, VIII. 625.

respects, they were on opposite sides in the battle about style and language. Like the Elizabethan poets, Nashe was in favour of the ornate and the artificial; as the passage I quoted earlier[20] demonstrates, he saw some similarity between his art and that of heraldry with its reliance on gilding and rich colouring to confer distinction on the undistinguished and antiquity on the new. By 'artificial' however, Nashe clearly understood 'clever'; the common word, or the colloquial phrase, not normally used in writing, were as proper to it as the 'huge word' or elaborate circumlocution.

Writing on a trivial subject, Nashe chooses a suitable dedicatee in the shape of a certain Humphrey King, about whom nothing is known except that he was the author of a pamphlet in verse entitled, *An halfe-penny-worth of wit, or the hermites tale*. His insignificance was, of course, in keeping with Nashe's burlesque purpose, but he also seems to have been chosen as patron because of his fondness for poetry and for drink. He may well represent the kind of audience Nashe had in mind. To the modern reader it may appear that that audience must have been a restricted one, for a nimble mind and the knowledge necessary to enjoy burlesque seem essential qualifications for the appreciation of this *jeu d'esprit*. Such an audience could, however, have been considerably larger than one is at first willing to imagine. Much of the clowning in Elizabethan drama makes similar demands, yet it was extremely popular, and *Lenten Stuff* is, above all else, clowning. The *rôle* was a familiar one for Nashe and he is fully conscious of it. Adapting the old fable of Midas to his purpose and giving it a distinctly fishy application, he writes:

> to shoote my fooles bolt amongst you, that fable of *Midas* eating gold had no other shadow or inclusiue pith in it, but he was of a queasie stomacke, and nothing hee could fancie but this newe found guilded fish, which *Bacchus* at his request gaue him, (though it were not knowne here two thousand yeare after, for it was the delicates of the gods, and no mortall foode til of late yeares.)[21]

*Lenten Stuff* is a whole sheaf of fool's bolts. The comic, but not on the face of it very fertile, topic of the kipper is made to yield some eighty pages of colourful writing by a skilful use of digression that anticipates the methods of Swift and of Sterne. Beginning with an account of the troubles over the *Isle of Dogs* which led him

[20] P. 238 above. [21] III. 193.

to seek refuge in Yarmouth, Nashe goes on to contrast the welcome he received there with the unfavourable reception Homer was supposed to have had in the cities of Greece that later vied with each other to claim him as their own. He makes it the occasion for a piece of mockery and writes as follows, deliberately putting Homer in the position of the professional writer in Elizabethan England:

> That good old blind bibber of *Helicon*, I wot well, came a begging to one of the chiefe citties of Greece, and promised them vast corpulent volumes of immortallity, if they would bestowe vpon him but a slender outbrothers annuity of mutton and broth, and a pallet to sleep on; and with derision they reiected him; wherupon he went to their enemies with the like proffer, who vsed him honourably, and whome hee vsed so honourably, that to this daye, though it be three thousand yeare since, their name and glorie florish greene in mens memory through his industry. I truste you make no question but those dull pated pennifathers, that in such dudgen scorne reiected him, drunck deep of the soure cup of repentance for it, when the high flight of his lines in common brute was ooyessed. Yea, in the worde of one no more wealthy then hee was, (wealthy saide I? nay I'le be sworne hee was a grande iurie man in respect of me,) those graybeard Huddle-duddles and crusty cum-twangs were strooke with such stinging remorse of their miserable Euclionisme and snudgery, that hee was not yet cold in his graue but they challenged him to be borne amongst them.[22]

As well as enabling Nashe to get in a slap at that old target of his, the niggardly patron, this digression is an excellent example of his method of using 'huge words' to 'enamell and hatch ouer' a device. In it there are no fewer than five words, *ooyessed*, *Huddle-duddle*, *cum-twang*, *Euclionisme* and *snudgery*, which seem to be nonce-words, since no other instance of their use is recorded in the *O.E.D.*, and one, *dudgen*, which appears to have been first used in this sense of *mean* or *contemptible* in the *Almond*. Yet, nonce-words though the five may be, all would have been immediately intelligible to the original audience for which *Lenten Stuff* was written. *Ooyessed* and *snudgery* are adapted from words in current use at the time, *Euclionisme* is derived from Euclio, the miser in Plautus's *Aulularia*, and *Huddle-duddles and crusty cum-twangs* is a picturesque variant on a phrase used by Lyly in *Euphues* to

[22] III. 155.

describe an old miser: 'Though Curio be olde huddle and twang, ipse.'[23] Much of the effect of *Lenten Stuff* derives directly from writing of this kind. The 'huge words' call attention to themselves by their originality, yet they have their roots in common speech or common knowledge. As a result they are striking without being obscure.

He uses something of the same technique in his account of the history of Yarmouth which, he openly states, he included in order to give more bulk to his trifling theme. His way of putting it, however, is characteristically figurative. He writes:

> There be of you, it may be, that will account me a paltrer, for hanging out the signe of the redde Herring in my title page, and no such feast towards for ought you can see. Soft and faire, my maisters, you must walke and talke before dinner an houre or two, the better to whet your appetites to taste of such a dainty dish as the redde Herring.[24]

The account of Yarmouth and its history is largely a collection of scraps drawn from other writers, though Nashe had, of course, local knowledge and his pride in the town and its achievement and standing is genuine enough. His handling of his second-hand material has much in common with the way he had already treated chronicle history in *The Unfortunate Traveller*. A comparison between the sober version of the 'Chronographycal table' given in the Manship Manuscript and Nashe's much livelier account is very instructive. The Manuscript describes the town as it was about the time of the Norman Conquest in the following terms:

> In the tymes of the Reygnes of Kinge Harrolde and of Kinge William the Conquerror, the saide sande did growe to be drye and was not overflowen by the Sea, but waxed in heighte, and also in greatnes, in so much as greate store of people of the Counties of Norffolke and Suffolke did resorte thither, and did pitche Tabernacles and Boothes for the enterteynenge of such Seafaringe men and Fishermen and Merchaunts as wold resorte unto that place, eyther to sell their Herringes, fish, and other comodoties, and for providenge suche things as those Seamen did neede and wante. The which thinge caused greate store of Seafaringe men to resorte thither; but especiallie the Fishermen of this Land; as also greate nombers of the Fishermen of Fraunce, Flaunders, and of Holland, Zealande, and all the lowe Contryes yerelie, from the feast of Sainte

[23] *Euphues*, ed. E. Arber, p. 106.
[24] III. 159.

> Michaell the Archangell untylle the feast of Sainte Martine, aboute the takinge, sellinge, and buyenge of Herringes, and at other tymes in the yere aboute other kindes of fishe.[25]

As a piece of prose this is about as bad as it could be, clumsy, flat and repetitive. Nashe takes it in hand, lops off the superfluous verbiage, tidies it up and enlivens it with dramatic imagery. In his version it becomes gay, quick-moving and vivid.

> In the time of King *Herrolde* and *William* the Conquerour, this sand of Yarmouth grew to a setled lumpe, and was as drie as the sands of Arabia, so that thronging theaters of people (as well Aliens as Englishmen) hiued thither about the selling of fish and Herring, from Saint Michael to Saint Martin, and there built sutlers booths and tabernacles, to canopie their heads in from the rhewme of the heauens, or the clouds dissoluing Cataracts.[26]

In particular, the rapid transition from 'thronging theaters' to the verb 'hiued', with its picture of bees swarming, conveys in a flash that sense of crowds of people which the Manuscript vainly seeks to get over by a process of enumeration. Nashe darts to the point while his source plods painfully around it.

The history of Yarmouth is in fact coherent as well as lively. Nashe does give an impression of the way in which the town had grown through the Middle Ages, of its wealth and of its civic pride, while never abandoning the general tone of banter and mockery which gives the whole work such unity as it has. The familiar and the ornately elaborate are deliberately played off against each other, especially in the passage where he makes the transition from Yarmouth to the red herring. Puzzled by the thriving dignity of the town, Nashe relates how he

> fell a communing herupon with a gentleman, a familiar of mine, and he eftsoones defined vnto mee that the redde herring was this old *Ticklecob*, or *Magister fac totum*, that brought in the red ruddocks and the grummell seed as thicke as oatmeale, and made Yarmouth for argent to put downe the citty of *Argentine*. Doe but conuert, said hee, the slenderest twinckling reflexe of your eie-sight to this flinty ringe that engirtes it, these towred walles, port-cullizd-gates, and gorgeous architectures that condecorate and adorne it, and then perponder of the red herringes priority and preualence, who is the onely unexhaustible mine that hath raisd and begot all this, and minutely to riper maturity fosters and cherisheth it.[27]

[25] IV. 382. [26] III. 162. [27] III. 174.

In its extravagant self-regard this passage prepares for the manner Nashe adopts in writing of the kipper. The burlesque intention is announced at once. He begins with a flourish, producing a long list of the *encomia* on trivial subjects which provide him with precedents: a list that begins with Homer's *Batrachomyomachia*, which is summed up in the phrase: 'Homer of rats and frogs hath heroiqut it'. The kipper is to be an epic hero and, therefore, has to be supplied with a proper classical ancestry. Nashe solves this problem by resorting to the Ovidian metamorphosis, so popular at the time in poetry. He makes two short trials of the method and then chooses as his target the most brilliant poem in this kind that the age had produced, Marlowe's *Hero and Leander*. No animus against Marlowe inspired Nashe's burlesque. On the contrary he admired the work he plays with and begins by voicing his praise of it:

> Let me see, hath anie bodie in Yarmouth heard of Leander and Hero, of whome diuine *Musaeus* sung, and a diuiner Muse than him, *Kit Marlow*?[28]

But admiration does not rule out criticism. *Hero and Leander* invited parody on several counts. First, it was extremely popular, as Nashe indicates by writing of the hero and heroine: 'Twoo faithfull louers they were, as euerie apprentise in Paules churchyard will tell you for your loue, and sel you for your mony.' A mocking version of it would, therefore, have a wide appeal and an immediate impact. Secondly, the very nature of the poem, with its stress on the fidelity of the lovers, its exaltation of passion into an absolute and its use of a rich exotic setting, was a challenge to common sense and common experience. Nashe was not alone in his realization of this. Shakespeare pays a great tribute to Marlowe and his poem in *As You Like It*, but in the same play Rosalind makes fun of the story, just as Mercutio and Benedick had done before her, when she says:

> Leander, he would have lived many a fair year, though Hero had turned nun, had it not been for a hot mid-summer-night; for, good youth, he went but forth to wash him in the Hellespont, and, being taken with the cramp, was drowned; and the foolish chroniclers of that age found it was—Hero of Sestos. But these are all lies; men have died from time to time, and worms have eaten them, but not for love. [IV. i.]

[28] III. 195.

Compared with the delicate, dancing irony of Rosalind's account, Nashe's rendering of the story is rough and swashbuckling, or, as he would have put it, boisterous, yet it rests on the same trick of reducing the rare and exotic to the ordinary and commonplace, of bringing the mythological down to the level of everyday life. His sense of decorum helps him. Knowing the proper way to handle such a story he carefully inverts it and creates studied indecorum. He uses the popular idiom, but enriches it with strange coinages of his own and develops the use of imagery to a point where it becomes absurd. His account of Leander's death is a good example of the method. Relating how violent storms kept the lovers apart for some seven days, he concludes:

> Hero wept as trickling as the heauens, to thinke that heauen should so diuorce them. Leander stormed worse than the stormes, that by them hee should be so restrained from his Cinthya. At Sestos was his soule, and hee coulde not abide to tarry in Abidos. Rayne, snowe, haile, or blowe it howe it could, into the pitchie Helespont he leapt, when the moone and all her torch-bearers were afraide to peepe out their heads; but he was peppered for it, hee hadde as good haue tooke meate, drinke, and leisure, for the churlish frampold waues gaue him his belly full of fish-broath, ere out of their laundry or washe-house they woulde graunt him his coquet or *transire*, and not onely that, but they sealde him his *quietus est* for curuetting any more to the mayden tower, and tossed his dead carcasse, well bathed or parboyled, to the sandy threshold of his leman or orenge, for a disiune or morning breakfast. All that liue long night could she not sleepe, she was so troubled with the rheume; which was a signe she should heare of some drowning: Yet towards cocke-crowing she caught a little slumber, and then shee dreamed that Leander and shee were playing at checkestone with pearles in the bottome of the sea.[29]

Here are the devices proper to the kind of narrative poem Nashe is guying: the similes relating the lovers' state of mind to the elements, the metaphors that endow the moon and stars with human attributes, the premonitory dream that Hero has. But it is all rendered ridiculous by being carried too far, by the commonplace context of cooking, washing and so forth in which it is set and by the colloquial phraseology in which it is cast. The device is an old one, but Nashe exploits it with verve and brilliance,

[29] III. 197.

carrying it right through to the final metamorphosis, in which the gods out of pity for the lovers turn Leander into the ling, Hero into a herring and, most striking of all, find an appropriate fate for the old nurse who looks after Hero; for in a burlesque of this kind it is the minor figure in the original story who ultimately emerges as the most important. Here Nashe is at his most outrageously comic:

> The nurse or mother Mampudding, that was a cowring on the backe side whiles these things were a tragedizing, led by the scritch or outcry to the prospect of this sorrowfull heigho, as soone as, through the raueld button holes of her bleare eyes, she had suckt in and receiued such a reuelation of Doomesday, and that she saw her mistris mounted a cockhorse, and hoysted away to hell or to heauen on the backs of those rough headed ruffians, down she sunk to the earth, as dead as a doore naile, and neuer mumpt crust after. Whereof their supernalities (hauing a drop or two of pitty left of the huge hogshead of teares they spent for *Hero* and *Leander*) seemed to be something sorie, though they could not weepe for it, and because they would bee sure to haue a medicine that should make them weep at all times, to that kinde of graine they turned her which wee call mustard seede, as well for shee was a shrewish snappish bawd, that wold bite off a mans nose with an answere and had rumatique sore eyes that ran alwaies, as that she might accompany *Hero* and *Leander* after death, as in hir life time: and hence it is that mustard bites a man so by the nose, and makes him weep and water his plants when he tasteth it; and that *Hero* and *Leander*, the red Herring and Ling, neuer come to the boord without mustard, their waiting maid: and if you marke it, mustard looks of the tanned wainscot hue of such a wrinklefaced beldam as she was that was altred thereinto.[30]

Quite apart from the ingenuity of the invention, the whole passage is a fine example of the vigour and close observation of which Nashe is capable. One sees the bleary eyes of the nurse, watches the motion of her toothless gums. Even the wrinkled appearance of old mustard has been caught. Nashe's images do their work, and so do his coinages, such as his bold use of the interjection 'heigh-ho' as a noun. This is the prose of a poet, handling the commonest and most trivial things in an imaginative manner. This reading of the story is a transmutation of gold into a baser metal, but not a vulgarization of it. To see what happened

[30] III. 200.

to *Hero and Leander* when it was vulgarized, it is only necessary to turn to Ben Jonson's *Bartholomew Fair*, where it is debased into a crude puppet-show by the stupid citizen John Littlewit.

The burlesque of *Hero and Leander* is the high-light of *Lenten Stuff*. Nashe tries to repeat his performance in it by inventing two more comic tales to explain 'how he [the herring] came to be king of fishes, and gradationately how from white to red he changed',[31] but the first of them fizzles out in a rather inconclusive fashion and the second amounts to little more than a bit of pope-baiting. The effort to spin out the trivial is painfully obvious. Paucity of material and debility of invention are everywhere apparent. Life only comes back into *Lenten Stuff* when he turns at last to a subject that really does interest him, because it is personal. Throughout his career he had been hampered by that pest, the professional informer, who made life so difficult for all who wrote about the life of the times. The allegory of the Bear and the Fox in *Pierce Penilesse* had led to trouble with some nobleman or other, who had committed 'it ouer to be prosecuted by a worse misconstruer then himselfe, *videlicet*, his learned counsaile';[32] his remarks about the Danes in the same work seem to have caused concern in high quarters;[33] a passage in *Christ's Tears* had so offended the citizens of London that it had had to be cancelled; and finally had come the outcry over *The Isle of Dogs* which had led to the play's suppression. It says much for Nashe's courage that in these circumstances he still protests against the intelligencers' activities in a vigorous and forthright fashion, presenting a ludicrous picture of their manner of going to work, which is probably not far removed from the truth, and even daring to challenge them to exercise their wits on some fantastic stories that he invents expressly as bait, red herrings in fact, for them. He writes:

> Let them looke to themselues as they will, for I am theirs to gull them better than euer I haue done; and this I am sure, I have destributed gudgeon dole amongst them, as Gods plenty as any stripling of my slender portion of witte, farre or neere. They needes will haue it so, much good do it them, I can not doe wythall: For if but carelesly betwixt sleeping and waking I write I knowe not what against plebeian Publicans and sinners (no better than the sworne brothers of candlesticke turners and tinkers) and leaue some

[31] III. 195. [32] III. 214.
[33] See Robert Beal's allusion quoted at V. 142.

> termes in suspence that my post-haste want of argent will not giue mee elbowe roome enough to explane or examine as I would, out steps me an infant squib of the Innes of Court, that hath not halfe greased his dining cappe, or scarce warmed his Lawyers cushion, and he, to approue hymselfe an extrauagant statesman, catcheth hold of a rush, and absolutely concludeth, it is meant of the Emperour of Ruscia, and that it will vtterly marre the traffike into that country if all the Pamphlets bee not called in and suppressed, wherein that libelling word is mentioned. An other, if but a head or a tayle of any beast he boasts of in his crest or his scutcheon be reckoned vp by chaunce in a volume where a man hath iust occasion to reckon vp all beasts in armory, he strait engageth hymselfe by the honor of his house, and his neuer reculed sword, to thresh downe the hayry roofe of that brayne that so seditiously mutined against hym, with the mortiferous bastinado, or cast such an vncurable Italian trench in his face, as not the basest creeper vpon pattens by the high way side but shall abhor him worse than the carrion of a dead corse, or a man hanged vp in gibbets.[34]

There is probably an element of exaggeration here, but Nashe's numerous brushes with authority are sufficient evidence that there is also a sub-stratum of truth in the picture. The lot of the satirist, whether prose-writer or dramatist, was not an easy one, particularly when his pen was sharp and he had no powerful patron to whom he could turn for protection. Nashe paid the penalty for his free-lance activities, and it is not unlikely that the unrepentant attitude he voices in the later part of *Lenten Stuff* may have contributed to the suppression of his writings by Whitgift and Bancroft in 1599. The pamphlet itself certainly suffers from the circumstances in which it was composed. It is a triumph over obstacles, but even Nashe's cleverness cannot compensate for the deficiency of material in it. Before he reaches the end he has grown tired with 'this playing with a shettlecocke, or tossing empty bladders in the ayre',[35] and the incipient Wellerism with which he encourages his readers to persevere may fairly be taken as an index of his own state of mind:

> Be of good cheere, my weary Readers, for I haue espied land, as *Diogenes* said to his weary Schollers when he had read to a waste leafe.[36]

*Lenten Stuff* is a bauble, a fool's bladder, flying hither and thither with every blow from the 'shettlecocke' of its author's wit and with

[34] III. 213. [35] III. 225. [36] III. 223.

every breeze that springs up from his miscellaneous reading. Kept aloft by sheer verbal dexterity, it never collapses or falls to earth. It is more like a circus turn, than anything else he wrote; but, also like the circus turn, there is nothing left when it is over. Only in the actual performance, the reading of it, does it exist as a thing in its own right. It is the ultimate and logical end of that narrowing down in the scope of experience Nashe handles, which begins with *Strange News* and the quarrel with Gabriel Harvey and for which the professional intelligencer was also responsible.

After completing *Lenten Stuff* Nashe wrote no more. He was still alive when it was going through the press early in 1599, but in Charles Fitzgeffrey's *Affaniae*, published in 1601, there is a Latin epigram on his death, which bears witness to the reputation he had achieved as a satirist.[37] The epitaph that would have pleased him best, however, is that which is found in *The Second Part of the Return from Parnassus*, which was first acted, according to Leishman, during the Christmas period of 1601–2.[38] In Act I Scene II of this play the following exchanges take place in the course of a review of the reputations of a list of authors prefixed to John Bodenham's *Belvedere*:

*Ingenioso.* *Thomas Nash.*
I, heer's a fellow, *Iudicio*, that carryed the deadly Stockado in his pen, whose muse was armed with a gagtooth, and his pen possest with *Hercules* furies.

*Iudicio.* Let all his faultes sleepe with his mournfull chest,
And there for euer with his ashes rest.
His stile was wittie, though it had some gal[l],
Some thing[s] he might haue mended, so may all.
Yet this I say, that for a mother witt,
Fewe men haue euer seene the like of it.[39]

[37] V. 149. [38] *The Three Parnassus Plays*, pp. 24–6.
[39] *Ibid.*, p. 245. Also quoted at V. 150.

# IX

# CONCLUSION

AT the beginning of this study I stated that Nashe is something of a puzzle. At the end of it I cannot say that the puzzle is much nearer to a solution. There is a tantalizing gap between the talents that were his and what he actually achieved with them. That his work was of considerable historical importance no one can doubt who considers the mark that he left on the writing of his time. He exerted a powerful influence not only on the work of subsequent pamphleteers, such as Dekker, but also on verse satire and on the drama. Nor is there any question about the qualities in his writing that made it influential. Men of the calibre of Shakespeare, Ben Jonson and Donne, to go no farther, found a stimulus in his lively exploitation and extension of the resources of the English language, in his wit and in his turn for depicting contemporary types with satirical sharpness. He was something of a pioneer in demonstrating how much raw material for the literary artist to work on lay ready to hand in the streets of London, in the multifarious activities and idiosyncracies of its inhabitants and in the phrases that fell from their lips. There was a potential Dickens in Nashe with his keen eye for oddities of speech, dress and behaviour, with his sense of humour, his social conscience and his fascinated interest in the grotesque, not to mention the deep attraction towards violence that is present in so much that he writes. Yet, gifted though he was, one cannot point to a single thing he wrote that is an achieved work of art in its own right and of which one can say with confidence that in it he has made full use of the capabilities that were indubitably his.

In part, Nashe's failure to do the work that he was born to do may be attributed to external factors. He could find no suitable place for himself in the literary organization of the day. In a world where the professional author who did not write for the stage still depended on patronage, his genius was not for producing the kind of thing that appealed to the great. Arcadia did not interest him. Nor was it for producing the kind of thing that appealed to the middle class. Deloney shared and approved of the attitudes and values of the citizens of London; Nashe scorned and criticized them and Deloney. The audience he seems to have had in mind for most of his writings, and with whom he was in closest sympathy, was that which had its nucleus in the Inns of Court and was made up of lively young men interested in letters and the arts, hostile to Puritanism and the middle-class ethos, witty, caustic and dissatisfied. But, while he was enjoyed and admired by this group, they were too few in numbers and too impecunious to ensure him a reasonable living.

Moreover, the literary forms in which Nashe might have excelled did not yet exist. His bent was for journalism and, perhaps, for the novel which was ultimately to grow out of journalism. But as yet there were no journals and no novel. All he could avail himself of was that accommodating but shapeless hold-all, the pamphlet, into which he bundled his essays, character-sketches, parodies, comic tales and social and literary criticism more or less higgledy-piggledy. Nor did he enjoy the freedom of comment that the journalist has since won for himself. As we have seen, his criticisms led him into trouble not only with the Privy Council, but also with the City fathers and, on at least one occasion, with some great man. The activities of the intelligencer were a constant threat to him. Unlike Pope, he could not 'stoop to Truth and moralize his song', though the impulse to do so was strong in him. Only about his fellow writers could he speak with complete frankness.

It was these external pressures, I think, that helped to force him into the literary *rôle* he eventually adopted, that of the jester, the professional fool, especially as that figure is depicted in the plays of Shakespeare. Indeed, it was in such terms that he thought of himself. We have seen him referring in *Lenten Stuff* to his sheaf of fool's bolts; one of his favourite devices throughout his work is the dialogue with himself that characters such as Launce and Launcelot Gobbo are also fond of; and in *Summer's Last Will and Testament* he clearly identifies himself with the figure of Will Summers, Henry VIII's fool. Now the jester, like the Elizabethan satirist, enjoyed a precarious freedom. The first qualification for the post was a ready wit. The fool must never be found lacking for an answer. No matter what the topic under discussion may be, he must be ready to contribute to it. He is allowed, and even expected, to tell the truth, though unwelcome, provided that he does it cleverly in an allusive and entertaining manner. If he becomes too blunt and outspoken, he is in danger of the whip, for his position is always that of a dependant. Puns, quibbles and the ambiguities of language generally are, therefore, his stock in trade. Like Feste in *Twelfth Night*, moreover, his attitude must be a double one. He has to show an equal ability both to laugh at and expose a fashionable pose, such as that of melancholy, and to adopt it and sing of it with conviction when to do so will put money in his purse. Nashe, or Pierce Penilesse, as he liked to think of himself, is such a jester. For each kind of company he may find himself in, for each kind of topic he deals with, he has an appropriate mask or *persona*. He lives wholly and only in society. Out of it he has neither function nor being. Even his private quarrels and animosities, like Feste's hatred of Malvolio, become the stuff of art and provide the material for a professional performance in which burlesque and parody play a large part.

Seeing the importance of the *rôle*, we see also why Nashe's writings are disappointing for the modern reader in another respect. At first glance they seem to offer far more in the way of personal revelation than do those of most of his contemporaries. He writes habitually in the first person, plucking the reader by the sleeve in a manner that appears to anticipate that of Laurence Sterne. He describes his financial difficulties, writes of his old college with affection and enthusiasm, springs to the defence of a friend and produces a brilliant little picture of him. Furthermore, he certainly impressed those who knew him by his personality. References to him are numerous and nearly always it is his biting satirical wit that is emphasized in them. The more one reads him, however, the more elusive the individual personality becomes, because his concern is not with self-expression but with effect. His eye is always on the audience and their reactions to what he is doing, it is never turned inwards on himself. His rapid changes of front can be interpreted, as C. S. Lewis interprets them,[1] as evidence of psychological unbalance in their author, his 'burliness' being 'only the "manic" peak, balanced in private by a "depressive" trough'. But such deductions seem to me to be dangerous, because, for the most part, Nashe's writings tell us nothing about Nashe. The things they do tell us about are the tastes, the sympathies and the prejudices of those he wrote for, or thought he was writing for. They are public rhetorical works, as remote from the confessional and self-revelatory kinds of literature, that later writers have accustomed us to, as anything well could be.

Nashe, in fact, had the qualities that his fellow writers were so fond of attributing to the chameleon, including the ability to 'eat the air, promise-crammed'. It was both his strength and his weakness. It enabled him to reflect his age and its tastes in an arresting manner, but it prevented him from doing more. Only two really passionate interests in something other than his own performance make themselves felt in his work, a thorough-going opposition to Puritanism in a broad general sense and, linked with it, a single-minded devotion to the cause of literature and of humane studies in general. As a social critic and as a literary critic he has something to say, but the great mass of his writing has rather the quality of a virtuoso turn in the circus or the music-hall. One marvels at the display of skill and ingenuity, at the way in which words beget words until a rope of them materializes up which the illusionist moves with a dazzling speed and dexterity. But when the trick has been accomplished nothing remains behind. There is more than a little of the Joyce of *Finnegans Wake* about Nashe. Fascinated by words, still more fascinated by the games he can play with them, he ultimately leaves the normal concerns of humanity behind. A work such as *Lenten Stuff* has no significance outside itself. It is a *jeu d'esprit* with no bearing on life. And, because it was towards this kind of thing that his work was always tending, Nashe is and will remain a minor author of genius, but still a minor author.

[1] *Op. cit.*, p. 414.

# APPENDIX

## NASHE'S COLLABORATION WITH GREENE

SINCE Chapter IV was written Donald J. McGinn, in an article entitled 'A Quip from Tom Nashe',[1] has argued that Nashe collaborated with Greene in the writing of *A Quip for an Upstart Courtier*, that it was this work Greene was alluding to in his *Groats-worth of Wit*, when he addressed Nashe as 'yong Iuuenall, that byting Satyrist, that lastlie with mee together writ a Comedie,' and that the attack on the Harveys, which was later cancelled, in the *Quip* was Nashe's main contribution to that work.

McGinn's argument, which rests mainly on stylistic resemblances between the *Quip* and some of Nashe's authentic works, particularly *Pierce Penilesse*, seems to me unacceptable for the following reasons:

1. In *Strange News* Nashe states quite explicitly that the passages in the *Quip* tilting at Gabriel and Richard Harvey were the work of Greene. He writes:

> *Tubalcan*, aliâs *Tuball*, first founder of Farriers Hall, heere is a great complaint made, that *vtriusque Academiae Robertus Greene* hath mockt thee, because hee saide, that as thou wert the first inuenter of Musicke, so *Gabriell Howliglasse* was the first inuenter of English Hexameter verses.[2]

[1] *Studies in the English Renaissance Drama*, edited by Bennett, Cargill and Hall, London, 1959, pp. 172–88.

[2] I. 298.

It might be argued that Nashe is merely quoting from the *Four Letters* here, but no such excuse can be made for a previous reference to Greene's authorship of the key passage in the *Quip*, where he states:

> *Greene*, beeing chiefe agent for the companie (for hee writ more than foure other, how well I will not say: but *Sat citò, si sat benè*) tooke occasion to canvaze him [Richard Harvey] a little in his Cloth-breeches and Veluet-breeches, and because by some probable collections hee gest the elder brothers hand was in it, he coupled them both in one yoake, and, to fulfill the prouerbe *Tria sunt omnia*, thrust in the third brother, who made a perfect parriall of Pamphleters.[3]

No statement could be plainer. Nashe says that not only the anti-Harvey passage, but also the entire pamphlet is Greene's work. He should have known.

2. While it is perfectly true that neither Greene nor Nashe restricted the word *comedy* to dramatic productions (Nashe calls *Have With You* a comedy), the whole context of the passage in Greene's *Groatsworth* demands that the word *Comedie* be given a dramatic interpretation. It is a warning to the three writers addressed in it to beware of actors, who will make profit and fame from their works with no sense of obligation. Greene writes:

> Is it not strange, that I, to whom they [the actors] all haue beene beholding: is it not like *that you, to whome they all haue beene beholding*, shall (were yee in that case as I am now) bee both at once of them forsaken?[4] [My italics.]

In other words Nashe had had a hand in a play which had been publicly performed and, since *Summer's Last Will and Testament* had not been acted when these words were written and was not, in any case, intended for the public theatre, the play in question can only have been the comedy which he had written together with Greene.

[3] I. 271.

[4] *Greene's Groats-worth of Witte*, ed. G. B. Harrison, London, 1923, p. 45.

# INDEX